Alex
KNOWS THE SCORE

CHARLES PEATTIE
AND
RUSSELL TAYLOR

HEADLINE

Also by Charles Peattie and Russell Taylor published by Headline
ALEX CALLS THE SHOTS
ALEX PLAYS THE GAME

Alex
KNOWS THE SCORE

RING RING
The Daily Telegraph

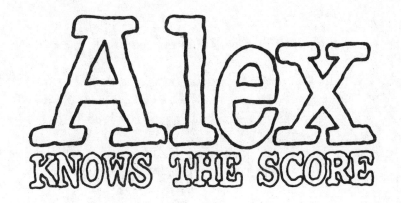

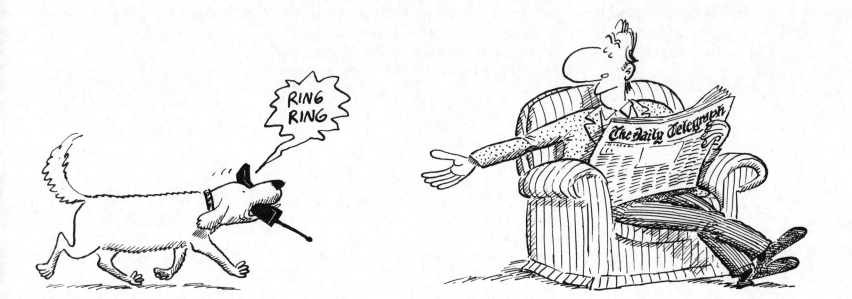

First published in 1995
by HEADLINE BOOK PUBLISHING

10 9 8 7 6 5 4 3 2 1

ISBN 0 7472 7796 6

Printed and bound in Great Britain by
BPC Hazell Books Ltd
A member of
The British Printing Company Ltd

HEADLINE BOOK PUBLISHING
A division of Hodder Headline PLC
338 Euston Road
London NW1 3BH

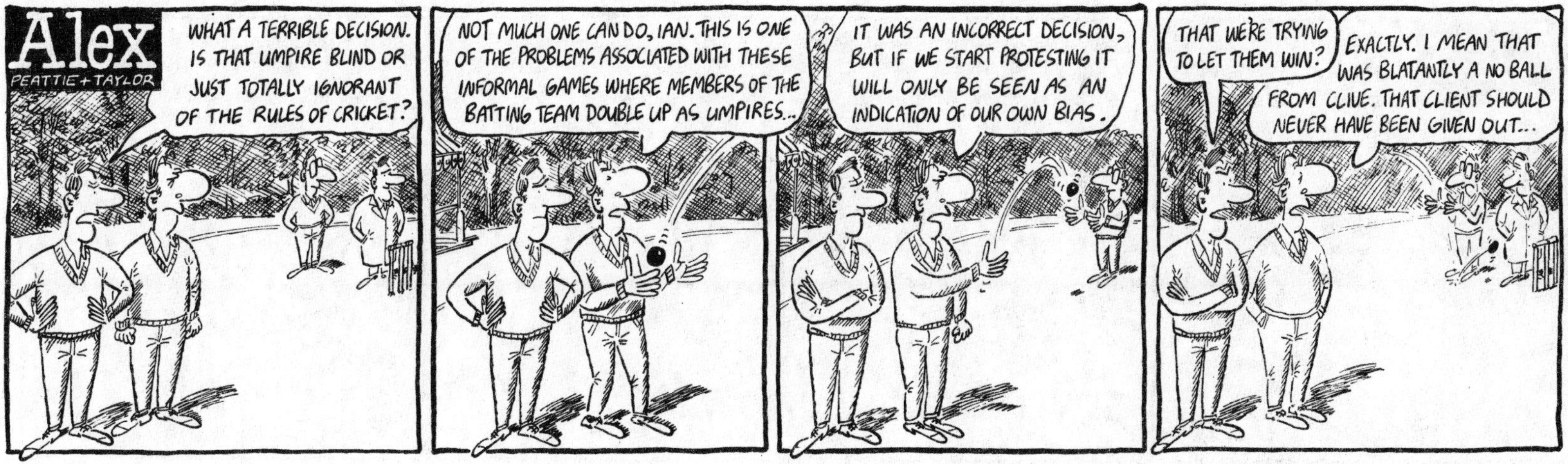
Alex
PEATTIE + TAYLOR
WHAT A TERRIBLE DECISION. IS THAT UMPIRE BLIND OR JUST TOTALLY IGNORANT OF THE RULES OF CRICKET?
NOT MUCH ONE CAN DO, IAN. THIS IS ONE OF THE PROBLEMS ASSOCIATED WITH THESE INFORMAL GAMES WHERE MEMBERS OF THE BATTING TEAM DOUBLE UP AS UMPIRES...
IT WAS AN INCORRECT DECISION, BUT IF WE START PROTESTING IT WILL ONLY BE SEEN AS AN INDICATION OF OUR OWN BIAS.
THAT WE'RE TRYING TO LET THEM WIN?
EXACTLY. I MEAN THAT WAS BLATANTLY A NO BALL FROM CLIVE. THAT CLIENT SHOULD NEVER HAVE BEEN GIVEN OUT...

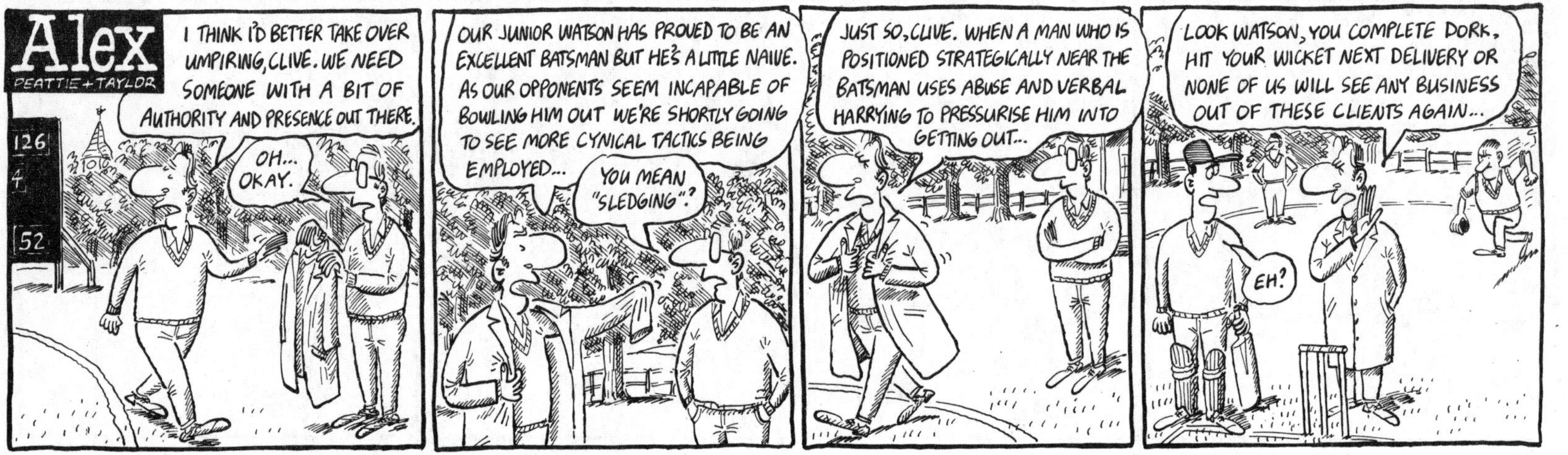
Alex
PEATTIE + TAYLOR
I THINK I'D BETTER TAKE OVER UMPIRING, CLIVE. WE NEED SOMEONE WITH A BIT OF AUTHORITY AND PRESENCE OUT THERE.
OH... OKAY.
126
4
52
OUR JUNIOR WATSON HAS PROVED TO BE AN EXCELLENT BATSMAN BUT HE'S A LITTLE NAIVE. AS OUR OPPONENTS SEEM INCAPABLE OF BOWLING HIM OUT WE'RE SHORTLY GOING TO SEE MORE CYNICAL TACTICS BEING EMPLOYED...
YOU MEAN "SLEDGING"?
JUST SO, CLIVE. WHEN A MAN WHO IS POSITIONED STRATEGICALLY NEAR THE BATSMAN USES ABUSE AND VERBAL HARRYING TO PRESSURISE HIM INTO GETTING OUT...
LOOK WATSON, YOU COMPLETE DORK. HIT YOUR WICKET NEXT DELIVERY OR NONE OF US WILL SEE ANY BUSINESS OUT OF THESE CLIENTS AGAIN...
EH?

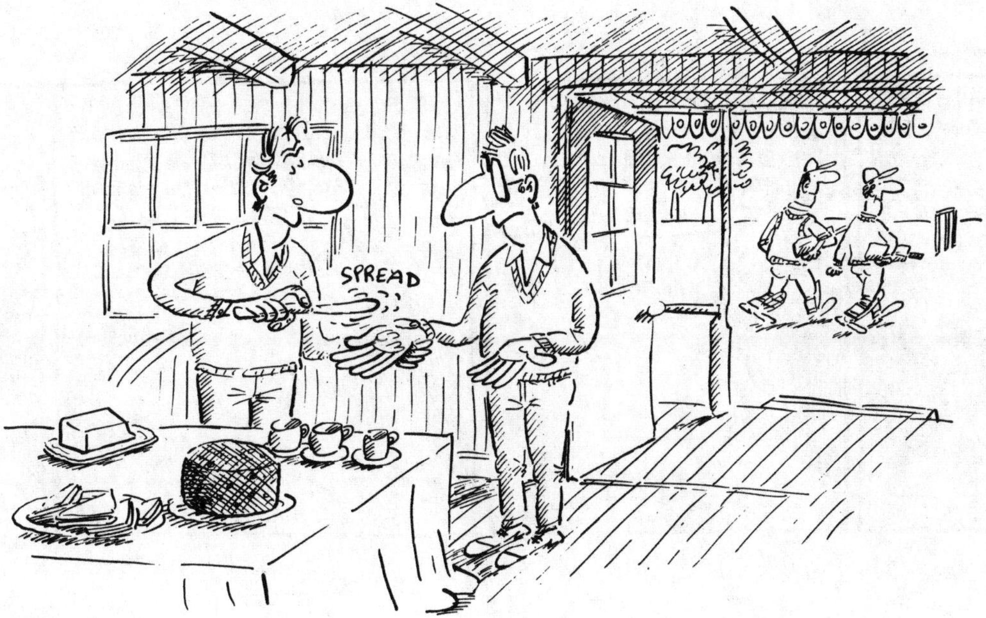
SPREAD

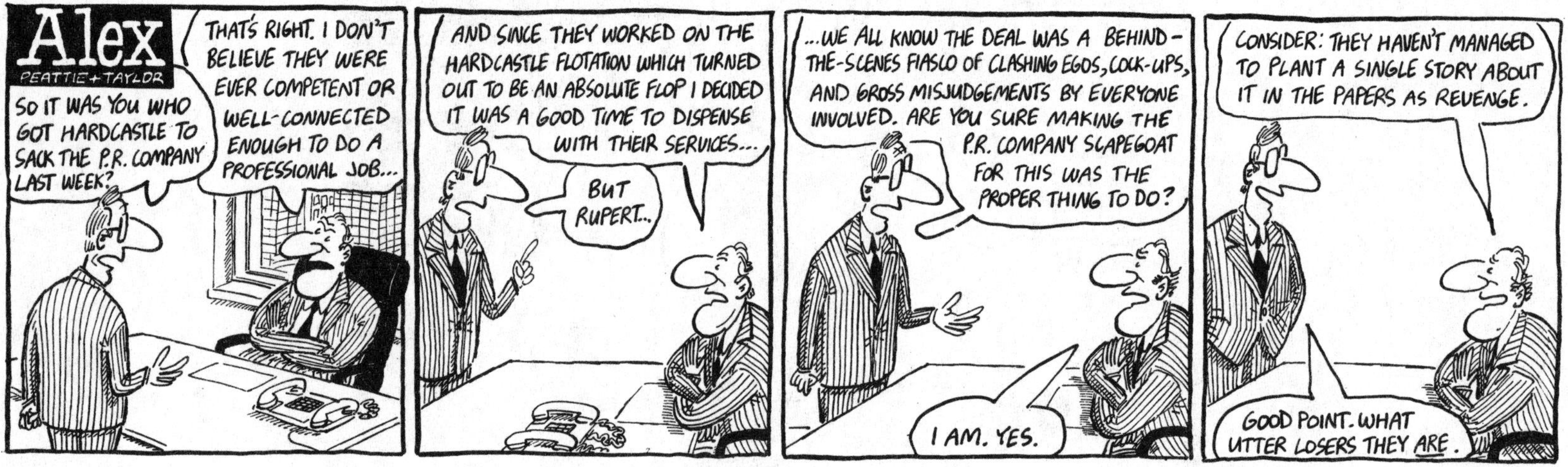
Alex
PEATTIE + TAYLOR
SO IT WAS YOU WHO GOT HARDCASTLE TO SACK THE P.R. COMPANY LAST WEEK?
THAT'S RIGHT. I DON'T BELIEVE THEY WERE EVER COMPETENT OR WELL-CONNECTED ENOUGH TO DO A PROFESSIONAL JOB...
AND SINCE THEY WORKED ON THE HARDCASTLE FLOTATION WHICH TURNED OUT TO BE AN ABSOLUTE FLOP I DECIDED IT WAS A GOOD TIME TO DISPENSE WITH THEIR SERVICES...
BUT RUPERT...
...WE ALL KNOW THE DEAL WAS A BEHIND-THE-SCENES FIASCO OF CLASHING EGOS, COCK-UPS, AND GROSS MISJUDGEMENTS BY EVERYONE INVOLVED. ARE YOU SURE MAKING THE P.R. COMPANY SCAPEGOAT FOR THIS WAS THE PROPER THING TO DO?
I AM. YES.
CONSIDER: THEY HAVEN'T MANAGED TO PLANT A SINGLE STORY ABOUT IT IN THE PAPERS AS REVENGE.
GOOD POINT. WHAT UTTER LOSERS THEY ARE.

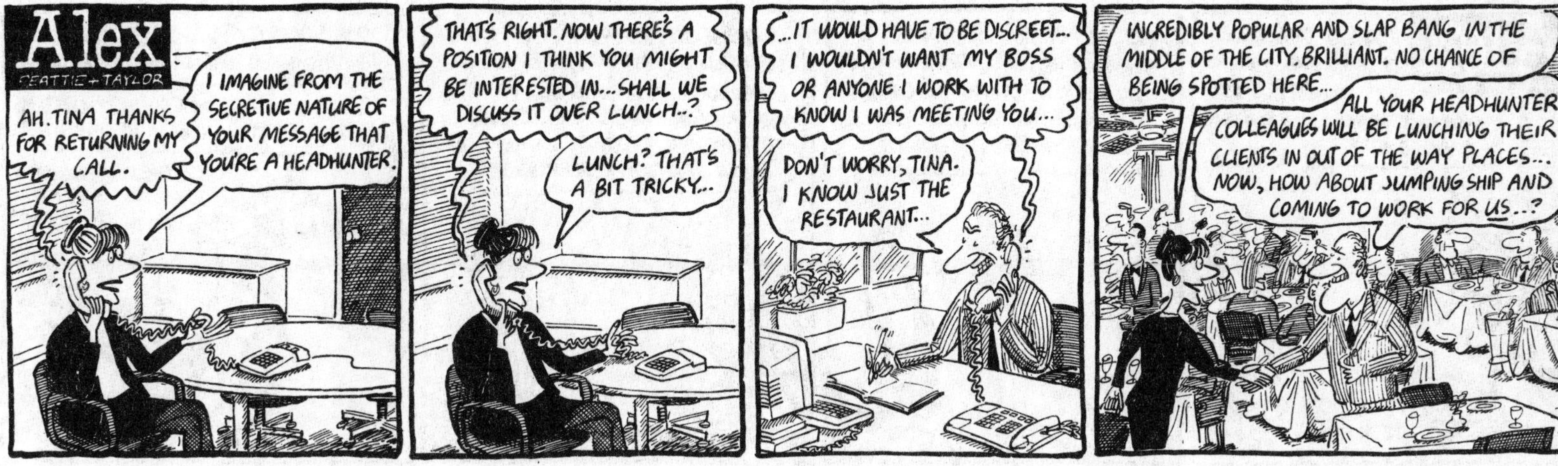
Alex
BEATTIE + TAYLOR
AH. TINA THANKS FOR RETURNING MY CALL.
I IMAGINE FROM THE SECRETIVE NATURE OF YOUR MESSAGE THAT YOU'RE A HEADHUNTER.
THAT'S RIGHT. NOW THERE'S A POSITION I THINK YOU MIGHT BE INTERESTED IN... SHALL WE DISCUSS IT OVER LUNCH..?
LUNCH? THAT'S A BIT TRICKY...
...IT WOULD HAVE TO BE DISCREET... I WOULDN'T WANT MY BOSS OR ANYONE I WORK WITH TO KNOW I WAS MEETING YOU...
DON'T WORRY, TINA. I KNOW JUST THE RESTAURANT...
INCREDIBLY POPULAR AND SLAP BANG IN THE MIDDLE OF THE CITY. BRILLIANT. NO CHANCE OF BEING SPOTTED HERE...
ALL YOUR HEADHUNTER COLLEAGUES WILL BE LUNCHING THEIR CLIENTS IN OUT OF THE WAY PLACES... NOW, HOW ABOUT JUMPING SHIP AND COMING TO WORK FOR US..?

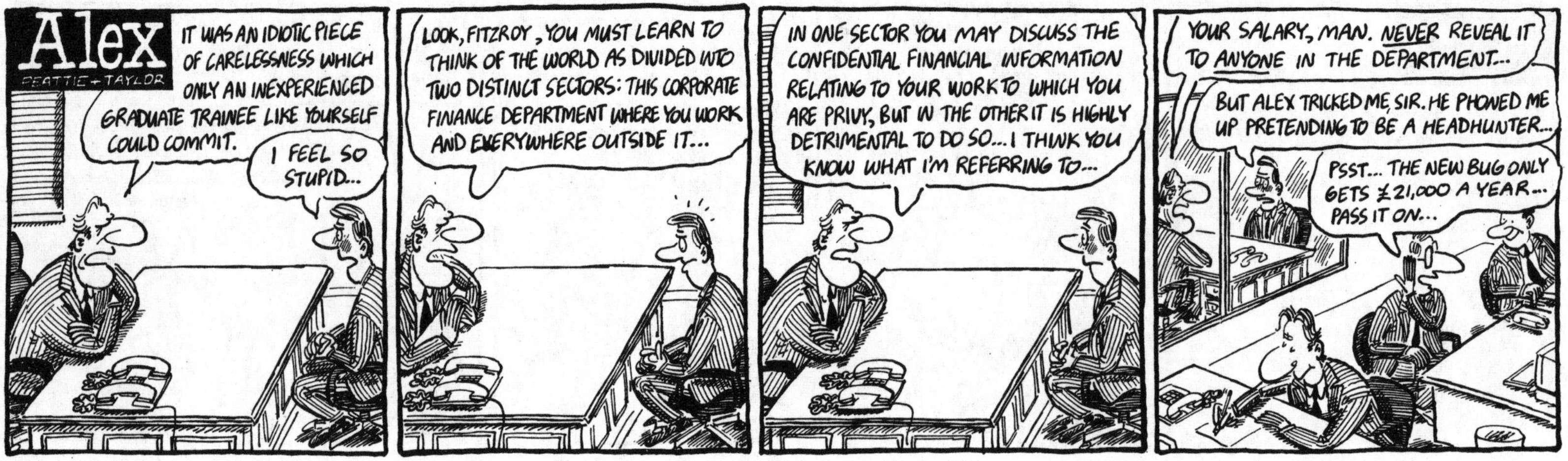

Alex
BEATTIE + TAYLOR
IT WAS AN IDIOTIC PIECE OF CARELESSNESS WHICH ONLY AN INEXPERIENCED GRADUATE TRAINEE LIKE YOURSELF COULD COMMIT.
I FEEL SO STUPID...
LOOK, FITZROY, YOU MUST LEARN TO THINK OF THE WORLD AS DIVIDED INTO TWO DISTINCT SECTORS: THIS CORPORATE FINANCE DEPARTMENT WHERE YOU WORK AND EVERYWHERE OUTSIDE IT...
IN ONE SECTOR YOU MAY DISCUSS THE CONFIDENTIAL FINANCIAL INFORMATION RELATING TO YOUR WORK TO WHICH YOU ARE PRIVY, BUT IN THE OTHER IT IS HIGHLY DETRIMENTAL TO DO SO... I THINK YOU KNOW WHAT I'M REFERRING TO...
YOUR SALARY, MAN. NEVER REVEAL IT TO ANYONE IN THE DEPARTMENT...
BUT ALEX TRICKED ME, SIR. HE PHONED ME UP PRETENDING TO BE A HEADHUNTER...
PSST... THE NEW BUG ONLY GETS £21,000 A YEAR... PASS IT ON...

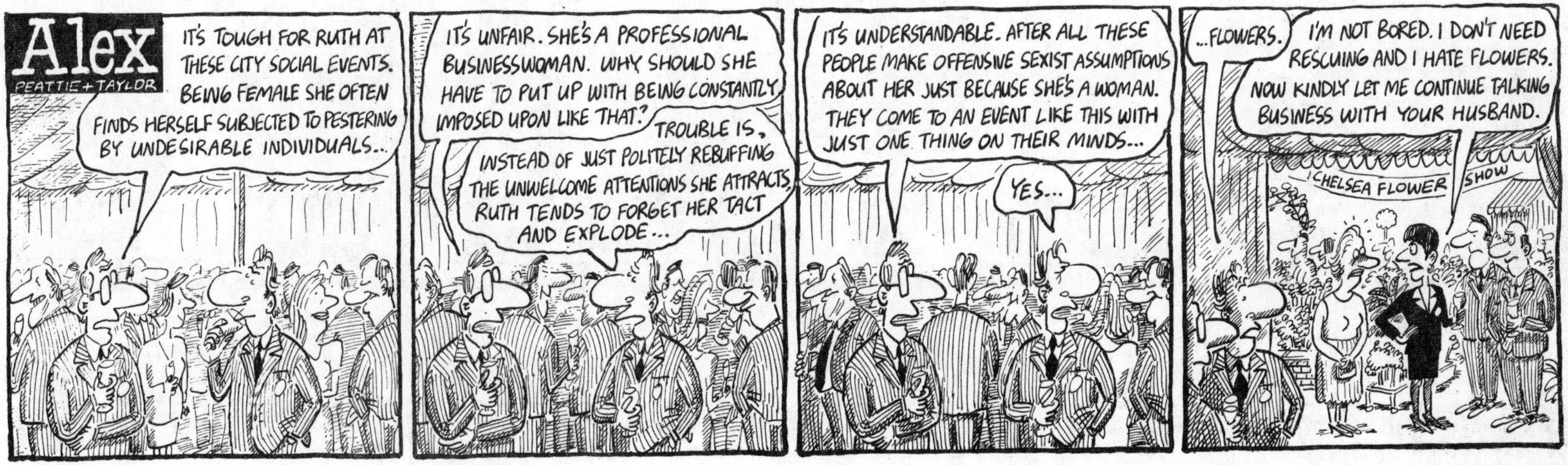
Alex
PEATTIE + TAYLOR
IT'S TOUGH FOR RUTH AT THESE CITY SOCIAL EVENTS. BEING FEMALE SHE OFTEN FINDS HERSELF SUBJECTED TO PESTERING BY UNDESIRABLE INDIVIDUALS...
IT'S UNFAIR. SHE'S A PROFESSIONAL BUSINESSWOMAN. WHY SHOULD SHE HAVE TO PUT UP WITH BEING CONSTANTLY IMPOSED UPON LIKE THAT?
TROUBLE IS, INSTEAD OF JUST POLITELY REBUFFING THE UNWELCOME ATTENTIONS SHE ATTRACTS, RUTH TENDS TO FORGET HER TACT AND EXPLODE...
IT'S UNDERSTANDABLE. AFTER ALL THESE PEOPLE MAKE OFFENSIVE SEXIST ASSUMPTIONS ABOUT HER JUST BECAUSE SHE'S A WOMAN. THEY COME TO AN EVENT LIKE THIS WITH JUST ONE THING ON THEIR MINDS...
YES...
...FLOWERS.
I'M NOT BORED. I DON'T NEED RESCUING AND I HATE FLOWERS. NOW KINDLY LET ME CONTINUE TALKING BUSINESS WITH YOUR HUSBAND.
CHELSEA FLOWER SHOW

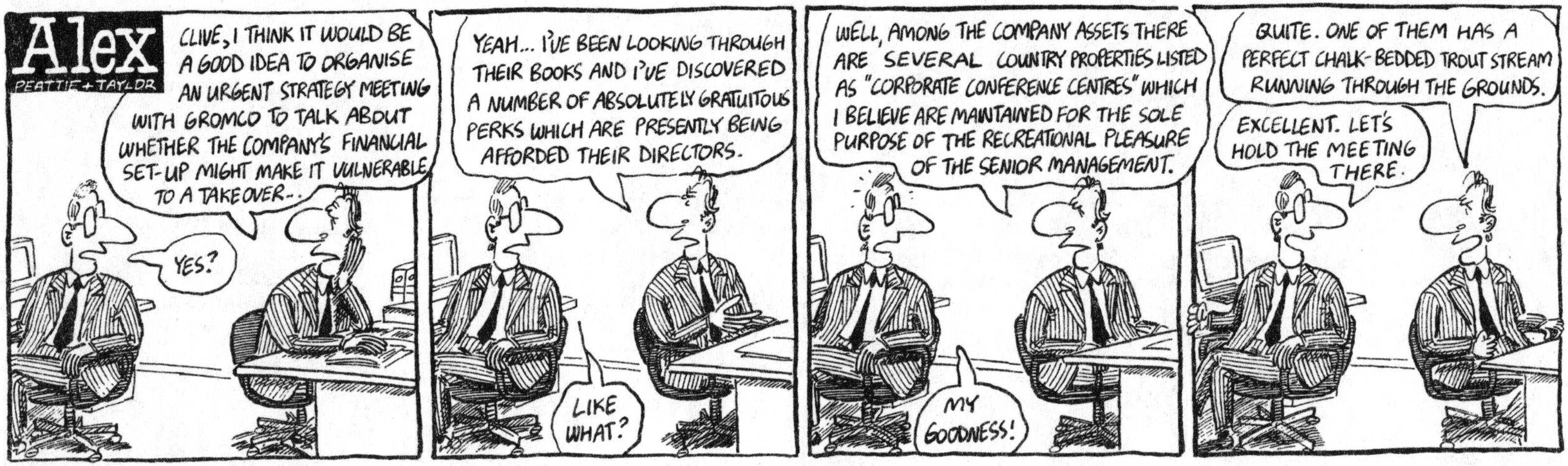
Alex
PEATTIE + TAYLOR
CLIVE, I THINK IT WOULD BE A GOOD IDEA TO ORGANISE AN URGENT STRATEGY MEETING WITH GROMCO TO TALK ABOUT WHETHER THE COMPANY'S FINANCIAL SET-UP MIGHT MAKE IT VULNERABLE TO A TAKEOVER...
YES?
YEAH... I'VE BEEN LOOKING THROUGH THEIR BOOKS AND I'VE DISCOVERED A NUMBER OF ABSOLUTELY GRATUITOUS PERKS WHICH ARE PRESENTLY BEING AFFORDED THEIR DIRECTORS.
LIKE WHAT?
WELL, AMONG THE COMPANY ASSETS THERE ARE SEVERAL COUNTRY PROPERTIES LISTED AS "CORPORATE CONFERENCE CENTRES" WHICH I BELIEVE ARE MAINTAINED FOR THE SOLE PURPOSE OF THE RECREATIONAL PLEASURE OF THE SENIOR MANAGEMENT.
MY GOODNESS!
QUITE. ONE OF THEM HAS A PERFECT CHALK-BEDDED TROUT STREAM RUNNING THROUGH THE GROUNDS.
EXCELLENT. LET'S HOLD THE MEETING THERE.

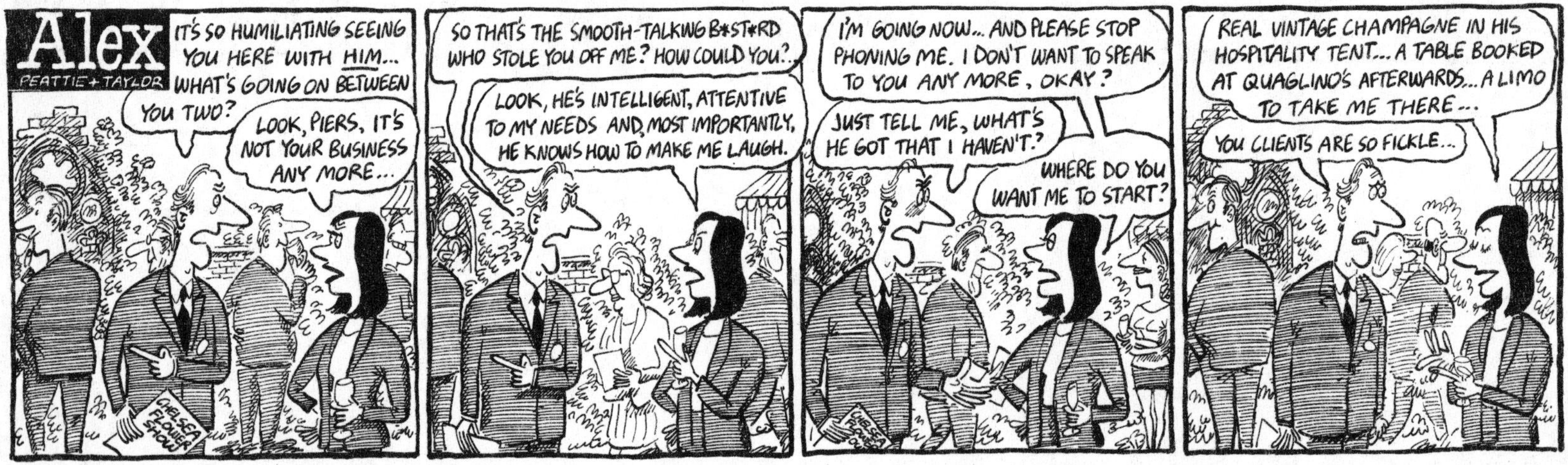
Alex
PEATTIE + TAYLOR
IT'S SO HUMILIATING SEEING YOU HERE WITH HIM... WHAT'S GOING ON BETWEEN YOU TWO?
LOOK, PIERS, IT'S NOT YOUR BUSINESS ANY MORE...
CHELSEA FLOWER SHOW
SO THAT'S THE SMOOTH-TALKING B*ST*RD WHO STOLE YOU OFF ME? HOW COULD YOU?..
LOOK, HE'S INTELLIGENT, ATTENTIVE TO MY NEEDS AND, MOST IMPORTANTLY, HE KNOWS HOW TO MAKE ME LAUGH.
I'M GOING NOW... AND PLEASE STOP PHONING ME. I DON'T WANT TO SPEAK TO YOU ANY MORE, OKAY?
JUST TELL ME, WHAT'S HE GOT THAT I HAVEN'T?
WHERE DO YOU WANT ME TO START?
REAL VINTAGE CHAMPAGNE IN HIS HOSPITALITY TENT... A TABLE BOOKED AT QUAGLINO'S AFTERWARDS... A LIMO TO TAKE ME THERE...
YOU CLIENTS ARE SO FICKLE...

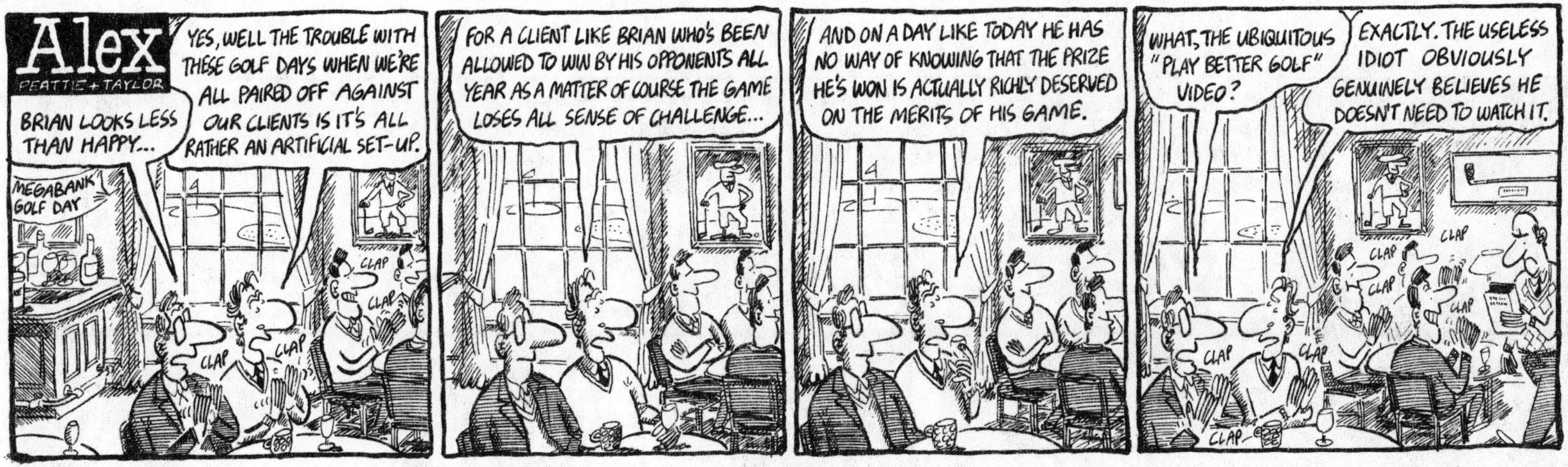
Alex
PEATTIE + TAYLOR
BRIAN LOOKS LESS THAN HAPPY...
YES, WELL THE TROUBLE WITH THESE GOLF DAYS WHEN WE'RE ALL PAIRED OFF AGAINST OUR CLIENTS IS IT'S ALL RATHER AN ARTIFICIAL SET-UP.
MEGABANK GOLF DAY
CLAP
CLAP
CLAP
CLAP
FOR A CLIENT LIKE BRIAN WHO'S BEEN ALLOWED TO WIN BY HIS OPPONENTS ALL YEAR AS A MATTER OF COURSE THE GAME LOSES ALL SENSE OF CHALLENGE...
AND ON A DAY LIKE TODAY HE HAS NO WAY OF KNOWING THAT THE PRIZE HE'S WON IS ACTUALLY RICHLY DESERVED ON THE MERITS OF HIS GAME.
WHAT, THE UBIQUITOUS "PLAY BETTER GOLF" VIDEO?
EXACTLY. THE USELESS IDIOT OBVIOUSLY GENUINELY BELIEVES HE DOESN'T NEED TO WATCH IT.
CLAP
CLAP
CLAP
CLAP
CLAP
CLAP
CLAP

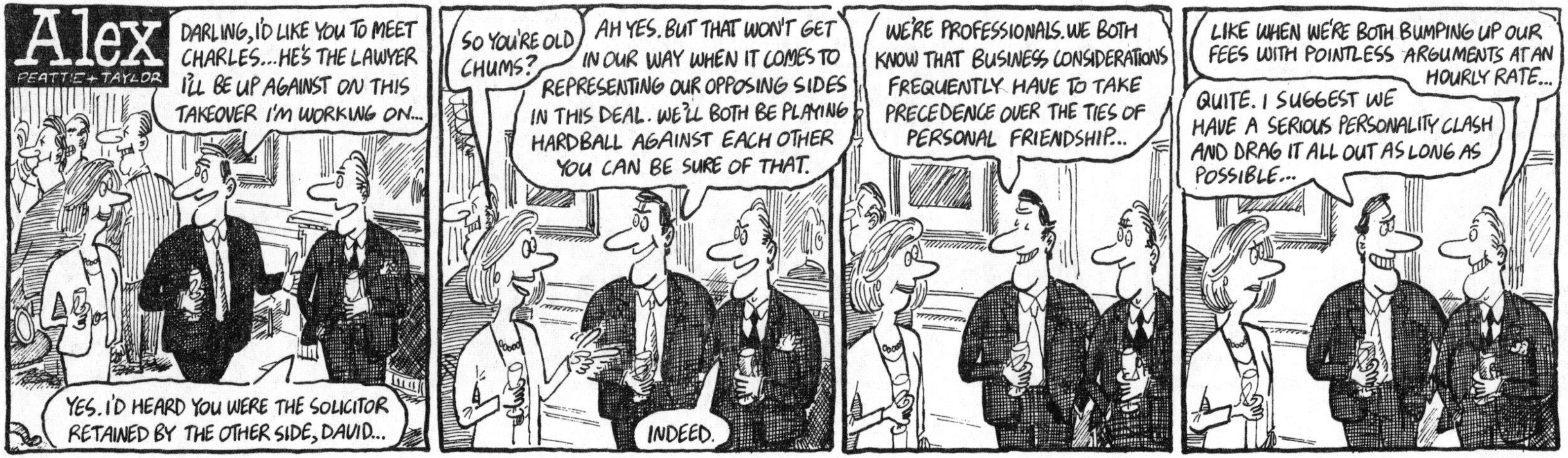
Alex
PEATTIE + TAYLOR
DARLING, I'D LIKE YOU TO MEET CHARLES...HE'S THE LAWYER I'LL BE UP AGAINST ON THIS TAKEOVER I'M WORKING ON...
YES. I'D HEARD YOU WERE THE SOLICITOR RETAINED BY THE OTHER SIDE, DAVID...
SO YOU'RE OLD CHUMS?
AH YES. BUT THAT WON'T GET IN OUR WAY WHEN IT COMES TO REPRESENTING OUR OPPOSING SIDES IN THIS DEAL. WE'LL BOTH BE PLAYING HARDBALL AGAINST EACH OTHER YOU CAN BE SURE OF THAT.
INDEED.
WE'RE PROFESSIONALS. WE BOTH KNOW THAT BUSINESS CONSIDERATIONS FREQUENTLY HAVE TO TAKE PRECEDENCE OVER THE TIES OF PERSONAL FRIENDSHIP...
LIKE WHEN WE'RE BOTH BUMPING UP OUR FEES WITH POINTLESS ARGUMENTS AT AN HOURLY RATE...
QUITE. I SUGGEST WE HAVE A SERIOUS PERSONALITY CLASH AND DRAG IT ALL OUT AS LONG AS POSSIBLE...

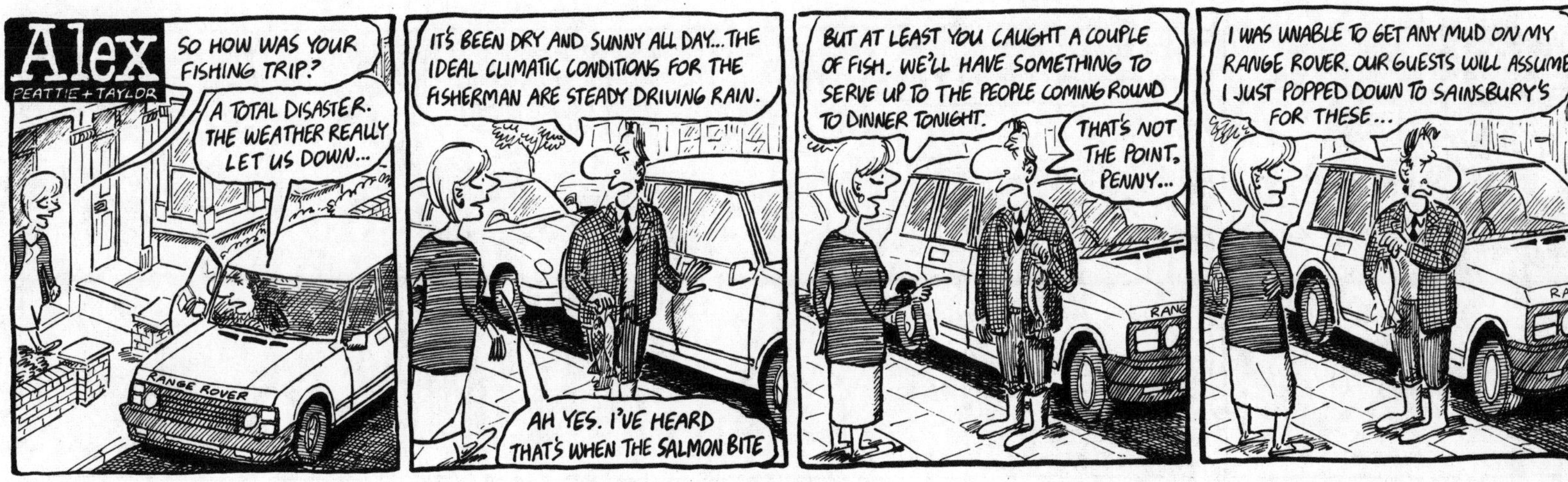
Alex
PEATTIE + TAYLOR
SO HOW WAS YOUR FISHING TRIP?
A TOTAL DISASTER. THE WEATHER REALLY LET US DOWN...
RANGE ROVER
IT'S BEEN DRY AND SUNNY ALL DAY... THE IDEAL CLIMATIC CONDITIONS FOR THE FISHERMAN ARE STEADY DRIVING RAIN.
AH YES. I'VE HEARD THAT'S WHEN THE SALMON BITE
BUT AT LEAST YOU CAUGHT A COUPLE OF FISH. WE'LL HAVE SOMETHING TO SERVE UP TO THE PEOPLE COMING ROUND TO DINNER TONIGHT.
THAT'S NOT THE POINT, PENNY...
I WAS UNABLE TO GET ANY MUD ON MY RANGE ROVER. OUR GUESTS WILL ASSUME I JUST POPPED DOWN TO SAINSBURY'S FOR THESE...

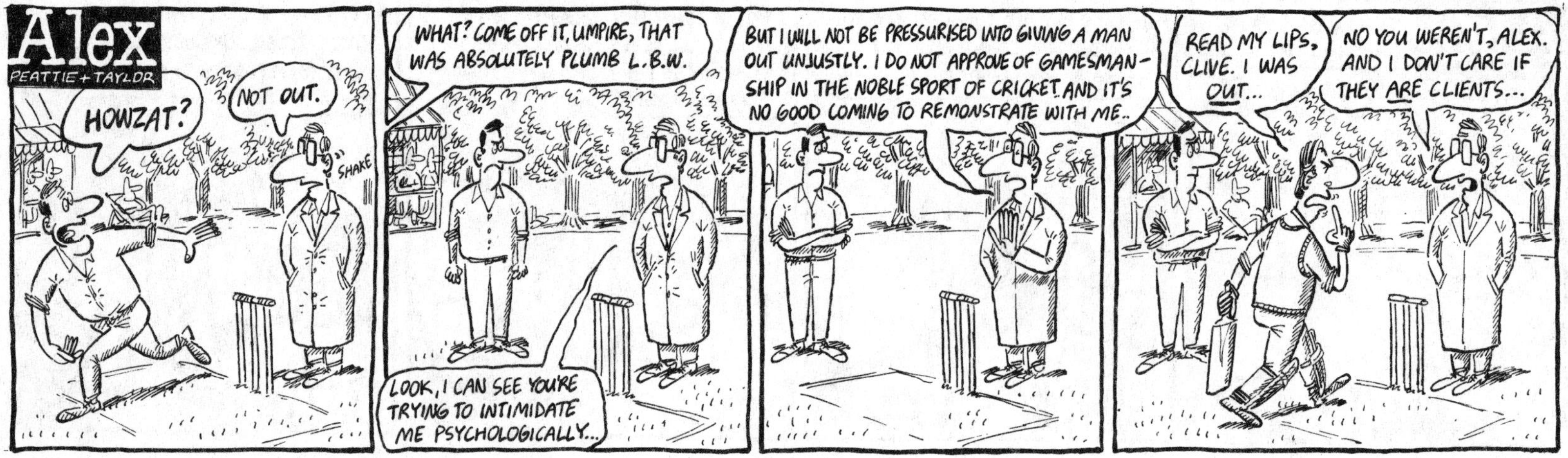
Alex
PEATTIE + TAYLOR
HOWZAT?
NOT OUT.
SHAKE
WHAT? COME OFF IT, UMPIRE, THAT WAS ABSOLUTELY PLUMB L.B.W.
LOOK, I CAN SEE YOU'RE TRYING TO INTIMIDATE ME PSYCHOLOGICALLY...
BUT I WILL NOT BE PRESSURISED INTO GIVING A MAN OUT UNJUSTLY. I DO NOT APPROVE OF GAMESMANSHIP IN THE NOBLE SPORT OF CRICKET. AND IT'S NO GOOD COMING TO REMONSTRATE WITH ME..
READ MY LIPS, CLIVE. I WAS OUT...
NO YOU WEREN'T, ALEX. AND I DON'T CARE IF THEY ARE CLIENTS...

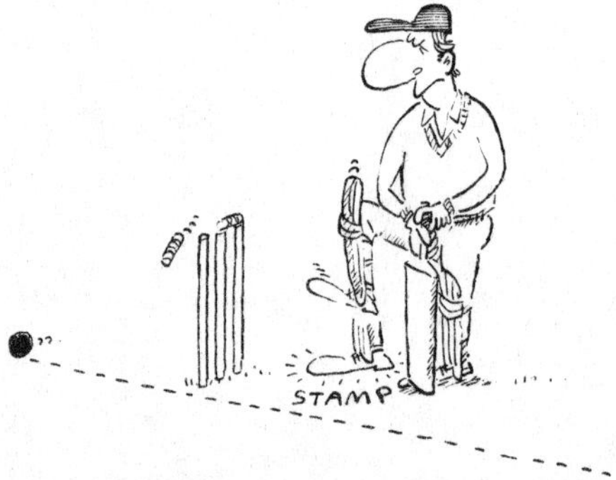
STAMP

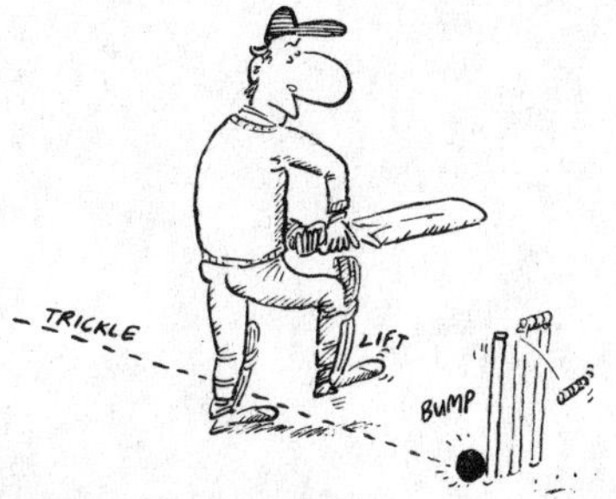
TRICKLE
LIFT
BUMP

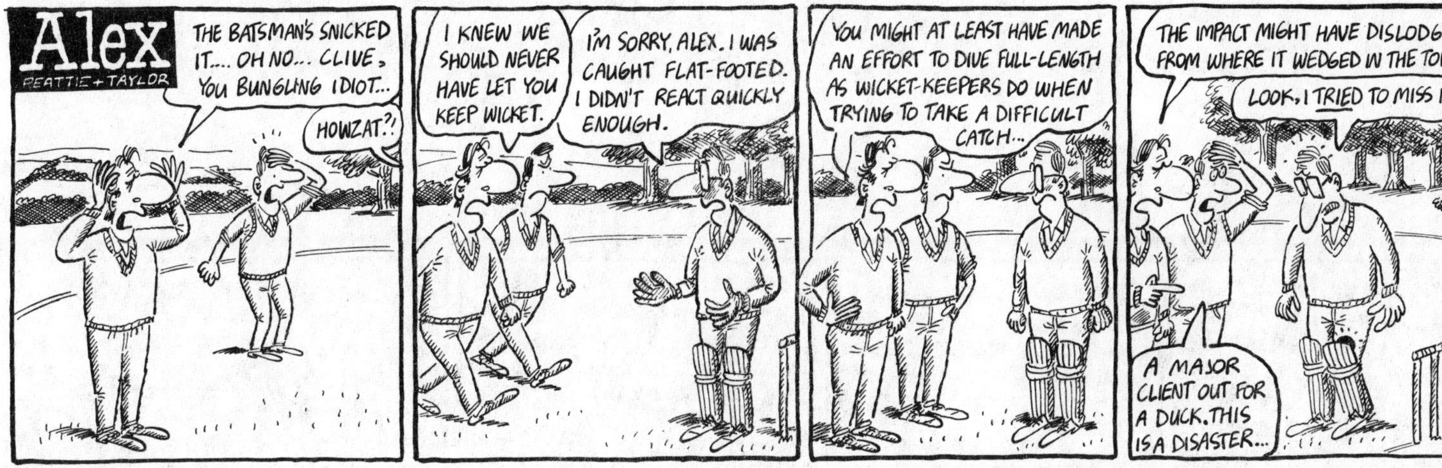
Alex
PEATTIE + TAYLOR
THE BATSMAN'S SNICKED IT.... OH NO... CLIVE, YOU BUNGLING IDIOT...
HOWZAT?!
I KNEW WE SHOULD NEVER HAVE LET YOU KEEP WICKET.
I'M SORRY, ALEX. I WAS CAUGHT FLAT-FOOTED. I DIDN'T REACT QUICKLY ENOUGH.
YOU MIGHT AT LEAST HAVE MADE AN EFFORT TO DIVE FULL-LENGTH AS WICKET-KEEPERS DO WHEN TRYING TO TAKE A DIFFICULT CATCH...
THE IMPACT MIGHT HAVE DISLODGED THE BALL FROM WHERE IT WEDGED IN THE TOP OF YOUR PAD...
LOOK, I TRIED TO MISS IT...
A MAJOR CLIENT OUT FOR A DUCK. THIS IS A DISASTER...

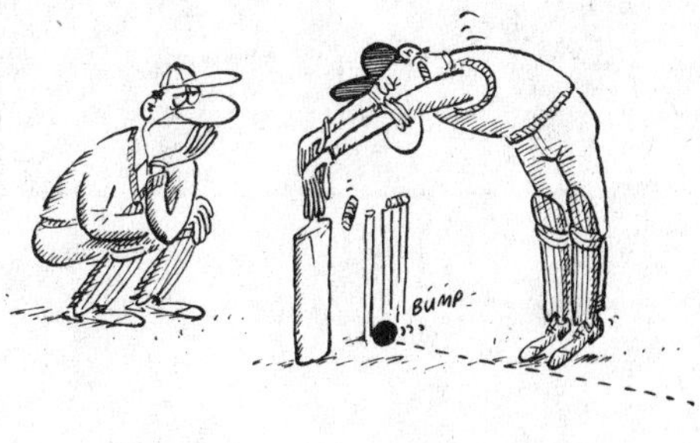
BUMP

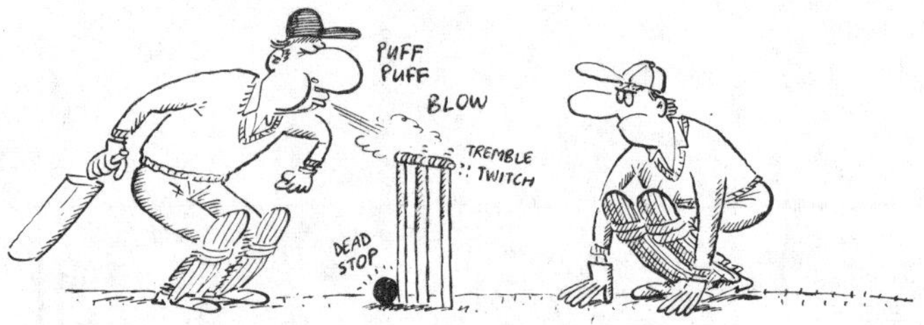
PUFF
PUFF
BLOW
TREMBLE
TWITCH
DEAD
STOP

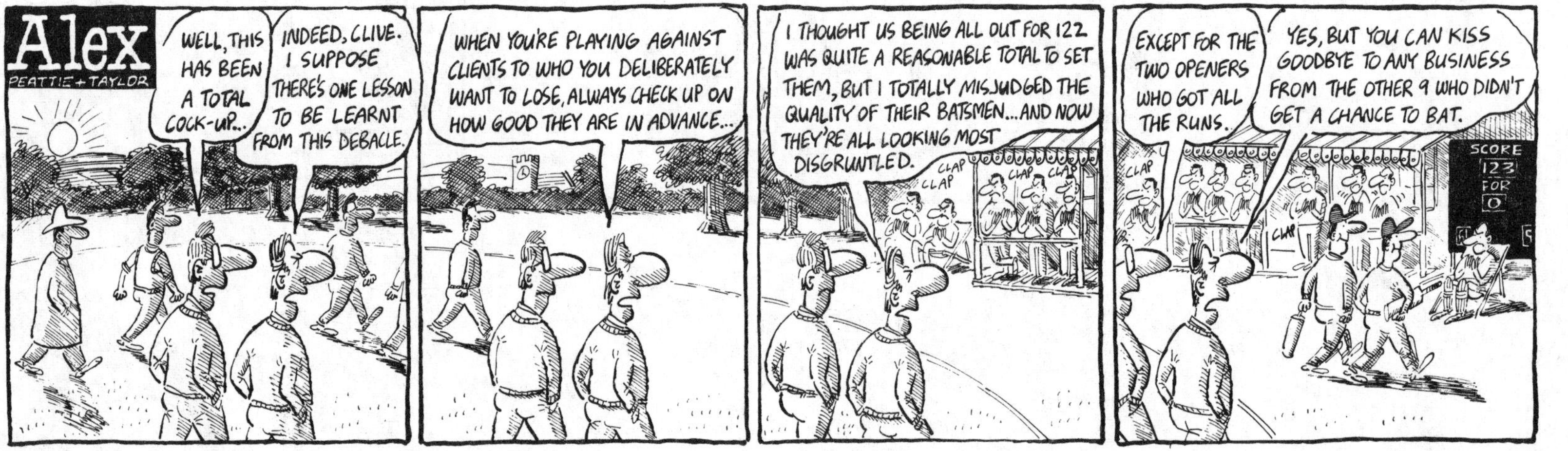
Alex
PEATTIE + TAYLOR
WELL, THIS HAS BEEN A TOTAL COCK-UP...
INDEED, CLIVE. I SUPPOSE THERE'S ONE LESSON TO BE LEARNT FROM THIS DEBACLE.
WHEN YOU'RE PLAYING AGAINST CLIENTS TO WHO YOU DELIBERATELY WANT TO LOSE, ALWAYS CHECK UP ON HOW GOOD THEY ARE IN ADVANCE...
I THOUGHT US BEING ALL OUT FOR 122 WAS QUITE A REASONABLE TOTAL TO SET THEM, BUT I TOTALLY MISJUDGED THE QUALITY OF THEIR BATSMEN... AND NOW THEY'RE ALL LOOKING MOST DISGRUNTLED.
CLAP
CLAP
CLAP
CLAP
EXCEPT FOR THE TWO OPENERS WHO GOT ALL THE RUNS.
YES, BUT YOU CAN KISS GOODBYE TO ANY BUSINESS FROM THE OTHER 9 WHO DIDN'T GET A CHANCE TO BAT.
CLAP
CLAP
SCORE
123
FOR
0
PEATTIE + TAYLOR

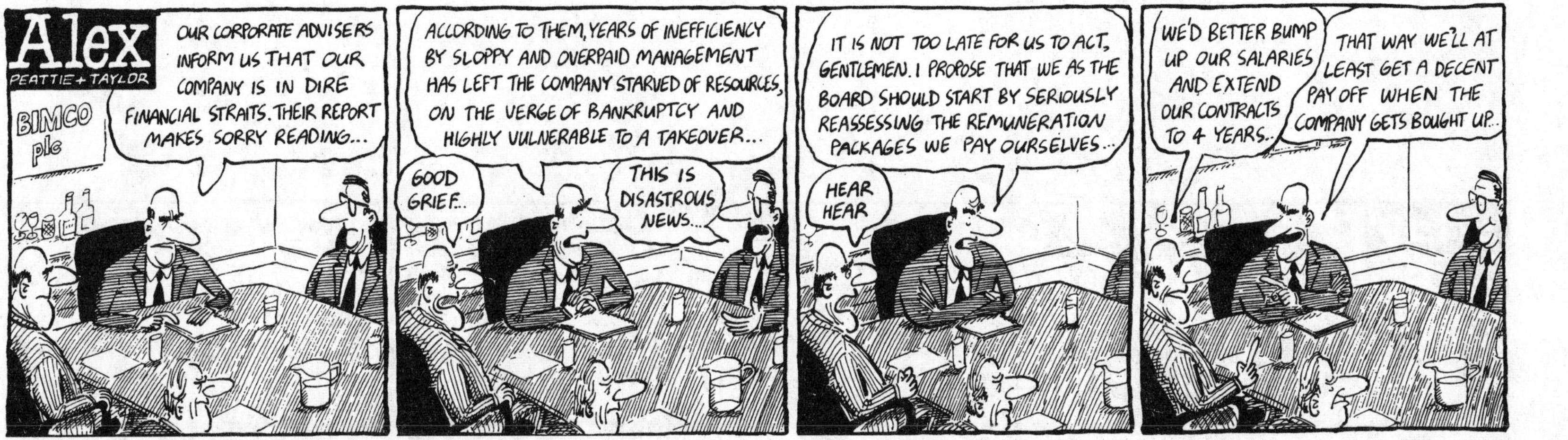
Alex
PEATTIE + TAYLOR
BIMCO plc
OUR CORPORATE ADVISERS INFORM US THAT OUR COMPANY IS IN DIRE FINANCIAL STRAITS. THEIR REPORT MAKES SORRY READING...
ACCORDING TO THEM, YEARS OF INEFFICIENCY BY SLOPPY AND OVERPAID MANAGEMENT HAS LEFT THE COMPANY STARVED OF RESOURCES, ON THE VERGE OF BANKRUPTCY AND HIGHLY VULNERABLE TO A TAKEOVER...
GOOD GRIEF..
THIS IS DISASTROUS NEWS...
IT IS NOT TOO LATE FOR US TO ACT, GENTLEMEN. I PROPOSE THAT WE AS THE BOARD SHOULD START BY SERIOUSLY REASSESSING THE REMUNERATION PACKAGES WE PAY OURSELVES...
HEAR HEAR
WE'D BETTER BUMP UP OUR SALARIES AND EXTEND OUR CONTRACTS TO 4 YEARS..
THAT WAY WE'LL AT LEAST GET A DECENT PAY OFF WHEN THE COMPANY GETS BOUGHT UP...

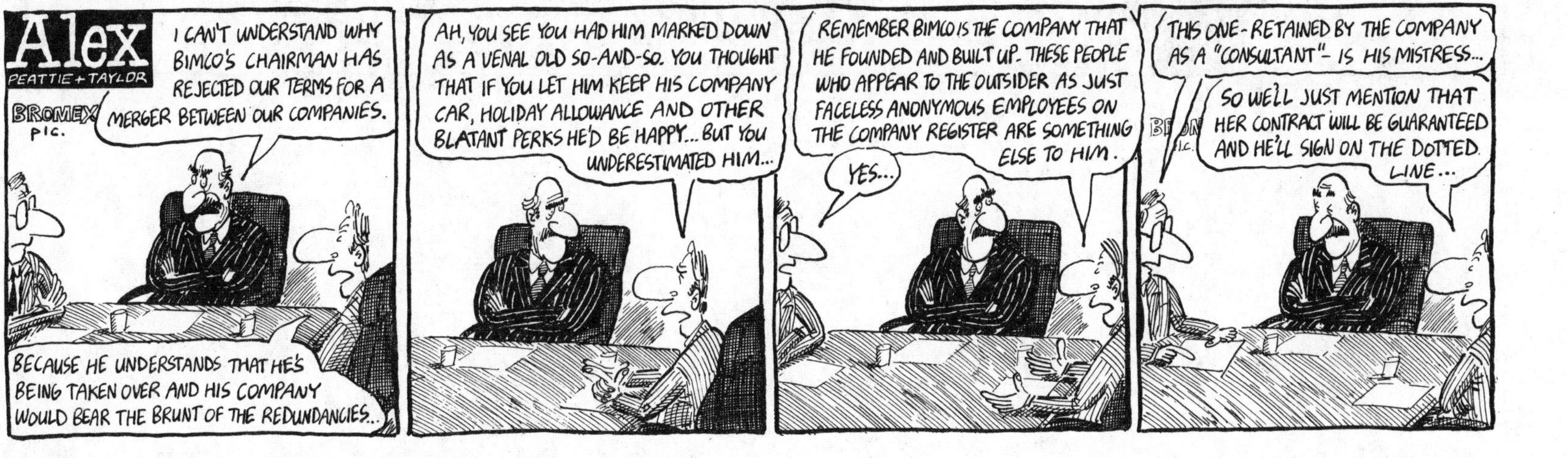
Alex
PEATTIE + TAYLOR
BROMEX plc.
I CAN'T UNDERSTAND WHY BIMCO'S CHAIRMAN HAS REJECTED OUR TERMS FOR A MERGER BETWEEN OUR COMPANIES.
BECAUSE HE UNDERSTANDS THAT HE'S BEING TAKEN OVER AND HIS COMPANY WOULD BEAR THE BRUNT OF THE REDUNDANCIES...
AH, YOU SEE YOU HAD HIM MARKED DOWN AS A VENAL OLD SO-AND-SO. YOU THOUGHT THAT IF YOU LET HIM KEEP HIS COMPANY CAR, HOLIDAY ALLOWANCE AND OTHER BLATANT PERKS HE'D BE HAPPY... BUT YOU UNDERESTIMATED HIM...
REMEMBER BIMCO IS THE COMPANY THAT HE FOUNDED AND BUILT UP. THESE PEOPLE WHO APPEAR TO THE OUTSIDER AS JUST FACELESS ANONYMOUS EMPLOYEES ON THE COMPANY REGISTER ARE SOMETHING ELSE TO HIM.
YES...
THIS ONE - RETAINED BY THE COMPANY AS A "CONSULTANT" - IS HIS MISTRESS...
SO WE'LL JUST MENTION THAT HER CONTRACT WILL BE GUARANTEED AND HE'LL SIGN ON THE DOTTED LINE...

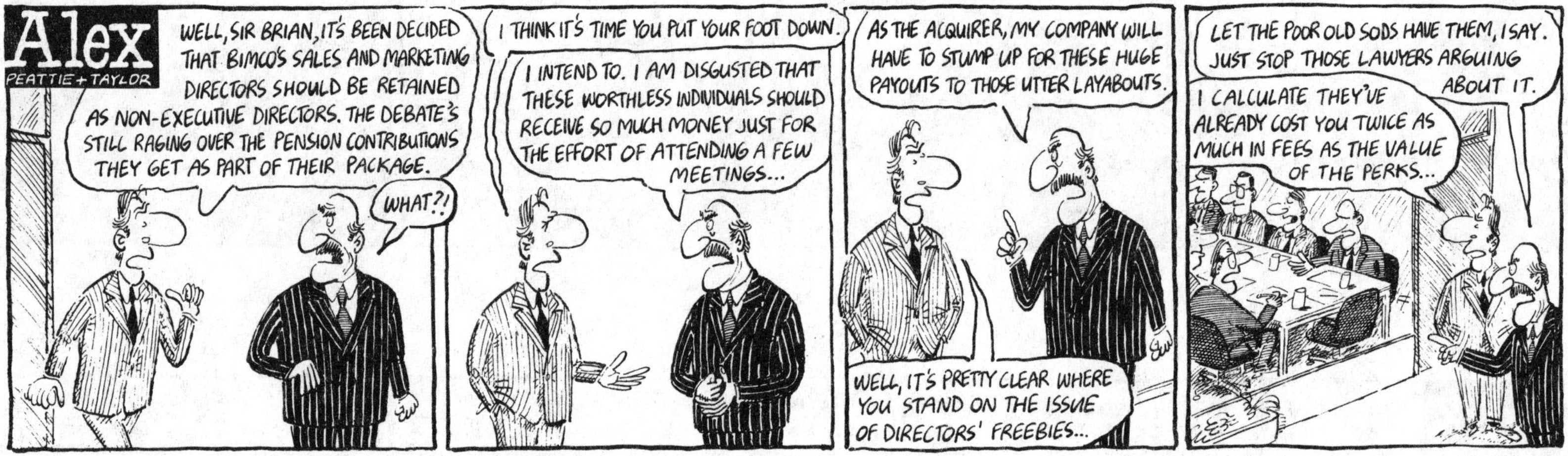
Alex
PEATTIE + TAYLOR
WELL, SIR BRIAN, IT'S BEEN DECIDED THAT BIMCO'S SALES AND MARKETING DIRECTORS SHOULD BE RETAINED AS NON-EXECUTIVE DIRECTORS. THE DEBATE'S STILL RAGING OVER THE PENSION CONTRIBUTIONS THEY GET AS PART OF THEIR PACKAGE.
WHAT?!
I THINK IT'S TIME YOU PUT YOUR FOOT DOWN.
I INTEND TO. I AM DISGUSTED THAT THESE WORTHLESS INDIVIDUALS SHOULD RECEIVE SO MUCH MONEY JUST FOR THE EFFORT OF ATTENDING A FEW MEETINGS...
AS THE ACQUIRER, MY COMPANY WILL HAVE TO STUMP UP FOR THESE HUGE PAYOUTS TO THOSE UTTER LAYABOUTS.
WELL, IT'S PRETTY CLEAR WHERE YOU STAND ON THE ISSUE OF DIRECTORS' FREEBIES...
LET THE POOR OLD SODS HAVE THEM, I SAY. JUST STOP THOSE LAWYERS ARGUING ABOUT IT.
I CALCULATE THEY'VE ALREADY COST YOU TWICE AS MUCH IN FEES AS THE VALUE OF THE PERKS...

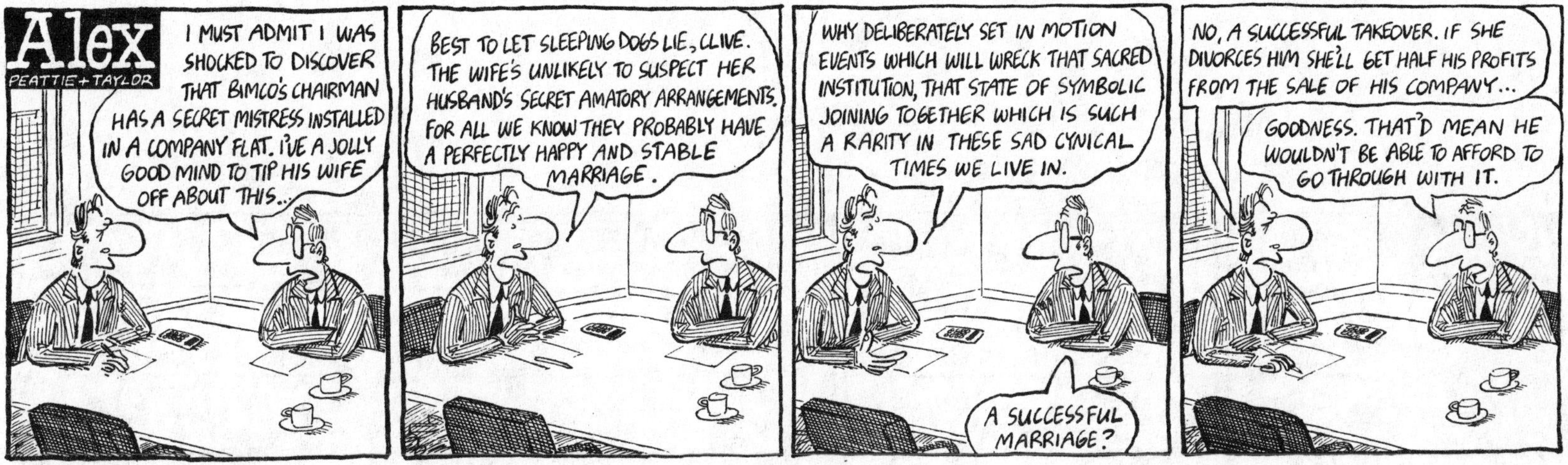
Alex
PEATTIE + TAYLOR
I MUST ADMIT I WAS SHOCKED TO DISCOVER THAT BIMCO'S CHAIRMAN HAS A SECRET MISTRESS INSTALLED IN A COMPANY FLAT. I'VE A JOLLY GOOD MIND TO TIP HIS WIFE OFF ABOUT THIS...
BEST TO LET SLEEPING DOGS LIE, CLIVE. THE WIFE'S UNLIKELY TO SUSPECT HER HUSBAND'S SECRET AMATORY ARRANGEMENTS. FOR ALL WE KNOW THEY PROBABLY HAVE A PERFECTLY HAPPY AND STABLE MARRIAGE.
WHY DELIBERATELY SET IN MOTION EVENTS WHICH WILL WRECK THAT SACRED INSTITUTION, THAT STATE OF SYMBOLIC JOINING TOGETHER WHICH IS SUCH A RARITY IN THESE SAD CYNICAL TIMES WE LIVE IN.
A SUCCESSFUL MARRIAGE?
NO, A SUCCESSFUL TAKEOVER. IF SHE DIVORCES HIM SHE'LL GET HALF HIS PROFITS FROM THE SALE OF HIS COMPANY...
GOODNESS. THAT'D MEAN HE WOULDN'T BE ABLE TO AFFORD TO GO THROUGH WITH IT.

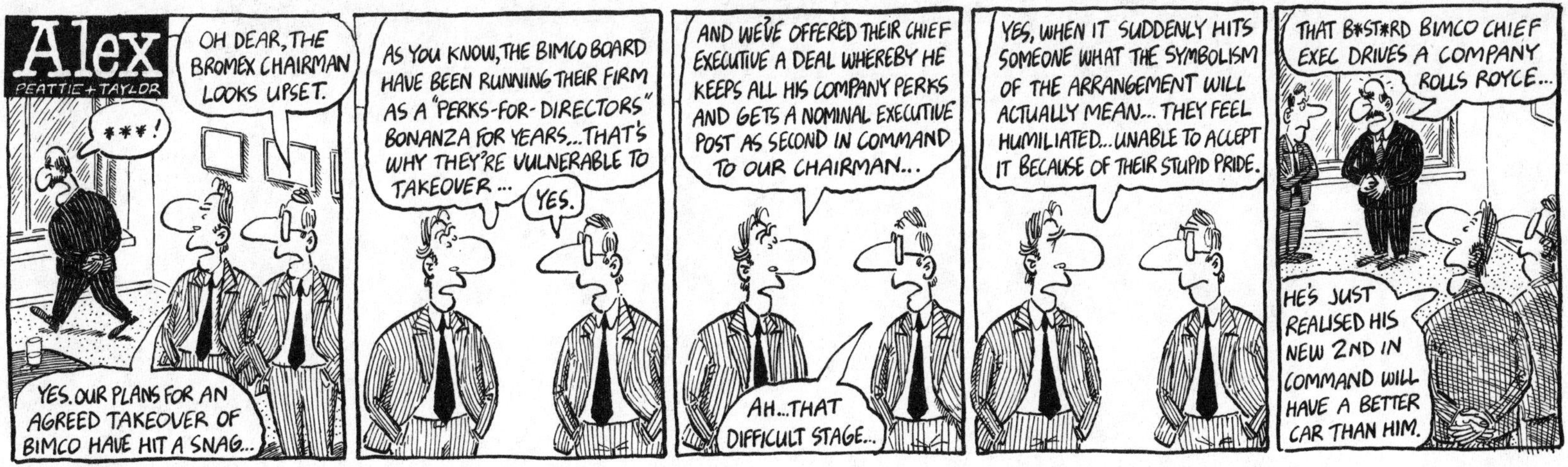
Alex
PEATTIE + TAYLOR
OH DEAR, THE BROMEX CHAIRMAN LOOKS UPSET.
***!
YES. OUR PLANS FOR AN AGREED TAKEOVER OF BIMCO HAVE HIT A SNAG...
AS YOU KNOW, THE BIMCO BOARD HAVE BEEN RUNNING THEIR FIRM AS A "PERKS-FOR-DIRECTORS" BONANZA FOR YEARS... THAT'S WHY THEY'RE VULNERABLE TO TAKEOVER...
YES.
AND WE'VE OFFERED THEIR CHIEF EXECUTIVE A DEAL WHEREBY HE KEEPS ALL HIS COMPANY PERKS AND GETS A NOMINAL EXECUTIVE POST AS SECOND IN COMMAND TO OUR CHAIRMAN...
AH... THAT DIFFICULT STAGE...
YES, WHEN IT SUDDENLY HITS SOMEONE WHAT THE SYMBOLISM OF THE ARRANGEMENT WILL ACTUALLY MEAN... THEY FEEL HUMILIATED... UNABLE TO ACCEPT IT BECAUSE OF THEIR STUPID PRIDE.
THAT B*ST*RD BIMCO CHIEF EXEC DRIVES A COMPANY ROLLS ROYCE...
HE'S JUST REALISED HIS NEW 2ND IN COMMAND WILL HAVE A BETTER CAR THAN HIM.

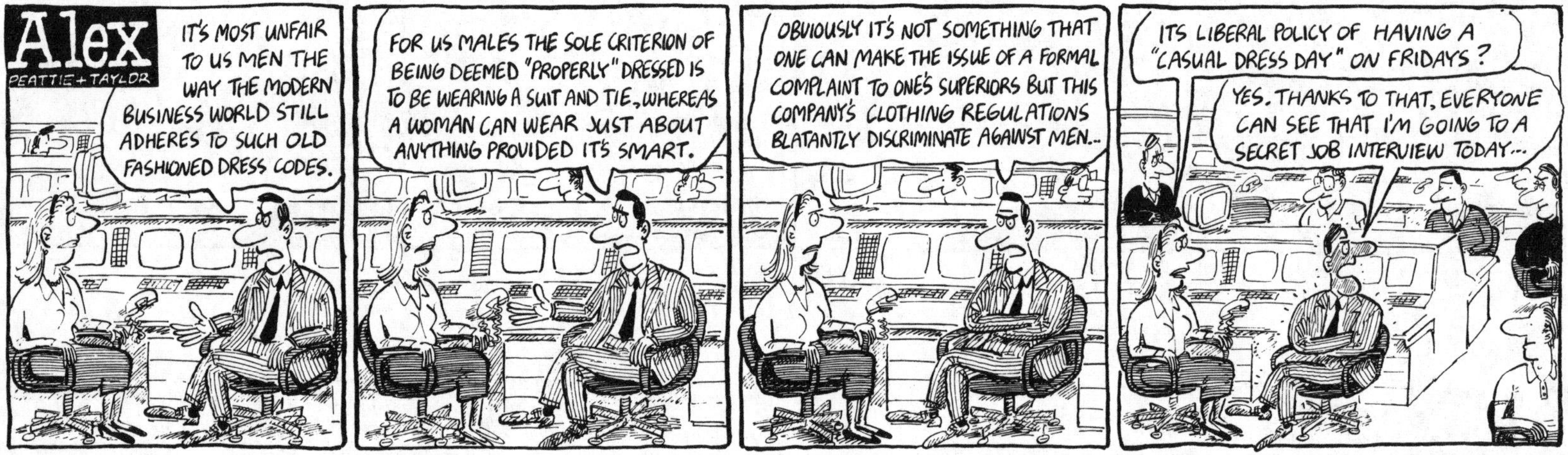
Alex
PEATTIE + TAYLOR
IT'S MOST UNFAIR TO US MEN THE WAY THE MODERN BUSINESS WORLD STILL ADHERES TO SUCH OLD FASHIONED DRESS CODES.
FOR US MALES THE SOLE CRITERION OF BEING DEEMED "PROPERLY" DRESSED IS TO BE WEARING A SUIT AND TIE, WHEREAS A WOMAN CAN WEAR JUST ABOUT ANYTHING PROVIDED IT'S SMART.
OBVIOUSLY IT'S NOT SOMETHING THAT ONE CAN MAKE THE ISSUE OF A FORMAL COMPLAINT TO ONE'S SUPERIORS BUT THIS COMPANY'S CLOTHING REGULATIONS BLATANTLY DISCRIMINATE AGAINST MEN...
ITS LIBERAL POLICY OF HAVING A "CASUAL DRESS DAY" ON FRIDAYS?
YES. THANKS TO THAT, EVERYONE CAN SEE THAT I'M GOING TO A SECRET JOB INTERVIEW TODAY...

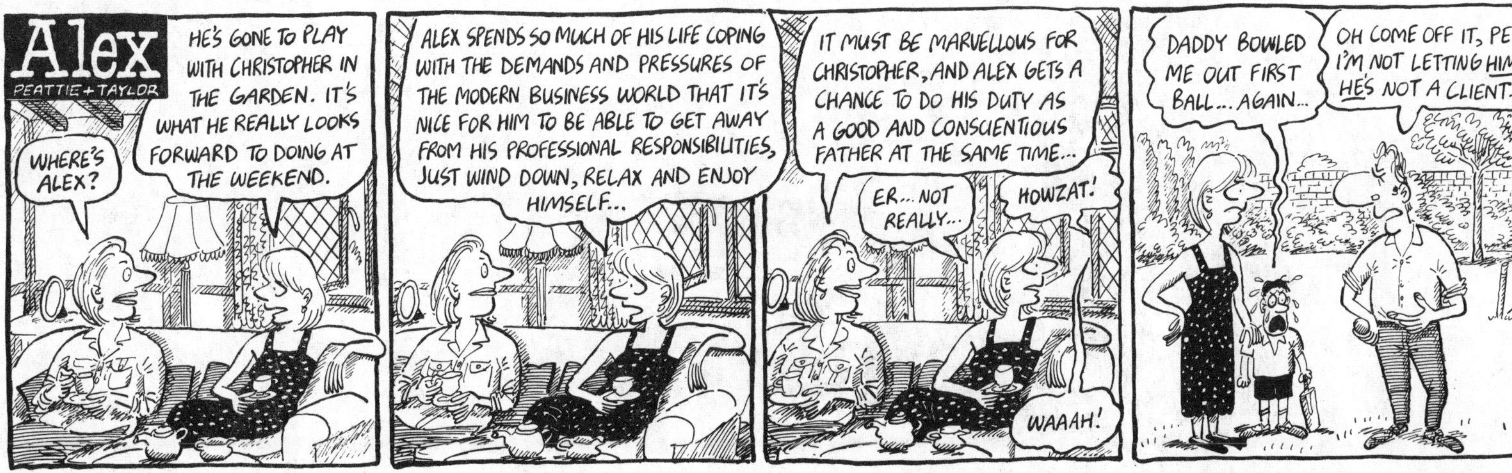
Alex
PEATTIE + TAYLOR
WHERE'S ALEX?
HE'S GONE TO PLAY WITH CHRISTOPHER IN THE GARDEN. IT'S WHAT HE REALLY LOOKS FORWARD TO DOING AT THE WEEKEND.
ALEX SPENDS SO MUCH OF HIS LIFE COPING WITH THE DEMANDS AND PRESSURES OF THE MODERN BUSINESS WORLD THAT IT'S NICE FOR HIM TO BE ABLE TO GET AWAY FROM HIS PROFESSIONAL RESPONSIBILITIES, JUST WIND DOWN, RELAX AND ENJOY HIMSELF...
IT MUST BE MARVELLOUS FOR CHRISTOPHER, AND ALEX GETS A CHANCE TO DO HIS DUTY AS A GOOD AND CONSCIENTIOUS FATHER AT THE SAME TIME...
ER... NOT REALLY...
HOWZAT!
WAAAH!
DADDY BOWLED ME OUT FIRST BALL... AGAIN...
OH COME OFF IT, PENNY. I'M NOT LETTING HIM WIN. HE'S NOT A CLIENT...

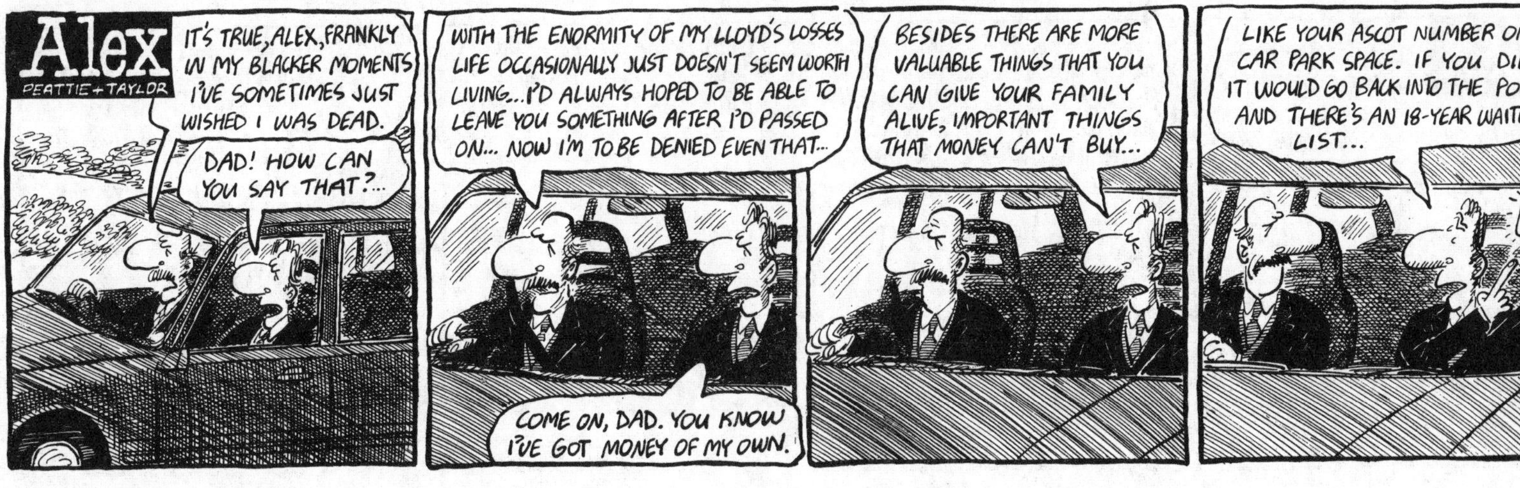
Alex
PEATTIE + TAYLOR
IT'S TRUE, ALEX, FRANKLY IN MY BLACKER MOMENTS I'VE SOMETIMES JUST WISHED I WAS DEAD.
DAD! HOW CAN YOU SAY THAT?...
WITH THE ENORMITY OF MY LLOYD'S LOSSES LIFE OCCASIONALLY JUST DOESN'T SEEM WORTH LIVING... I'D ALWAYS HOPED TO BE ABLE TO LEAVE YOU SOMETHING AFTER I'D PASSED ON... NOW I'M TO BE DENIED EVEN THAT...
COME ON, DAD. YOU KNOW I'VE GOT MONEY OF MY OWN.
BESIDES THERE ARE MORE VALUABLE THINGS THAT YOU CAN GIVE YOUR FAMILY ALIVE, IMPORTANT THINGS THAT MONEY CAN'T BUY...
LIKE YOUR ASCOT NUMBER ONE CAR PARK SPACE. IF YOU DIED IT WOULD GO BACK INTO THE POOL AND THERE'S AN 18-YEAR WAITING LIST...
ASCOT No 1

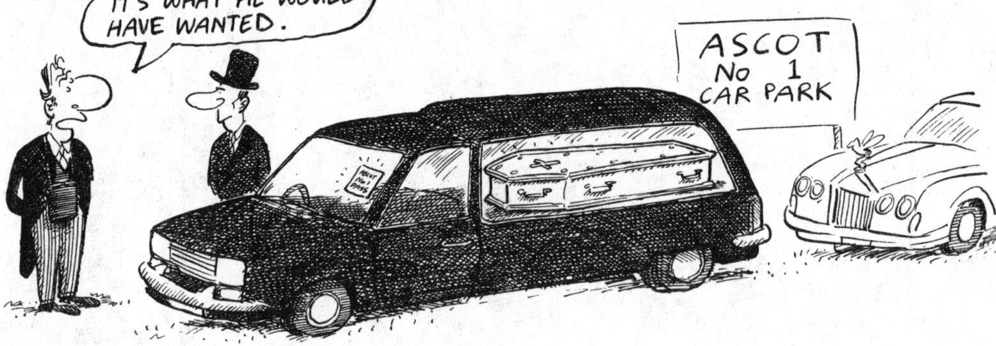
IT'S WHAT HE WOULD HAVE WANTED.
ASCOT No 1 CAR PARK

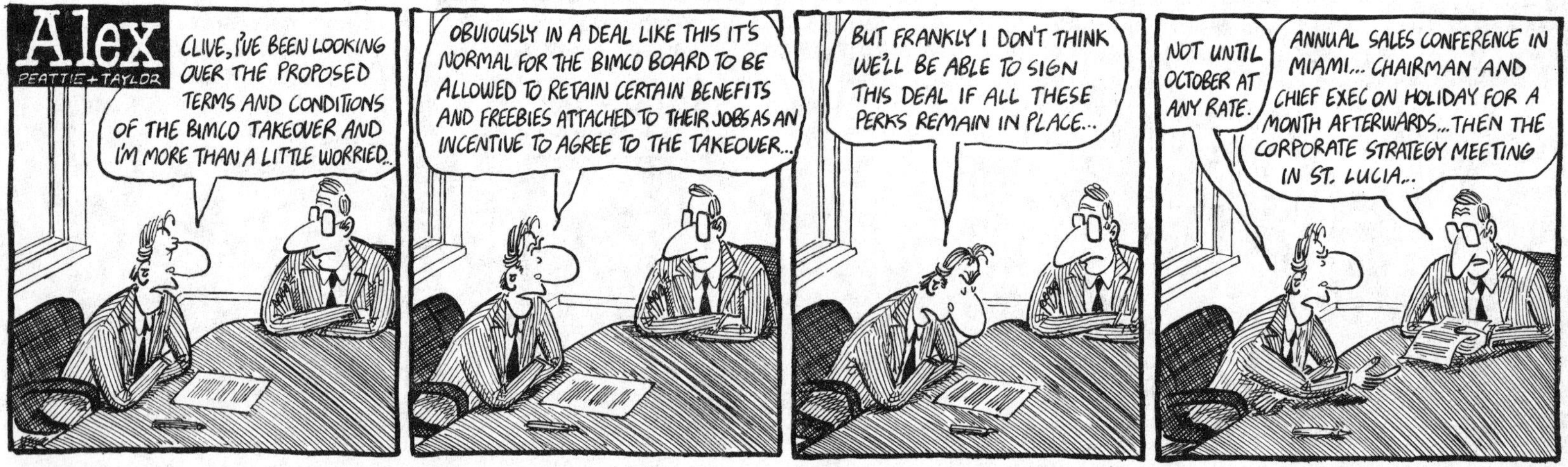
Alex
PEATTIE + TAYLOR
CLIVE, I'VE BEEN LOOKING OVER THE PROPOSED TERMS AND CONDITIONS OF THE BIMCO TAKEOVER AND I'M MORE THAN A LITTLE WORRIED...
OBVIOUSLY IN A DEAL LIKE THIS IT'S NORMAL FOR THE BIMCO BOARD TO BE ALLOWED TO RETAIN CERTAIN BENEFITS AND FREEBIES ATTACHED TO THEIR JOBS AS AN INCENTIVE TO AGREE TO THE TAKEOVER...
BUT FRANKLY I DON'T THINK WE'LL BE ABLE TO SIGN THIS DEAL IF ALL THESE PERKS REMAIN IN PLACE...
NOT UNTIL OCTOBER AT ANY RATE.
ANNUAL SALES CONFERENCE IN MIAMI... CHAIRMAN AND CHIEF EXEC ON HOLIDAY FOR A MONTH AFTERWARDS... THEN THE CORPORATE STRATEGY MEETING IN ST. LUCIA...

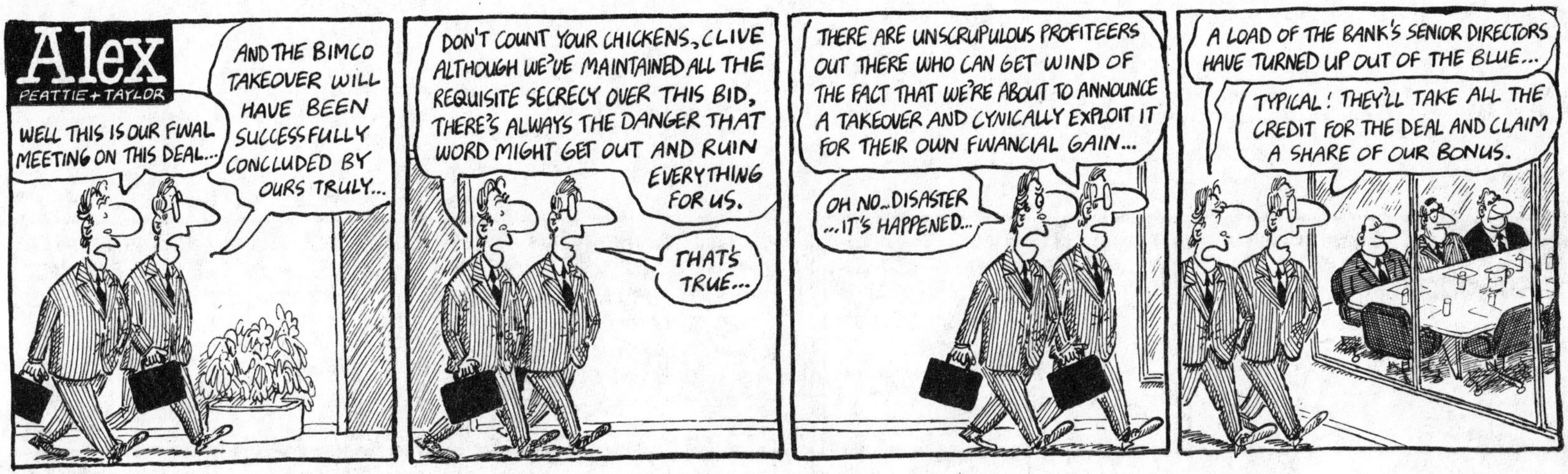
Alex
PEATTIE + TAYLOR
WELL THIS IS OUR FINAL MEETING ON THIS DEAL...
AND THE BIMCO TAKEOVER WILL HAVE BEEN SUCCESSFULLY CONCLUDED BY OURS TRULY...
DON'T COUNT YOUR CHICKENS, CLIVE ALTHOUGH WE'VE MAINTAINED ALL THE REQUISITE SECRECY OVER THIS BID, THERE'S ALWAYS THE DANGER THAT WORD MIGHT GET OUT AND RUIN EVERYTHING FOR US.
THAT'S TRUE...
THERE ARE UNSCRUPULOUS PROFITEERS OUT THERE WHO CAN GET WIND OF THE FACT THAT WE'RE ABOUT TO ANNOUNCE A TAKEOVER AND CYNICALLY EXPLOIT IT FOR THEIR OWN FINANCIAL GAIN...
OH NO...DISASTER ...IT'S HAPPENED...
A LOAD OF THE BANK'S SENIOR DIRECTORS HAVE TURNED UP OUT OF THE BLUE...
TYPICAL! THEY'LL TAKE ALL THE CREDIT FOR THE DEAL AND CLAIM A SHARE OF OUR BONUS.

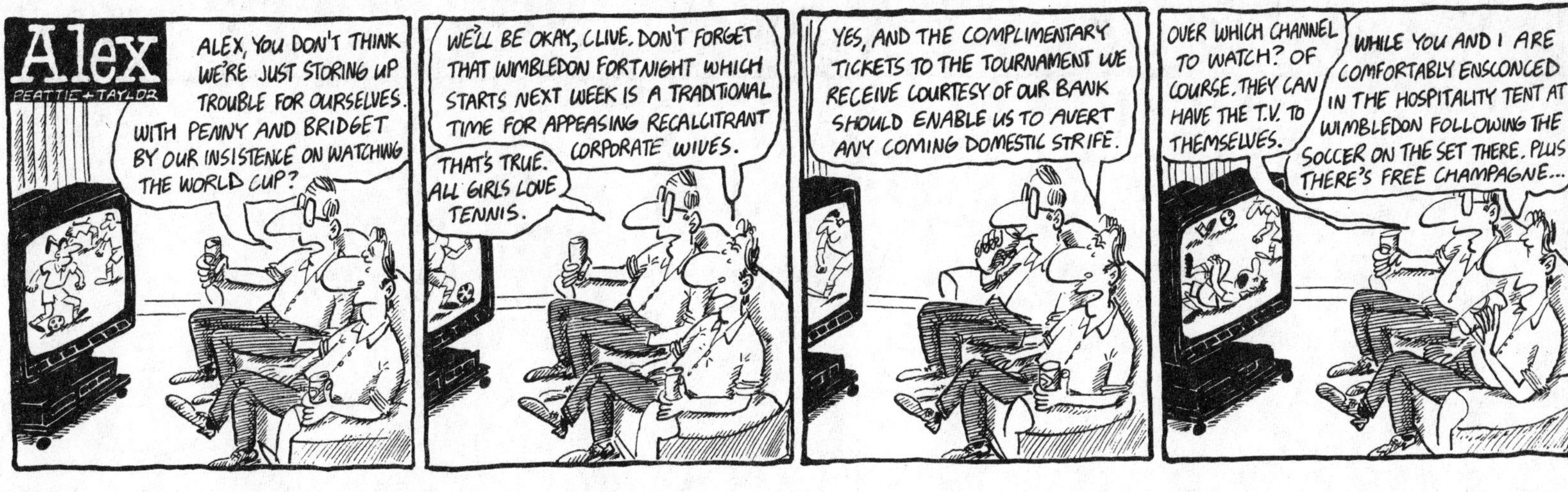
Alex
PEATTIE + TAYLOR
ALEX, YOU DON'T THINK WE'RE JUST STORING UP TROUBLE FOR OURSELVES. WITH PENNY AND BRIDGET BY OUR INSISTENCE ON WATCHING THE WORLD CUP?
WE'LL BE OKAY, CLIVE. DON'T FORGET THAT WIMBLEDON FORTNIGHT WHICH STARTS NEXT WEEK IS A TRADITIONAL TIME FOR APPEASING RECALCITRANT CORPORATE WIVES.
THAT'S TRUE. ALL GIRLS LOVE TENNIS.
YES, AND THE COMPLIMENTARY TICKETS TO THE TOURNAMENT WE RECEIVE COURTESY OF OUR BANK SHOULD ENABLE US TO AVERT ANY COMING DOMESTIC STRIFE.
OVER WHICH CHANNEL TO WATCH? OF COURSE, THEY CAN HAVE THE T.V. TO THEMSELVES.
WHILE YOU AND I ARE COMFORTABLY ENSCONCED IN THE HOSPITALITY TENT AT WIMBLEDON FOLLOWING THE SOCCER ON THE SET THERE. PLUS THERE'S FREE CHAMPAGNE...

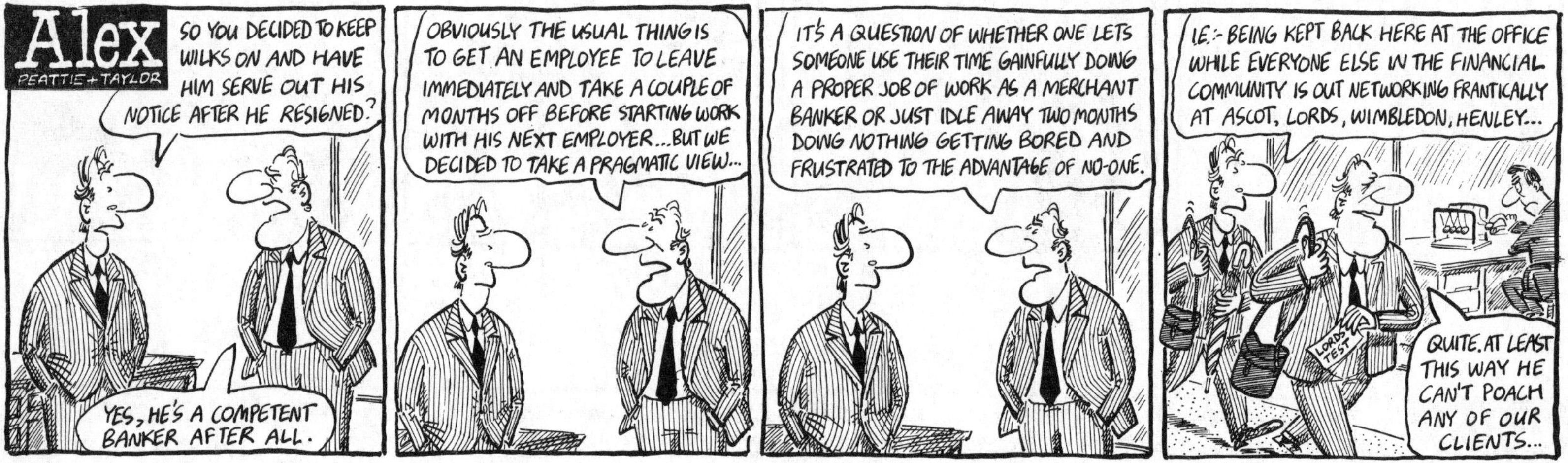
Alex
PEATTIE + TAYLOR
SO YOU DECIDED TO KEEP WILKS ON AND HAVE HIM SERVE OUT HIS NOTICE AFTER HE RESIGNED?
YES, HE'S A COMPETENT BANKER AFTER ALL.
OBVIOUSLY THE USUAL THING IS TO GET AN EMPLOYEE TO LEAVE IMMEDIATELY AND TAKE A COUPLE OF MONTHS OFF BEFORE STARTING WORK WITH HIS NEXT EMPLOYER... BUT WE DECIDED TO TAKE A PRAGMATIC VIEW...
IT'S A QUESTION OF WHETHER ONE LETS SOMEONE USE THEIR TIME GAINFULLY DOING A PROPER JOB OF WORK AS A MERCHANT BANKER OR JUST IDLE AWAY TWO MONTHS DOING NOTHING GETTING BORED AND FRUSTRATED TO THE ADVANTAGE OF NO-ONE.
I.E.:- BEING KEPT BACK HERE AT THE OFFICE WHILE EVERYONE ELSE IN THE FINANCIAL COMMUNITY IS OUT NETWORKING FRANTICALLY AT ASCOT, LORDS, WIMBLEDON, HENLEY...
LORDS TEST
QUITE. AT LEAST THIS WAY HE CAN'T POACH ANY OF OUR CLIENTS...

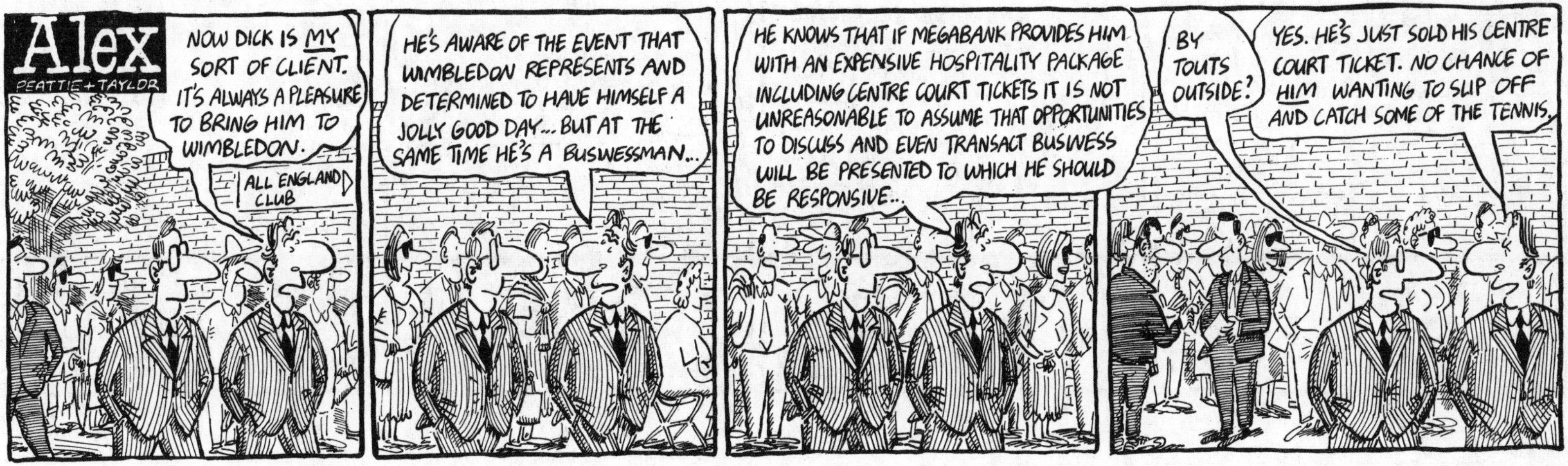
Alex
PEATTIE + TAYLOR
NOW DICK IS MY SORT OF CLIENT. IT'S ALWAYS A PLEASURE TO BRING HIM TO WIMBLEDON.
ALL ENGLAND CLUB
HE'S AWARE OF THE EVENT THAT WIMBLEDON REPRESENTS AND DETERMINED TO HAVE HIMSELF A JOLLY GOOD DAY... BUT AT THE SAME TIME HE'S A BUSINESSMAN...
HE KNOWS THAT IF MEGABANK PROVIDES HIM WITH AN EXPENSIVE HOSPITALITY PACKAGE INCLUDING CENTRE COURT TICKETS IT IS NOT UNREASONABLE TO ASSUME THAT OPPORTUNITIES TO DISCUSS AND EVEN TRANSACT BUSINESS WILL BE PRESENTED TO WHICH HE SHOULD BE RESPONSIVE...
BY TOUTS OUTSIDE?
YES. HE'S JUST SOLD HIS CENTRE COURT TICKET. NO CHANCE OF HIM WANTING TO SLIP OFF AND CATCH SOME OF THE TENNIS.

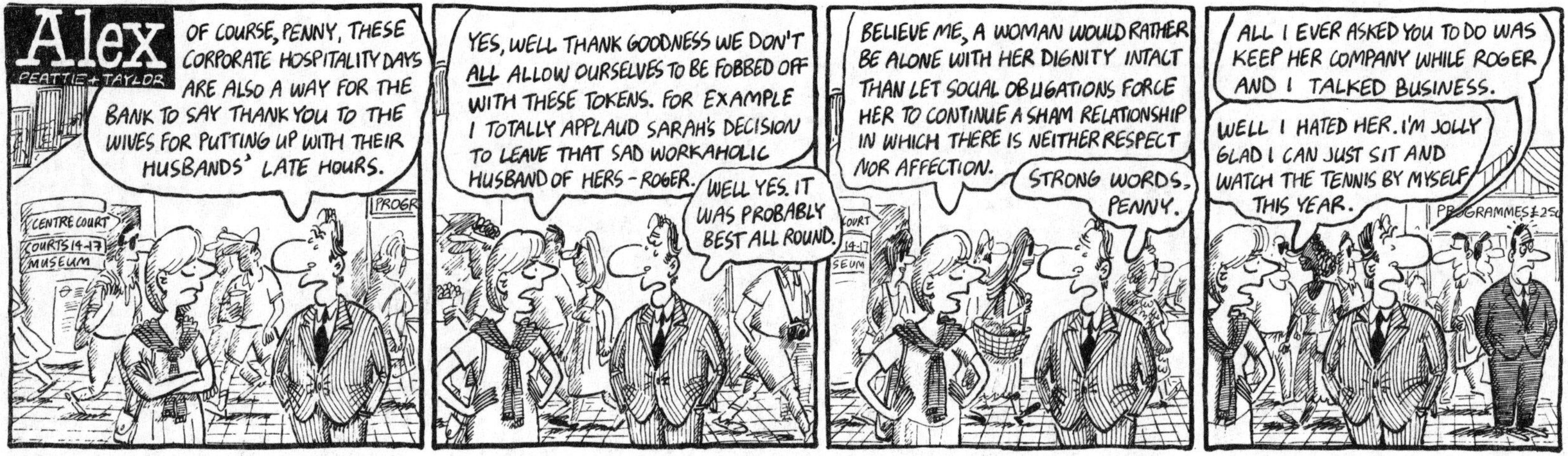
Alex
PEATTIE + TAYLOR
OF COURSE, PENNY, THESE CORPORATE HOSPITALITY DAYS ARE ALSO A WAY FOR THE BANK TO SAY THANK YOU TO THE WIVES FOR PUTTING UP WITH THEIR HUSBANDS' LATE HOURS.
CENTRE COURT
COURTS 14-17
MUSEUM
YES, WELL THANK GOODNESS WE DON'T ALL ALLOW OURSELVES TO BE FOBBED OFF WITH THESE TOKENS. FOR EXAMPLE I TOTALLY APPLAUD SARAH'S DECISION TO LEAVE THAT SAD WORKAHOLIC HUSBAND OF HERS - ROGER.
WELL YES. IT WAS PROBABLY BEST ALL ROUND.
BELIEVE ME, A WOMAN WOULD RATHER BE ALONE WITH HER DIGNITY INTACT THAN LET SOCIAL OBLIGATIONS FORCE HER TO CONTINUE A SHAM RELATIONSHIP IN WHICH THERE IS NEITHER RESPECT NOR AFFECTION.
STRONG WORDS, PENNY.
ALL I EVER ASKED YOU TO DO WAS KEEP HER COMPANY WHILE ROGER AND I TALKED BUSINESS.
WELL I HATED HER. I'M JOLLY GLAD I CAN JUST SIT AND WATCH THE TENNIS BY MYSELF THIS YEAR.

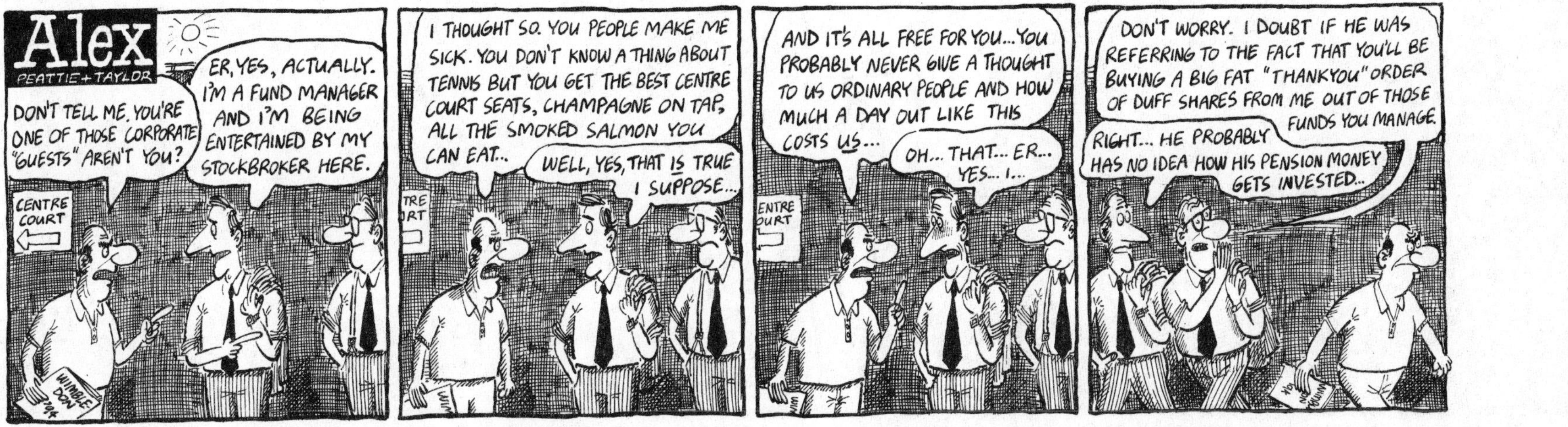

Alex
PEATTIE + TAYLOR
DON'T TELL ME. YOU'RE ONE OF THOSE CORPORATE "GUESTS" AREN'T YOU?
ER, YES, ACTUALLY. I'M A FUND MANAGER AND I'M BEING ENTERTAINED BY MY STOCKBROKER HERE.
CENTRE COURT
I THOUGHT SO. YOU PEOPLE MAKE ME SICK. YOU DON'T KNOW A THING ABOUT TENNIS BUT YOU GET THE BEST CENTRE COURT SEATS, CHAMPAGNE ON TAP, ALL THE SMOKED SALMON YOU CAN EAT...
WELL, YES, THAT IS TRUE I SUPPOSE...
AND IT'S ALL FREE FOR YOU... YOU PROBABLY NEVER GIVE A THOUGHT TO US ORDINARY PEOPLE AND HOW MUCH A DAY OUT LIKE THIS COSTS US...
OH... THAT... ER... YES... I...
DON'T WORRY. I DOUBT IF HE WAS REFERRING TO THE FACT THAT YOU'LL BE BUYING A BIG FAT "THANKYOU" ORDER OF DUFF SHARES FROM ME OUT OF THOSE FUNDS YOU MANAGE.
RIGHT... HE PROBABLY HAS NO IDEA HOW HIS PENSION MONEY GETS INVESTED...

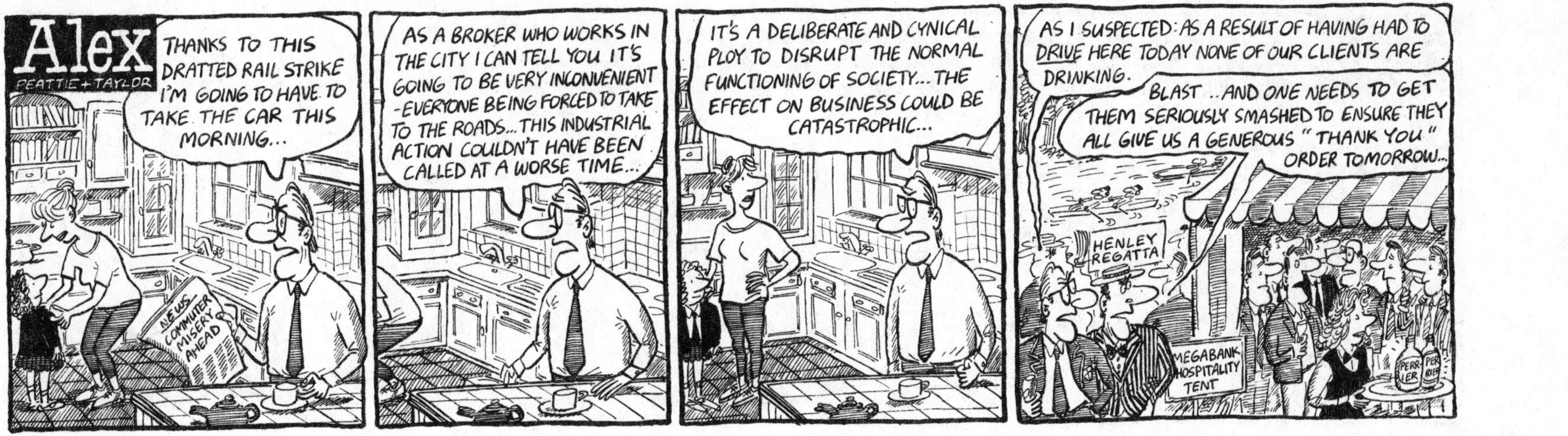

Alex
PEATTIE + TAYLOR
THANKS TO THIS DRATTED RAIL STRIKE I'M GOING TO HAVE TO TAKE THE CAR THIS MORNING...
NEWS COMMUTER MISERY AHEAD
AS A BROKER WHO WORKS IN THE CITY I CAN TELL YOU IT'S GOING TO BE VERY INCONVENIENT - EVERYONE BEING FORCED TO TAKE TO THE ROADS... THIS INDUSTRIAL ACTION COULDN'T HAVE BEEN CALLED AT A WORSE TIME...
IT'S A DELIBERATE AND CYNICAL PLOY TO DISRUPT THE NORMAL FUNCTIONING OF SOCIETY... THE EFFECT ON BUSINESS COULD BE CATASTROPHIC...
AS I SUSPECTED: AS A RESULT OF HAVING HAD TO DRIVE HERE TODAY NONE OF OUR CLIENTS ARE DRINKING.
BLAST .. AND ONE NEEDS TO GET THEM SERIOUSLY SMASHED TO ENSURE THEY ALL GIVE US A GENEROUS "THANK YOU" ORDER TOMORROW...
HENLEY REGATTA
MEGABANK HOSPITALITY TENT
PERRIER
PERRIER

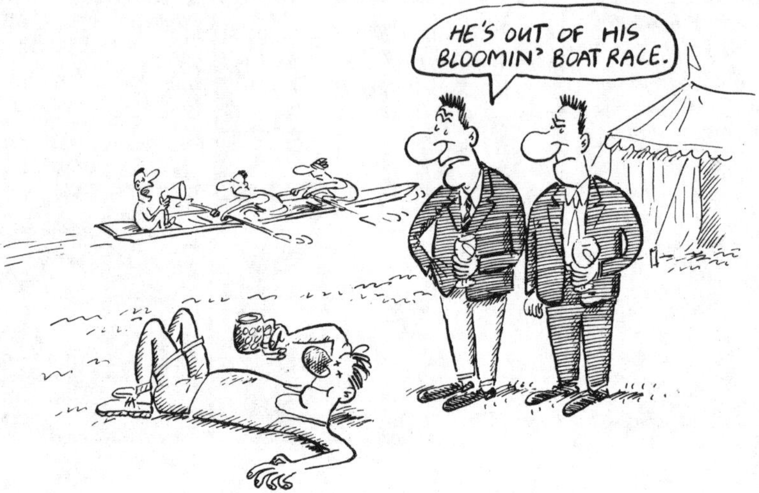
HE'S OUT OF HIS BLOOMIN' BOAT RACE.

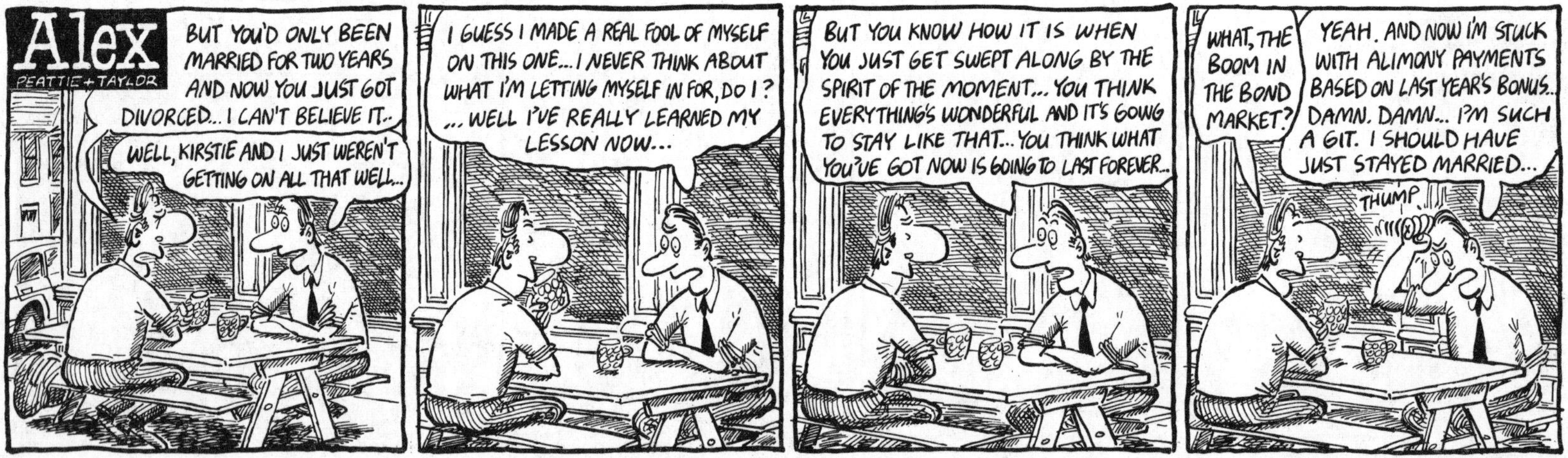
Alex
PEATTIE + TAYLOR
BUT YOU'D ONLY BEEN MARRIED FOR TWO YEARS AND NOW YOU JUST GOT DIVORCED... I CAN'T BELIEVE IT..
WELL, KIRSTIE AND I JUST WEREN'T GETTING ON ALL THAT WELL...
I GUESS I MADE A REAL FOOL OF MYSELF ON THIS ONE... I NEVER THINK ABOUT WHAT I'M LETTING MYSELF IN FOR, DO I? ... WELL I'VE REALLY LEARNED MY LESSON NOW...
BUT YOU KNOW HOW IT IS WHEN YOU JUST GET SWEPT ALONG BY THE SPIRIT OF THE MOMENT... YOU THINK EVERYTHING'S WONDERFUL AND IT'S GOING TO STAY LIKE THAT... YOU THINK WHAT YOU'VE GOT NOW IS GOING TO LAST FOREVER...
WHAT, THE BOOM IN THE BOND MARKET?
YEAH. AND NOW I'M STUCK WITH ALIMONY PAYMENTS BASED ON LAST YEAR'S BONUS... DAMN. DAMN... I'M SUCH A GIT. I SHOULD HAVE JUST STAYED MARRIED...
THUMP

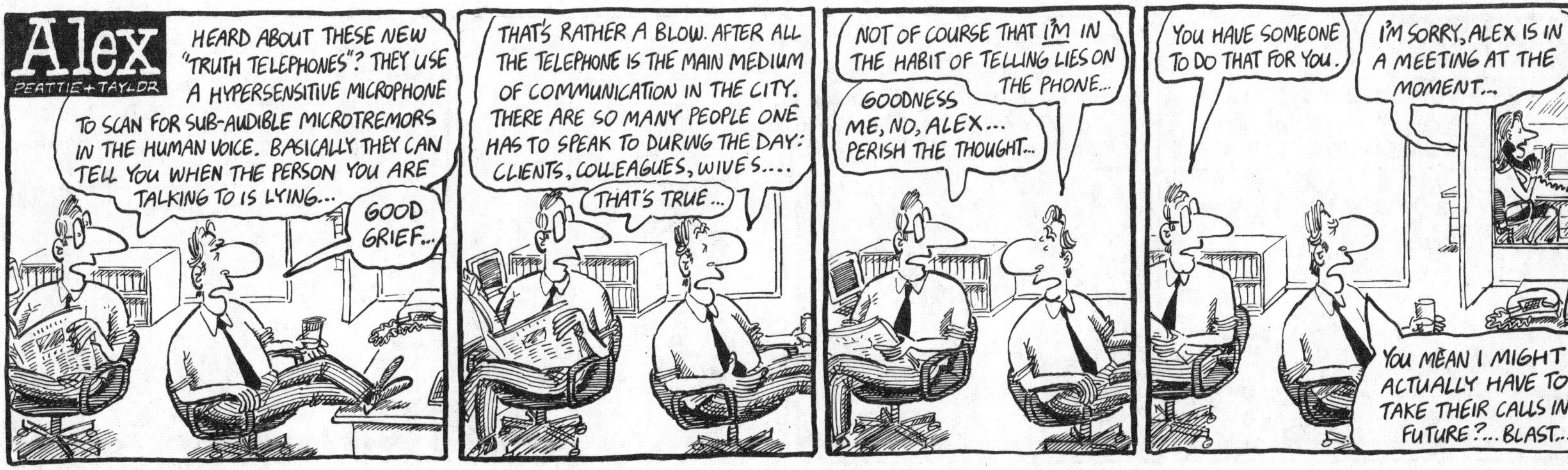
Alex
PEATTIE + TAYLOR
HEARD ABOUT THESE NEW "TRUTH TELEPHONES"? THEY USE A HYPERSENSITIVE MICROPHONE TO SCAN FOR SUB-AUDIBLE MICROTREMORS IN THE HUMAN VOICE. BASICALLY THEY CAN TELL YOU WHEN THE PERSON YOU ARE TALKING TO IS LYING...
GOOD GRIEF...
THAT'S RATHER A BLOW. AFTER ALL THE TELEPHONE IS THE MAIN MEDIUM OF COMMUNICATION IN THE CITY. THERE ARE SO MANY PEOPLE ONE HAS TO SPEAK TO DURING THE DAY: CLIENTS, COLLEAGUES, WIVES....
THAT'S TRUE...
NOT OF COURSE THAT I'M IN THE HABIT OF TELLING LIES ON THE PHONE...
GOODNESS ME, NO, ALEX... PERISH THE THOUGHT...
YOU HAVE SOMEONE TO DO THAT FOR YOU.
I'M SORRY, ALEX IS IN A MEETING AT THE MOMENT...
YOU MEAN I MIGHT ACTUALLY HAVE TO TAKE THEIR CALLS IN FUTURE?... BLAST...

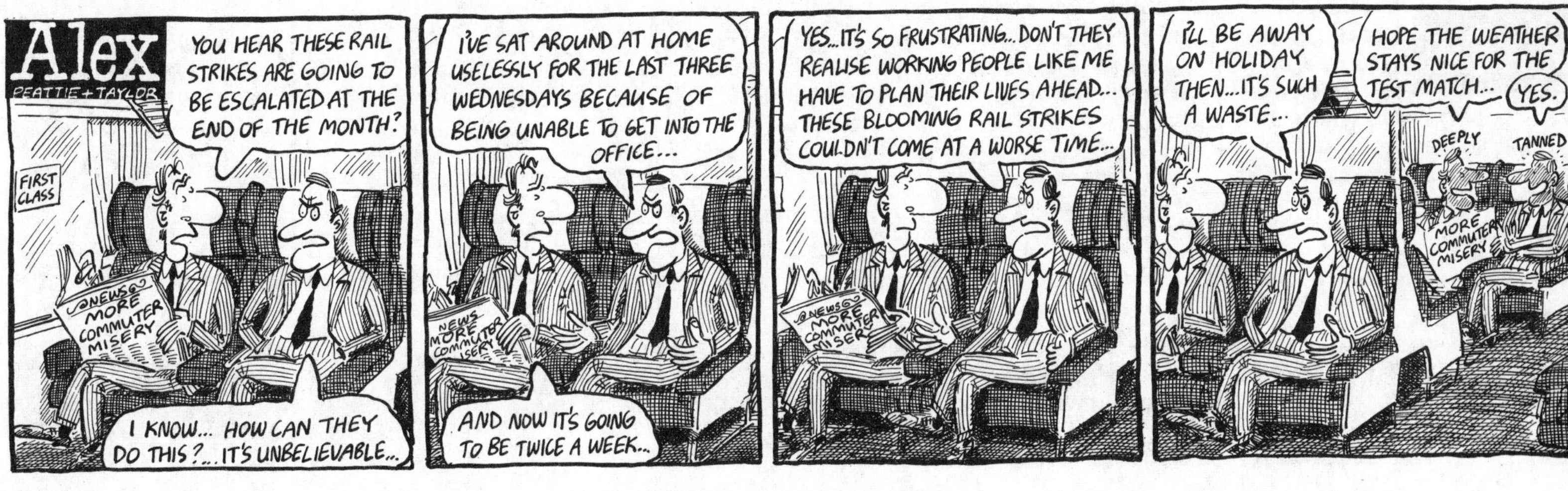
Alex
PEATTIE + TAYLOR
YOU HEAR THESE RAIL STRIKES ARE GOING TO BE ESCALATED AT THE END OF THE MONTH?
FIRST CLASS
NEWS MORE COMMUTER MISERY
I KNOW... HOW CAN THEY DO THIS?... IT'S UNBELIEVABLE...
I'VE SAT AROUND AT HOME USELESSLY FOR THE LAST THREE WEDNESDAYS BECAUSE OF BEING UNABLE TO GET INTO THE OFFICE...
AND NOW IT'S GOING TO BE TWICE A WEEK...
YES... IT'S SO FRUSTRATING... DON'T THEY REALISE WORKING PEOPLE LIKE ME HAVE TO PLAN THEIR LIVES AHEAD... THESE BLOOMING RAIL STRIKES COULDN'T COME AT A WORSE TIME...
I'LL BE AWAY ON HOLIDAY THEN... IT'S SUCH A WASTE...
HOPE THE WEATHER STAYS NICE FOR THE TEST MATCH...
YES.
DEEPLY
TANNED
MORE COMMUTER MISERY

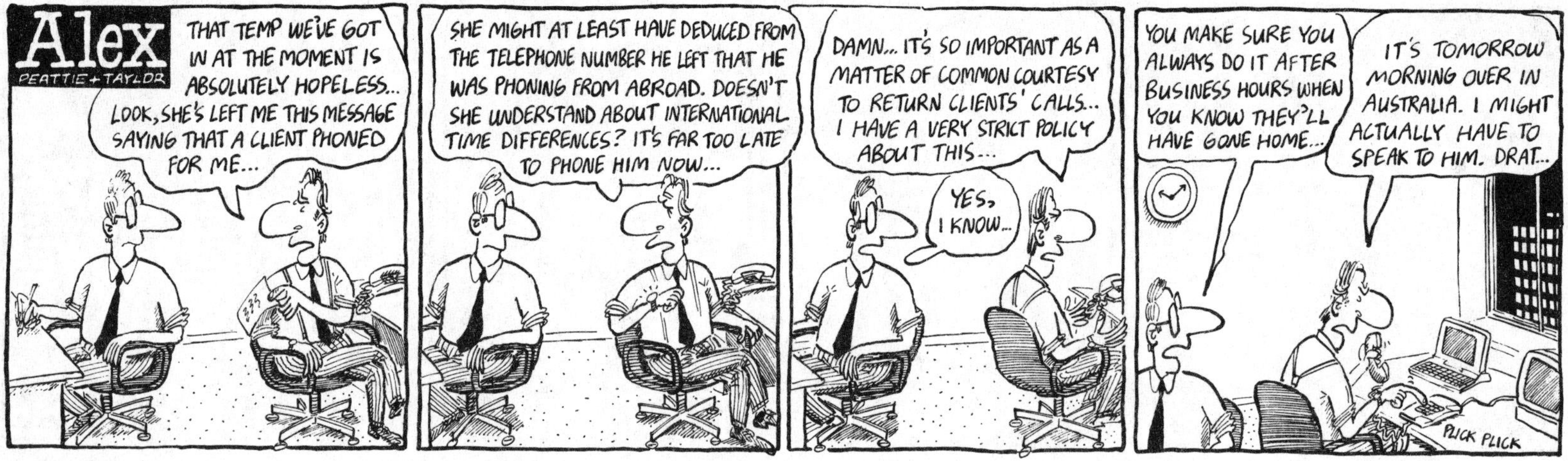
Alex
PEATTIE + TAYLOR
THAT TEMP WE'VE GOT IN AT THE MOMENT IS ABSOLUTELY HOPELESS... LOOK, SHE'S LEFT ME THIS MESSAGE SAYING THAT A CLIENT PHONED FOR ME...
SHE MIGHT AT LEAST HAVE DEDUCED FROM THE TELEPHONE NUMBER HE LEFT THAT HE WAS PHONING FROM ABROAD. DOESN'T SHE UNDERSTAND ABOUT INTERNATIONAL TIME DIFFERENCES? IT'S FAR TOO LATE TO PHONE HIM NOW...
DAMN... IT'S SO IMPORTANT AS A MATTER OF COMMON COURTESY TO RETURN CLIENTS' CALLS... I HAVE A VERY STRICT POLICY ABOUT THIS...
YES, I KNOW...
YOU MAKE SURE YOU ALWAYS DO IT AFTER BUSINESS HOURS WHEN YOU KNOW THEY'LL HAVE GONE HOME...
IT'S TOMORROW MORNING OVER IN AUSTRALIA. I MIGHT ACTUALLY HAVE TO SPEAK TO HIM. DRAT...
PLICK PLICK

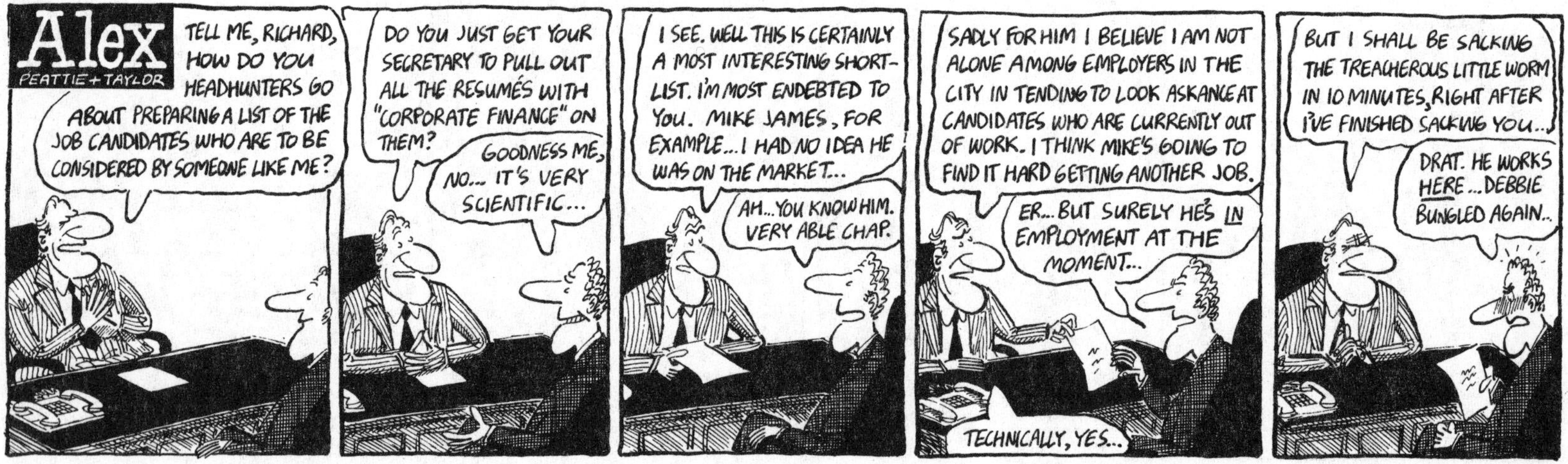
Alex
PEATTIE + TAYLOR
TELL ME, RICHARD, HOW DO YOU HEADHUNTERS GO ABOUT PREPARING A LIST OF THE JOB CANDIDATES WHO ARE TO BE CONSIDERED BY SOMEONE LIKE ME?
DO YOU JUST GET YOUR SECRETARY TO PULL OUT ALL THE RESUMÉS WITH "CORPORATE FINANCE" ON THEM?
GOODNESS ME, NO... IT'S VERY SCIENTIFIC...
I SEE. WELL THIS IS CERTAINLY A MOST INTERESTING SHORT-LIST. I'M MOST ENDEBTED TO YOU. MIKE JAMES, FOR EXAMPLE... I HAD NO IDEA HE WAS ON THE MARKET...
AH... YOU KNOW HIM. VERY ABLE CHAP.
SADLY FOR HIM I BELIEVE I AM NOT ALONE AMONG EMPLOYERS IN THE CITY IN TENDING TO LOOK ASKANCE AT CANDIDATES WHO ARE CURRENTLY OUT OF WORK. I THINK MIKE'S GOING TO FIND IT HARD GETTING ANOTHER JOB.
ER... BUT SURELY HE'S IN EMPLOYMENT AT THE MOMENT...
TECHNICALLY, YES...
BUT I SHALL BE SACKING THE TREACHEROUS LITTLE WORM IN 10 MINUTES, RIGHT AFTER I'VE FINISHED SACKING YOU...
DRAT. HE WORKS HERE... DEBBIE BUNGLED AGAIN...

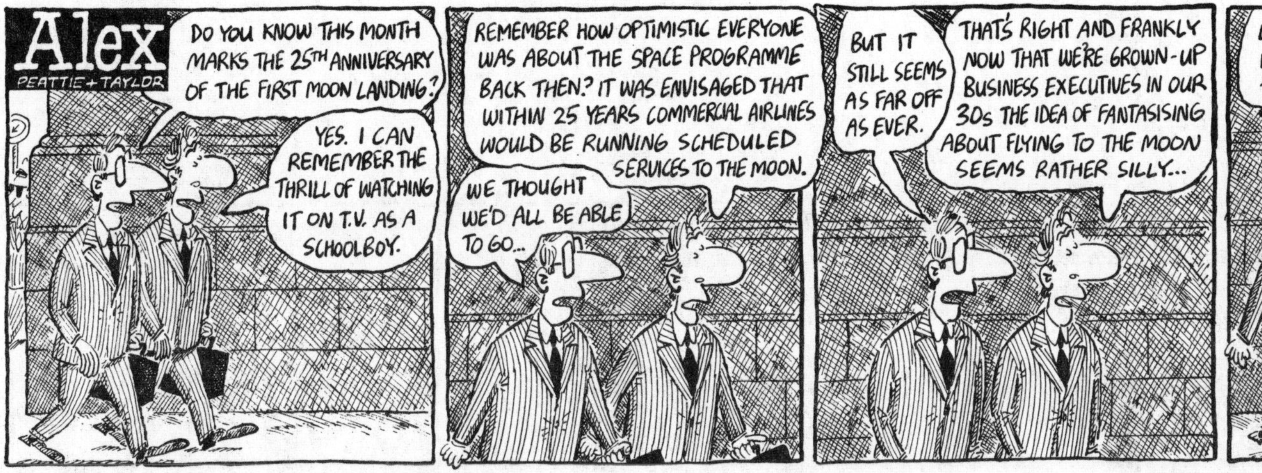
Alex
PEATTIE + TAYLOR
DO YOU KNOW THIS MONTH MARKS THE 25TH ANNIVERSARY OF THE FIRST MOON LANDING?
YES. I CAN REMEMBER THE THRILL OF WATCHING IT ON T.V. AS A SCHOOLBOY.
REMEMBER HOW OPTIMISTIC EVERYONE WAS ABOUT THE SPACE PROGRAMME BACK THEN? IT WAS ENVISAGED THAT WITHIN 25 YEARS COMMERCIAL AIRLINES WOULD BE RUNNING SCHEDULED SERVICES TO THE MOON.
WE THOUGHT WE'D ALL BE ABLE TO GO...
BUT IT STILL SEEMS AS FAR OFF AS EVER.
THAT'S RIGHT AND FRANKLY NOW THAT WE'RE GROWN-UP BUSINESS EXECUTIVES IN OUR 30s THE IDEA OF FANTASISING ABOUT FLYING TO THE MOON SEEMS RATHER SILLY...
EXACTLY. IT'S ONLY 250,000 MILES. I'VE GOT ENOUGH AIR MILES TO GO THERE 2 OR 3 TIMES ALREADY...
ME TOO. I'M HOLDING OUT FOR MARS.
B.A. GOLD
B.A. GOLD

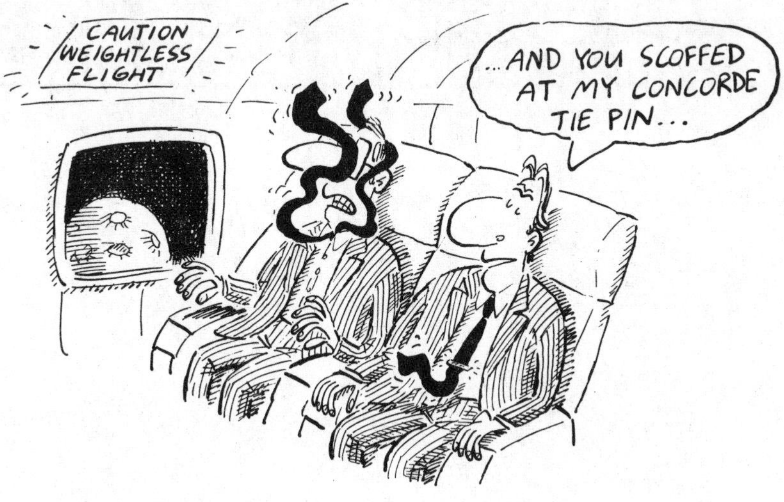
CAUTION WEIGHTLESS FLIGHT
...AND YOU SCOFFED AT MY CONCORDE TIE PIN...

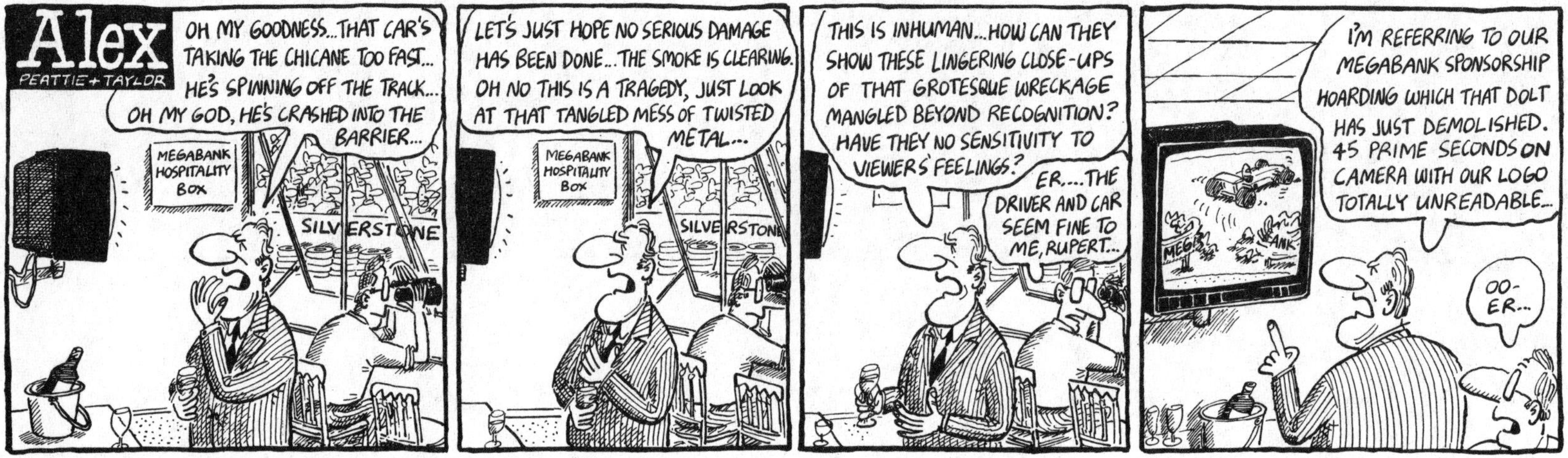
Alex
PEATTIE + TAYLOR
OH MY GOODNESS... THAT CAR'S TAKING THE CHICANE TOO FAST... HE'S SPINNING OFF THE TRACK... OH MY GOD, HE'S CRASHED INTO THE BARRIER...
MEGABANK HOSPITALITY BOX
SILVERSTONE
LET'S JUST HOPE NO SERIOUS DAMAGE HAS BEEN DONE... THE SMOKE IS CLEARING. OH NO THIS IS A TRAGEDY, JUST LOOK AT THAT TANGLED MESS OF TWISTED METAL...
MEGABANK HOSPITALITY BOX
SILVERSTONE
THIS IS INHUMAN... HOW CAN THEY SHOW THESE LINGERING CLOSE-UPS OF THAT GROTESQUE WRECKAGE MANGLED BEYOND RECOGNITION? HAVE THEY NO SENSITIVITY TO VIEWERS' FEELINGS?
ER.... THE DRIVER AND CAR SEEM FINE TO ME, RUPERT...
I'M REFERRING TO OUR MEGABANK SPONSORSHIP HOARDING WHICH THAT DOLT HAS JUST DEMOLISHED. 45 PRIME SECONDS ON CAMERA WITH OUR LOGO TOTALLY UNREADABLE...
MEG
ANK
OO- ER...

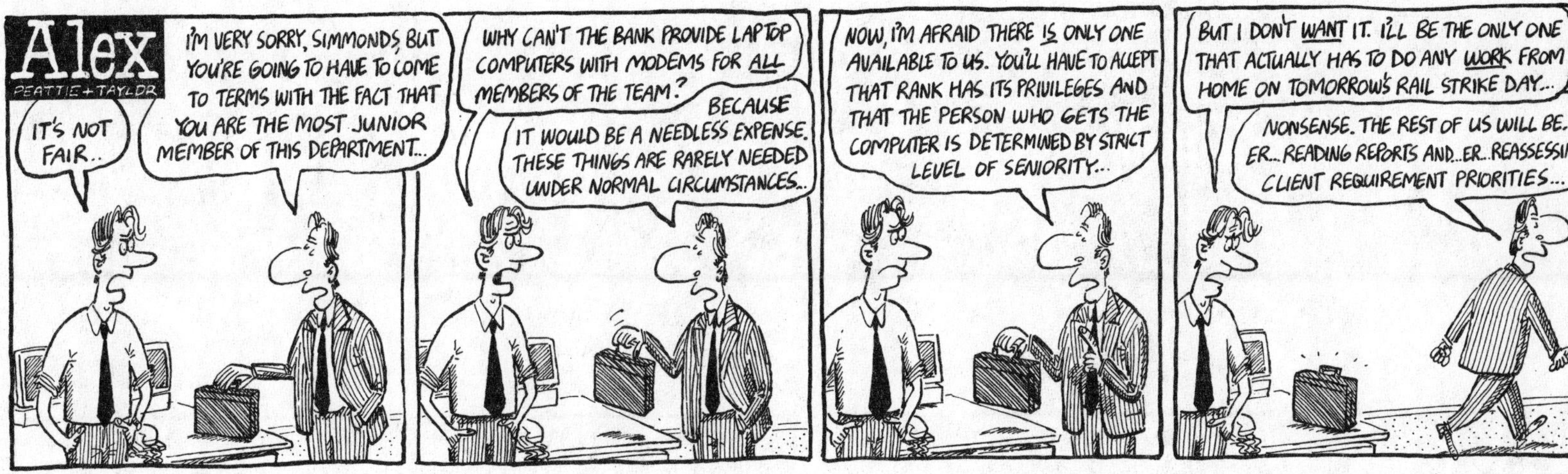
Alex
PEATTIE + TAYLOR
I'M VERY SORRY, SIMMONDS, BUT YOU'RE GOING TO HAVE TO COME TO TERMS WITH THE FACT THAT YOU ARE THE MOST JUNIOR MEMBER OF THIS DEPARTMENT...
IT'S NOT FAIR...
WHY CAN'T THE BANK PROVIDE LAPTOP COMPUTERS WITH MODEMS FOR ALL MEMBERS OF THE TEAM?
BECAUSE IT WOULD BE A NEEDLESS EXPENSE. THESE THINGS ARE RARELY NEEDED UNDER NORMAL CIRCUMSTANCES...
NOW, I'M AFRAID THERE IS ONLY ONE AVAILABLE TO US. YOU'LL HAVE TO ACCEPT THAT RANK HAS ITS PRIVILEGES AND THAT THE PERSON WHO GETS THE COMPUTER IS DETERMINED BY STRICT LEVEL OF SENIORITY...
BUT I DON'T WANT IT. I'LL BE THE ONLY ONE THAT ACTUALLY HAS TO DO ANY WORK FROM HOME ON TOMORROW'S RAIL STRIKE DAY...
NONSENSE. THE REST OF US WILL BE... ER... READING REPORTS AND... ER... REASSESSING CLIENT REQUIREMENT PRIORITIES...

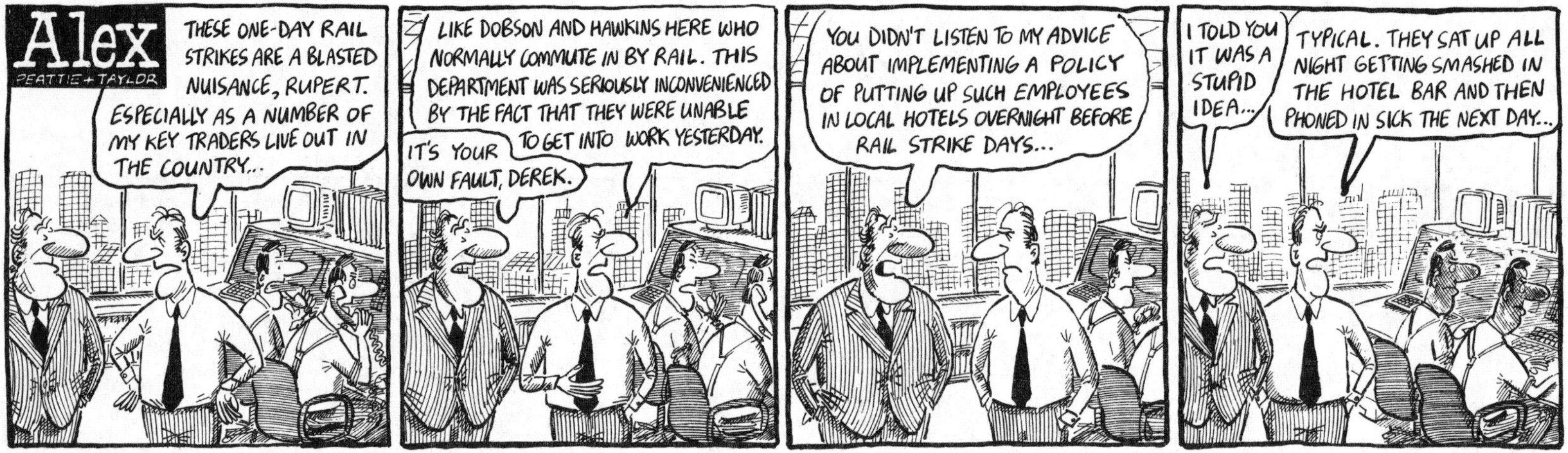
Alex
PEATTIE + TAYLOR
THESE ONE-DAY RAIL STRIKES ARE A BLASTED NUISANCE, RUPERT. ESPECIALLY AS A NUMBER OF MY KEY TRADERS LIVE OUT IN THE COUNTRY...
LIKE DOBSON AND HAWKINS HERE WHO NORMALLY COMMUTE IN BY RAIL. THIS DEPARTMENT WAS SERIOUSLY INCONVENIENCED BY THE FACT THAT THEY WERE UNABLE TO GET INTO WORK YESTERDAY.
IT'S YOUR OWN FAULT, DEREK.
YOU DIDN'T LISTEN TO MY ADVICE ABOUT IMPLEMENTING A POLICY OF PUTTING UP SUCH EMPLOYEES IN LOCAL HOTELS OVERNIGHT BEFORE RAIL STRIKE DAYS...
I TOLD YOU IT WAS A STUPID IDEA...
TYPICAL. THEY SAT UP ALL NIGHT GETTING SMASHED IN THE HOTEL BAR AND THEN PHONED IN SICK THE NEXT DAY...

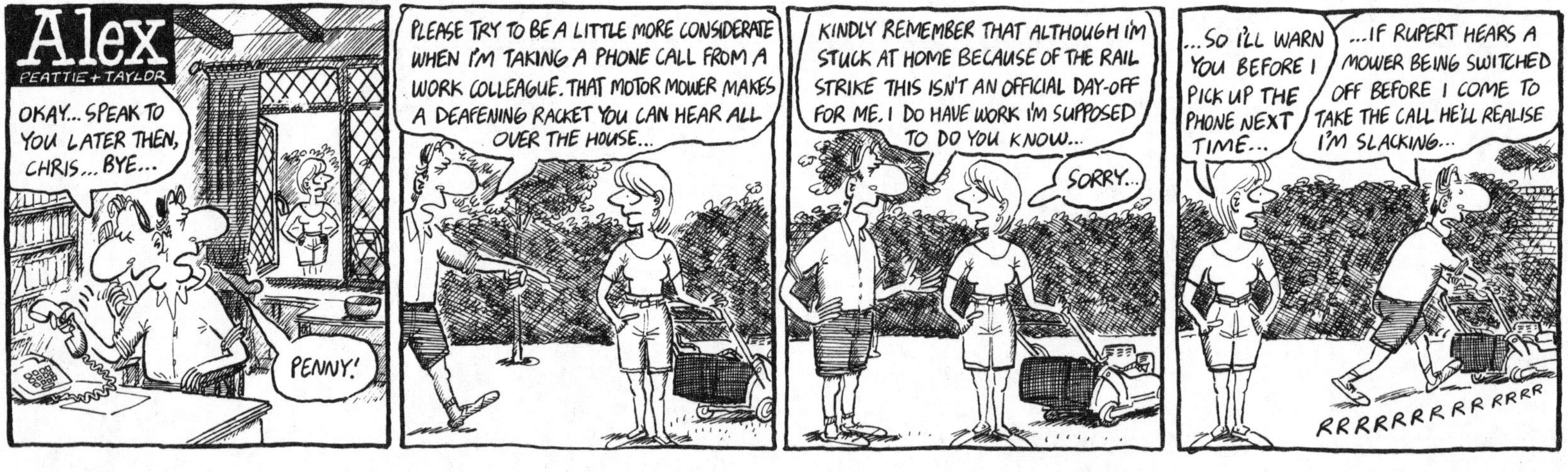
Alex
PEATTIE + TAYLOR
OKAY... SPEAK TO YOU LATER THEN, CHRIS... BYE...
PENNY!
PLEASE TRY TO BE A LITTLE MORE CONSIDERATE WHEN I'M TAKING A PHONE CALL FROM A WORK COLLEAGUE. THAT MOTOR MOWER MAKES A DEAFENING RACKET YOU CAN HEAR ALL OVER THE HOUSE...
KINDLY REMEMBER THAT ALTHOUGH I'M STUCK AT HOME BECAUSE OF THE RAIL STRIKE THIS ISN'T AN OFFICIAL DAY-OFF FOR ME. I DO HAVE WORK I'M SUPPOSED TO DO YOU KNOW...
SORRY...
...SO I'LL WARN YOU BEFORE I PICK UP THE PHONE NEXT TIME...
...IF RUPERT HEARS A MOWER BEING SWITCHED OFF BEFORE I COME TO TAKE THE CALL HE'LL REALISE I'M SLACKING...
RRRRRRRRRRRRR

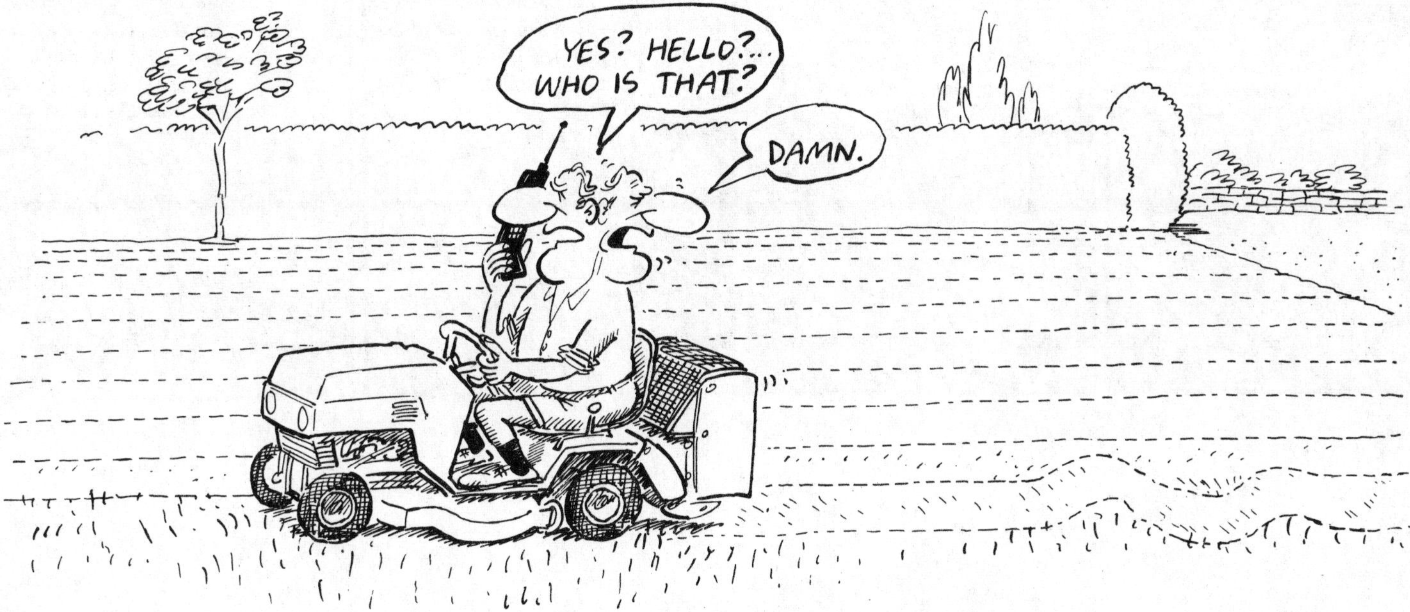
YES? HELLO?...
WHO IS THAT?
DAMN.

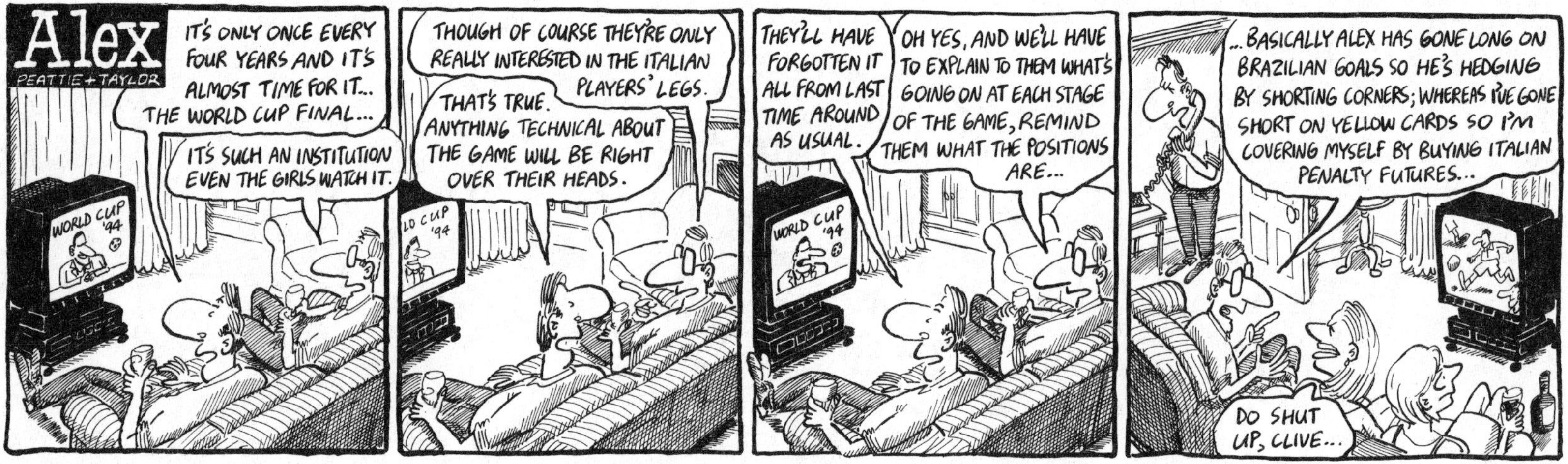
Alex
PEATTIE + TAYLOR
IT'S ONLY ONCE EVERY FOUR YEARS AND IT'S ALMOST TIME FOR IT... THE WORLD CUP FINAL...
IT'S SUCH AN INSTITUTION EVEN THE GIRLS WATCH IT.
WORLD CUP '94
THOUGH OF COURSE THEY'RE ONLY REALLY INTERESTED IN THE ITALIAN PLAYERS' LEGS.
THAT'S TRUE. ANYTHING TECHNICAL ABOUT THE GAME WILL BE RIGHT OVER THEIR HEADS.
THEY'LL HAVE FORGOTTEN IT ALL FROM LAST TIME AROUND AS USUAL.
OH YES, AND WE'LL HAVE TO EXPLAIN TO THEM WHAT'S GOING ON AT EACH STAGE OF THE GAME, REMIND THEM WHAT THE POSITIONS ARE...
WORLD CUP '94
...BASICALLY ALEX HAS GONE LONG ON BRAZILIAN GOALS SO HE'S HEDGING BY SHORTING CORNERS; WHEREAS I'VE GONE SHORT ON YELLOW CARDS SO I'M COVERING MYSELF BY BUYING ITALIAN PENALTY FUTURES...
DO SHUT UP, CLIVE...

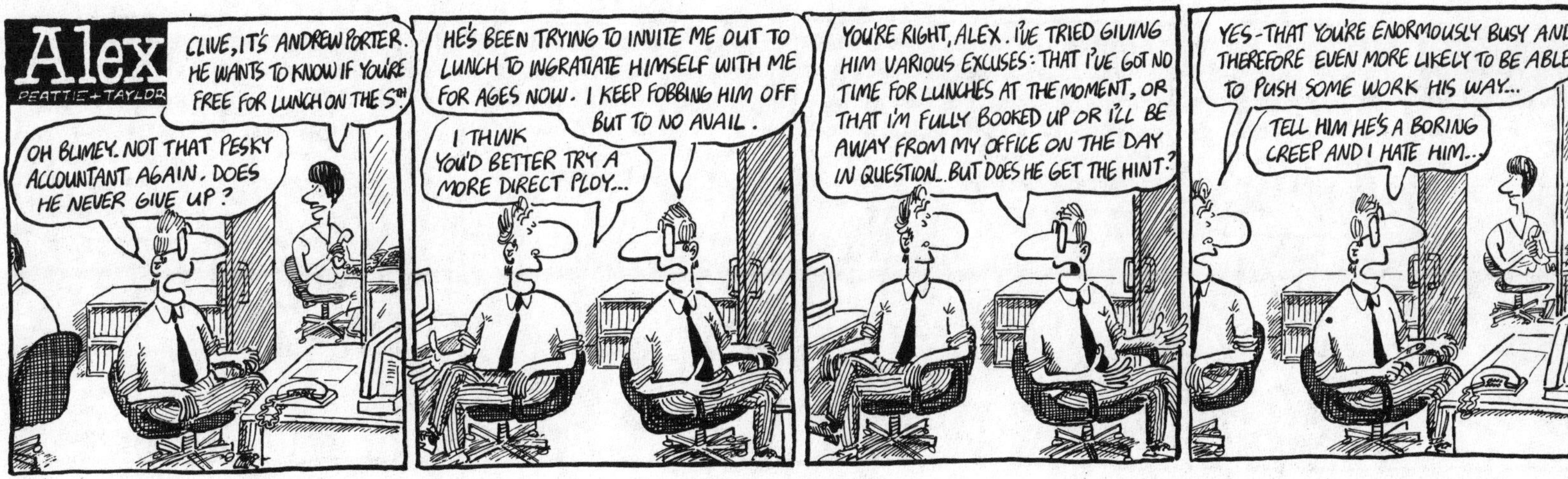
Alex
BEATTIE + TAYLOR
CLIVE, IT'S ANDREW PORTER. HE WANTS TO KNOW IF YOU'RE FREE FOR LUNCH ON THE 5TH
OH BLIMEY. NOT THAT PESKY ACCOUNTANT AGAIN. DOES HE NEVER GIVE UP?
HE'S BEEN TRYING TO INVITE ME OUT TO LUNCH TO INGRATIATE HIMSELF WITH ME FOR AGES NOW. I KEEP FOBBING HIM OFF BUT TO NO AVAIL.
I THINK YOU'D BETTER TRY A MORE DIRECT PLOY...
YOU'RE RIGHT, ALEX. I'VE TRIED GIVING HIM VARIOUS EXCUSES: THAT I'VE GOT NO TIME FOR LUNCHES AT THE MOMENT, OR THAT I'M FULLY BOOKED UP OR I'LL BE AWAY FROM MY OFFICE ON THE DAY IN QUESTION... BUT DOES HE GET THE HINT?
YES - THAT YOU'RE ENORMOUSLY BUSY AND THEREFORE EVEN MORE LIKELY TO BE ABLE TO PUSH SOME WORK HIS WAY...
TELL HIM HE'S A BORING CREEP AND I HATE HIM...

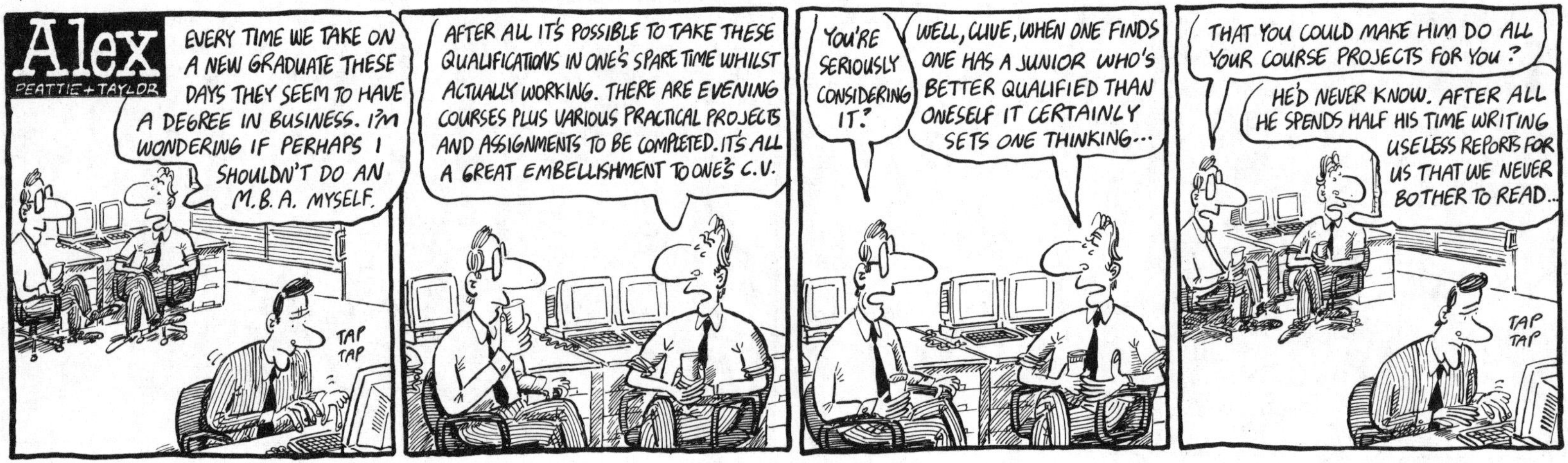
Alex
PEATTIE + TAYLOR
EVERY TIME WE TAKE ON A NEW GRADUATE THESE DAYS THEY SEEM TO HAVE A DEGREE IN BUSINESS. I'M WONDERING IF PERHAPS I SHOULDN'T DO AN M.B.A. MYSELF.
TAP TAP
AFTER ALL IT'S POSSIBLE TO TAKE THESE QUALIFICATIONS IN ONE'S SPARE TIME WHILST ACTUALLY WORKING. THERE ARE EVENING COURSES PLUS VARIOUS PRACTICAL PROJECTS AND ASSIGNMENTS TO BE COMPLETED. IT'S ALL A GREAT EMBELLISHMENT TO ONE'S C.V.
YOU'RE SERIOUSLY CONSIDERING IT?
WELL, CLIVE, WHEN ONE FINDS ONE HAS A JUNIOR WHO'S BETTER QUALIFIED THAN ONESELF IT CERTAINLY SETS ONE THINKING...
THAT YOU COULD MAKE HIM DO ALL YOUR COURSE PROJECTS FOR YOU?
HE'D NEVER KNOW. AFTER ALL HE SPENDS HALF HIS TIME WRITING USELESS REPORTS FOR US THAT WE NEVER BOTHER TO READ...
TAP TAP

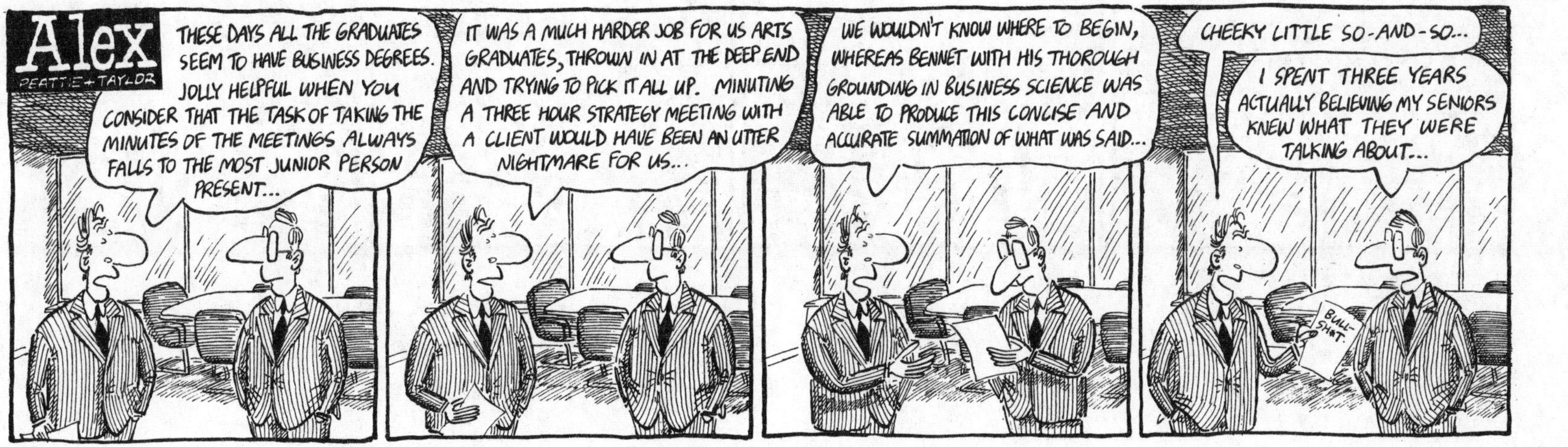
Alex
BEATTIE + TAYLOR
THESE DAYS ALL THE GRADUATES SEEM TO HAVE BUSINESS DEGREES. JOLLY HELPFUL WHEN YOU CONSIDER THAT THE TASK OF TAKING THE MINUTES OF THE MEETINGS ALWAYS FALLS TO THE MOST JUNIOR PERSON PRESENT...
IT WAS A MUCH HARDER JOB FOR US ARTS GRADUATES, THROWN IN AT THE DEEP END AND TRYING TO PICK IT ALL UP. MINUTING A THREE HOUR STRATEGY MEETING WITH A CLIENT WOULD HAVE BEEN AN UTTER NIGHTMARE FOR US...
WE WOULDN'T KNOW WHERE TO BEGIN, WHEREAS BENNET WITH HIS THOROUGH GROUNDING IN BUSINESS SCIENCE WAS ABLE TO PRODUCE THIS CONCISE AND ACCURATE SUMMATION OF WHAT WAS SAID...
CHEEKY LITTLE SO-AND-SO...
I SPENT THREE YEARS ACTUALLY BELIEVING MY SENIORS KNEW WHAT THEY WERE TALKING ABOUT...
BULL-SHIT.

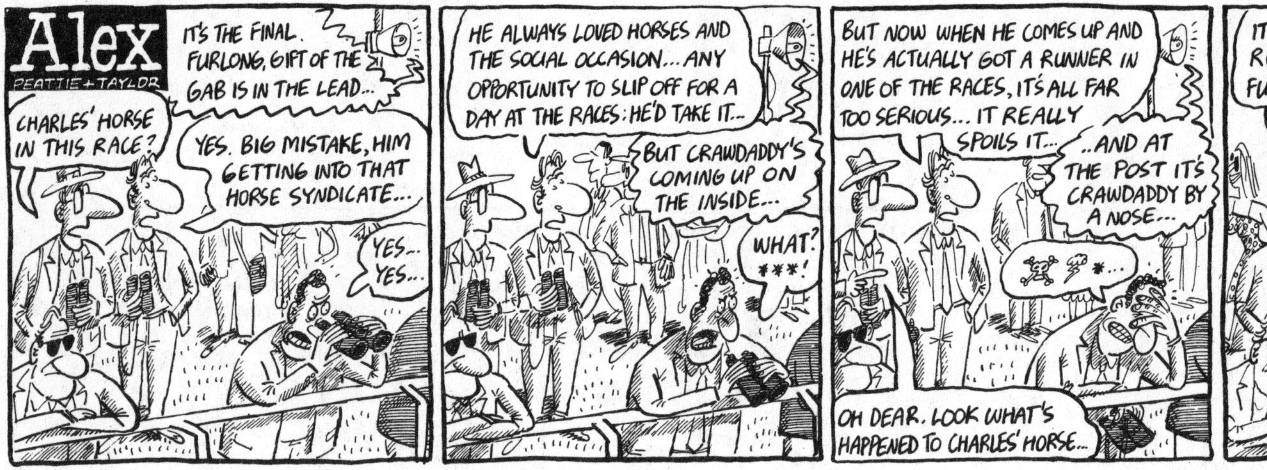
Alex
PEATTIE + TAYLOR
IT'S THE FINAL FURLONG, GIFT OF THE GAB IS IN THE LEAD...
CHARLES' HORSE IN THIS RACE?
YES. BIG MISTAKE, HIM GETTING INTO THAT HORSE SYNDICATE...
YES.. YES...
HE ALWAYS LOVED HORSES AND THE SOCIAL OCCASION... ANY OPPORTUNITY TO SLIP OFF FOR A DAY AT THE RACES: HE'D TAKE IT...
BUT CRAWDADDY'S COMING UP ON THE INSIDE...
WHAT? ***!
BUT NOW WHEN HE COMES UP AND HE'S ACTUALLY GOT A RUNNER IN ONE OF THE RACES, IT'S ALL FAR TOO SERIOUS... IT REALLY SPOILS IT...
..AND AT THE POST IT'S CRAWDADDY BY A NOSE...
OH DEAR. LOOK WHAT'S HAPPENED TO CHARLES' HORSE...
IT'S WON... SO HE'LL HAVE TO LEAD IT ROUND THE WINNER'S ENCLOSURE IN FULL VIEW OF THE T.V. CAMERAS...
LET'S HOPE HIS BOSS ISN'T WATCHING. CHARLES USUALLY PHONES IN SICK ON RACE DAYS...

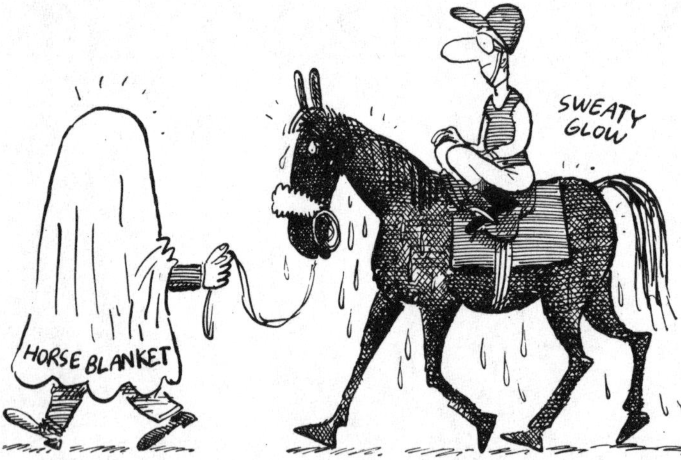
SWEATY GLOW
HORSE BLANKET

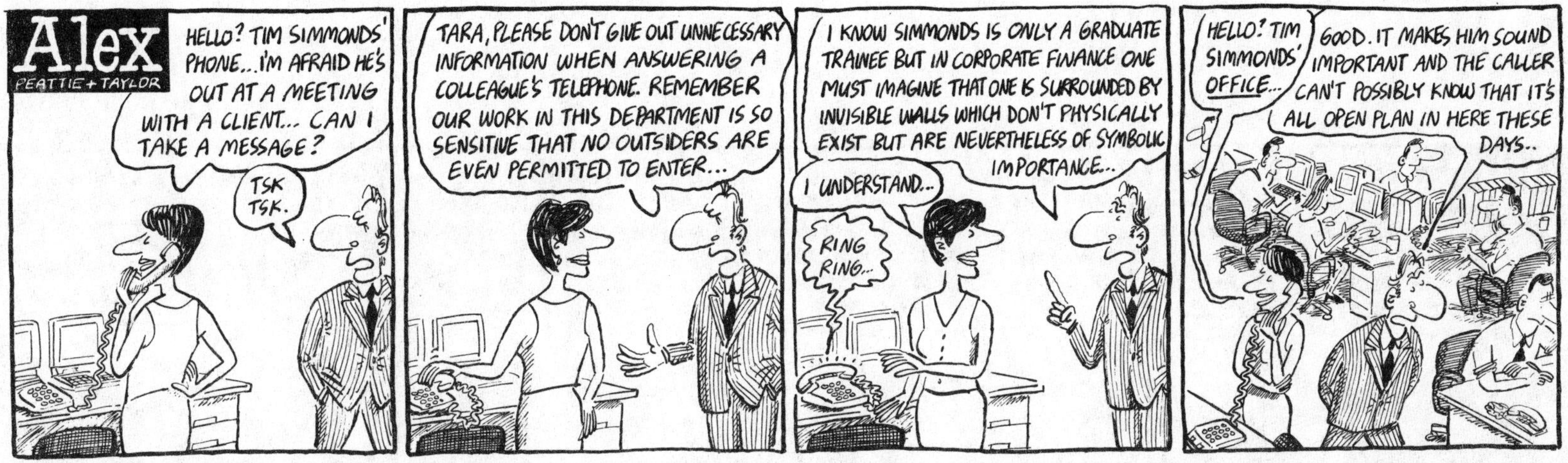
Alex
PEATTIE + TAYLOR
HELLO? TIM SIMMONDS' PHONE... I'M AFRAID HE'S OUT AT A MEETING WITH A CLIENT... CAN I TAKE A MESSAGE?
TSK TSK.
TARA, PLEASE DON'T GIVE OUT UNNECESSARY INFORMATION WHEN ANSWERING A COLLEAGUE'S TELEPHONE. REMEMBER OUR WORK IN THIS DEPARTMENT IS SO SENSITIVE THAT NO OUTSIDERS ARE EVEN PERMITTED TO ENTER...
I KNOW SIMMONDS IS ONLY A GRADUATE TRAINEE BUT IN CORPORATE FINANCE ONE MUST IMAGINE THAT ONE IS SURROUNDED BY INVISIBLE WALLS WHICH DON'T PHYSICALLY EXIST BUT ARE NEVERTHELESS OF SYMBOLIC IMPORTANCE...
I UNDERSTAND...
RING RING...
HELLO? TIM SIMMONDS' OFFICE...
GOOD. IT MAKES HIM SOUND IMPORTANT AND THE CALLER CAN'T POSSIBLY KNOW THAT IT'S ALL OPEN PLAN IN HERE THESE DAYS..

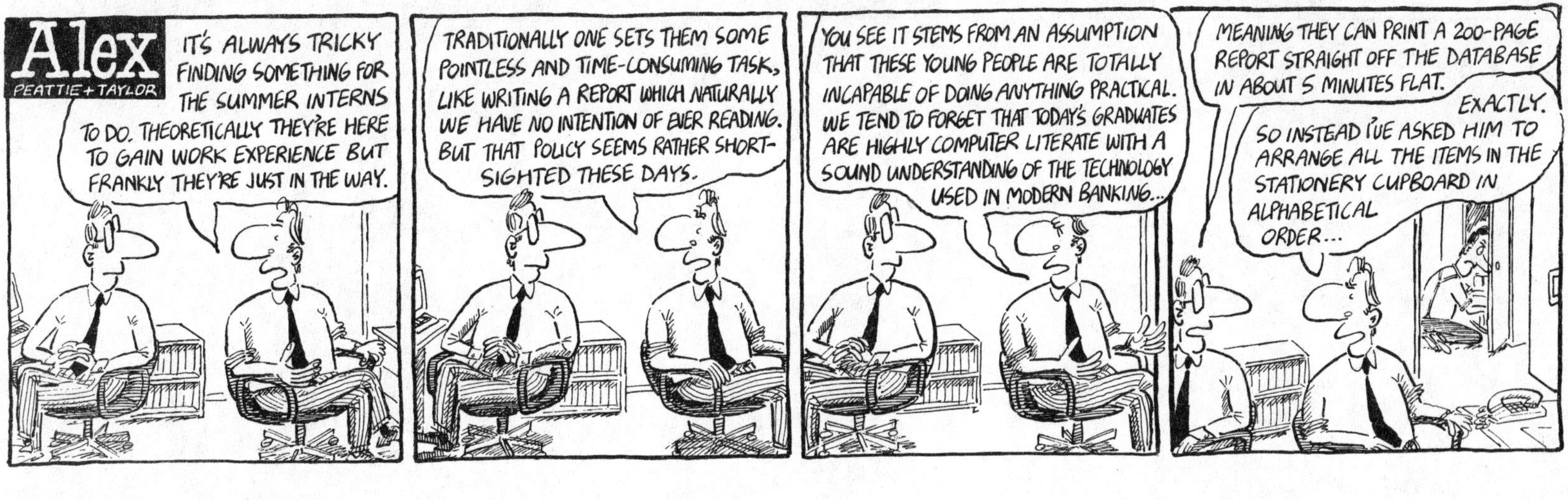
Alex
PEATTIE + TAYLOR
IT'S ALWAYS TRICKY FINDING SOMETHING FOR THE SUMMER INTERNS TO DO. THEORETICALLY THEY'RE HERE TO GAIN WORK EXPERIENCE BUT FRANKLY THEY'RE JUST IN THE WAY.
TRADITIONALLY ONE SETS THEM SOME POINTLESS AND TIME-CONSUMING TASK, LIKE WRITING A REPORT WHICH NATURALLY WE HAVE NO INTENTION OF EVER READING. BUT THAT POLICY SEEMS RATHER SHORT-SIGHTED THESE DAYS.
YOU SEE IT STEMS FROM AN ASSUMPTION THAT THESE YOUNG PEOPLE ARE TOTALLY INCAPABLE OF DOING ANYTHING PRACTICAL. WE TEND TO FORGET THAT TODAY'S GRADUATES ARE HIGHLY COMPUTER LITERATE WITH A SOUND UNDERSTANDING OF THE TECHNOLOGY USED IN MODERN BANKING...
MEANING THEY CAN PRINT A 200-PAGE REPORT STRAIGHT OFF THE DATABASE IN ABOUT 5 MINUTES FLAT.
EXACTLY.
SO INSTEAD I'VE ASKED HIM TO ARRANGE ALL THE ITEMS IN THE STATIONERY CUPBOARD IN ALPHABETICAL ORDER...

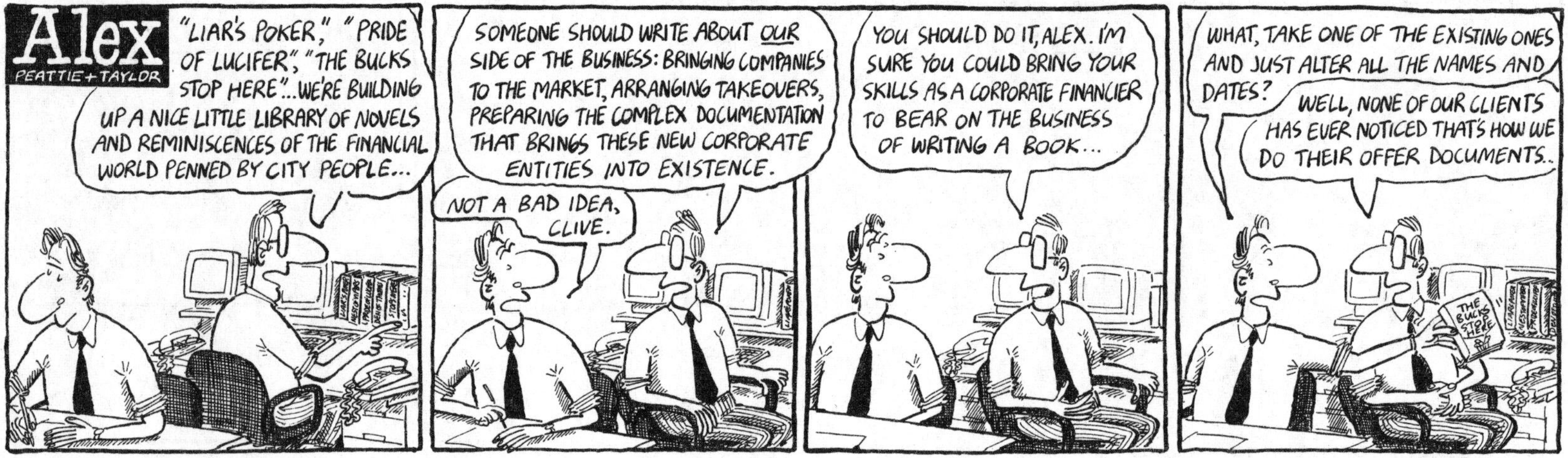
Alex
PEATTIE + TAYLOR
"LIAR'S POKER," "PRIDE OF LUCIFER", "THE BUCKS STOP HERE"... WE'RE BUILDING UP A NICE LITTLE LIBRARY OF NOVELS AND REMINISCENCES OF THE FINANCIAL WORLD PENNED BY CITY PEOPLE...
SOMEONE SHOULD WRITE ABOUT OUR SIDE OF THE BUSINESS: BRINGING COMPANIES TO THE MARKET, ARRANGING TAKEOVERS, PREPARING THE COMPLEX DOCUMENTATION THAT BRINGS THESE NEW CORPORATE ENTITIES INTO EXISTENCE.
NOT A BAD IDEA, CLIVE.
YOU SHOULD DO IT, ALEX. I'M SURE YOU COULD BRING YOUR SKILLS AS A CORPORATE FINANCIER TO BEAR ON THE BUSINESS OF WRITING A BOOK...
WHAT, TAKE ONE OF THE EXISTING ONES AND JUST ALTER ALL THE NAMES AND DATES?
WELL, NONE OF OUR CLIENTS HAS EVER NOTICED THAT'S HOW WE DO THEIR OFFER DOCUMENTS..
THE BUCKS STOP HERE

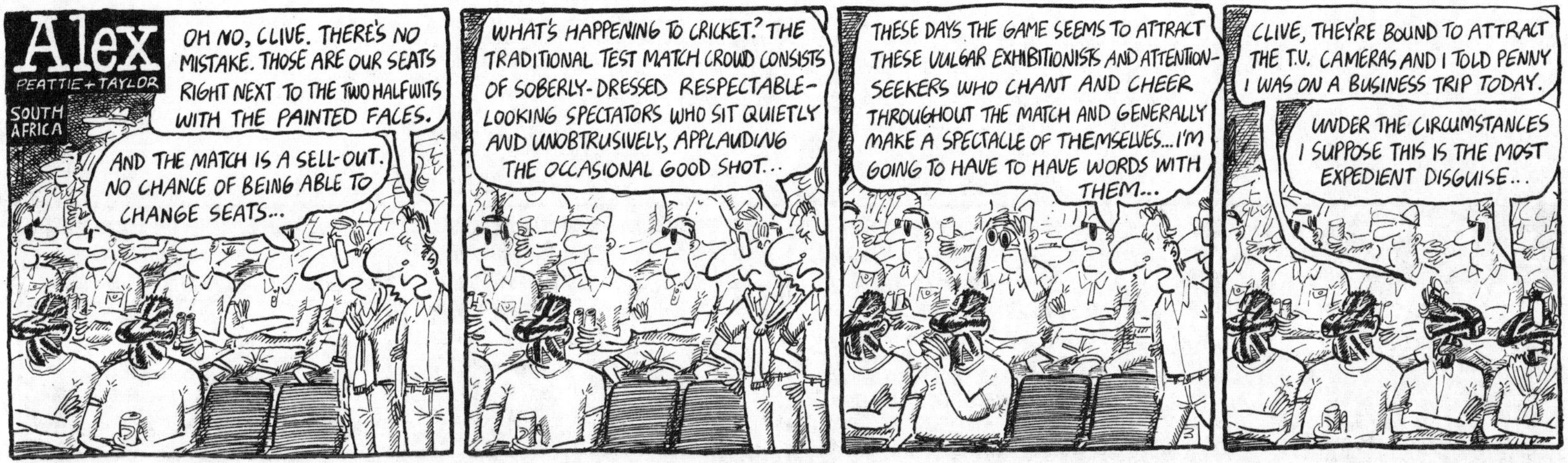
Alex
PEATTIE + TAYLOR
SOUTH AFRICA
OH NO, CLIVE. THERE'S NO MISTAKE. THOSE ARE OUR SEATS RIGHT NEXT TO THE TWO HALFWITS WITH THE PAINTED FACES.
AND THE MATCH IS A SELL-OUT. NO CHANCE OF BEING ABLE TO CHANGE SEATS...
WHAT'S HAPPENING TO CRICKET? THE TRADITIONAL TEST MATCH CROWD CONSISTS OF SOBERLY-DRESSED RESPECTABLE-LOOKING SPECTATORS WHO SIT QUIETLY AND UNOBTRUSIVELY, APPLAUDING THE OCCASIONAL GOOD SHOT...
THESE DAYS THE GAME SEEMS TO ATTRACT THESE VULGAR EXHIBITIONISTS AND ATTENTION-SEEKERS WHO CHANT AND CHEER THROUGHOUT THE MATCH AND GENERALLY MAKE A SPECTACLE OF THEMSELVES... I'M GOING TO HAVE TO HAVE WORDS WITH THEM...
CLIVE, THEY'RE BOUND TO ATTRACT THE T.V. CAMERAS AND I TOLD PENNY I WAS ON A BUSINESS TRIP TODAY.
UNDER THE CIRCUMSTANCES I SUPPOSE THIS IS THE MOST EXPEDIENT DISGUISE...

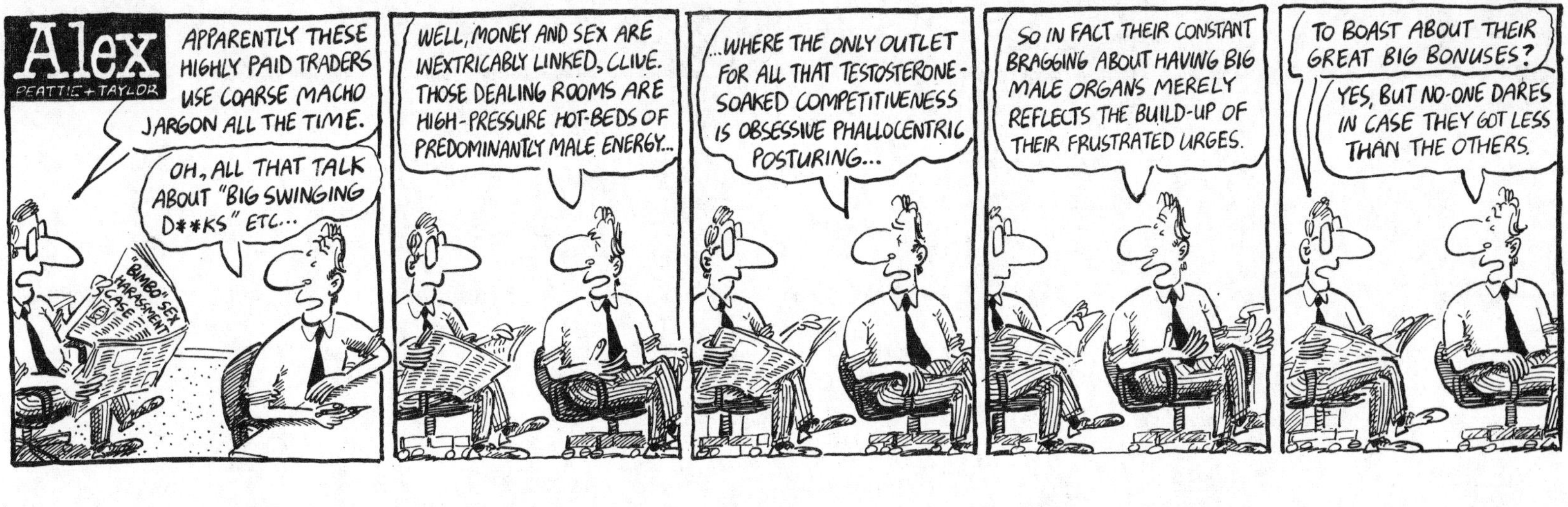
Alex
PEATTIE + TAYLOR
APPARENTLY THESE HIGHLY PAID TRADERS USE COARSE MACHO JARGON ALL THE TIME.
OH, ALL THAT TALK ABOUT "BIG SWINGING D**KS" ETC...
"BIMBO" SEX HARASSMENT CASE
WELL, MONEY AND SEX ARE INEXTRICABLY LINKED, CLIVE. THOSE DEALING ROOMS ARE HIGH-PRESSURE HOT-BEDS OF PREDOMINANTLY MALE ENERGY...
...WHERE THE ONLY OUTLET FOR ALL THAT TESTOSTERONE-SOAKED COMPETITIVENESS IS OBSESSIVE PHALLOCENTRIC POSTURING...
SO IN FACT THEIR CONSTANT BRAGGING ABOUT HAVING BIG MALE ORGANS MERELY REFLECTS THE BUILD-UP OF THEIR FRUSTRATED URGES.
TO BOAST ABOUT THEIR GREAT BIG BONUSES?
YES, BUT NO-ONE DARES IN CASE THEY GOT LESS THAN THE OTHERS.

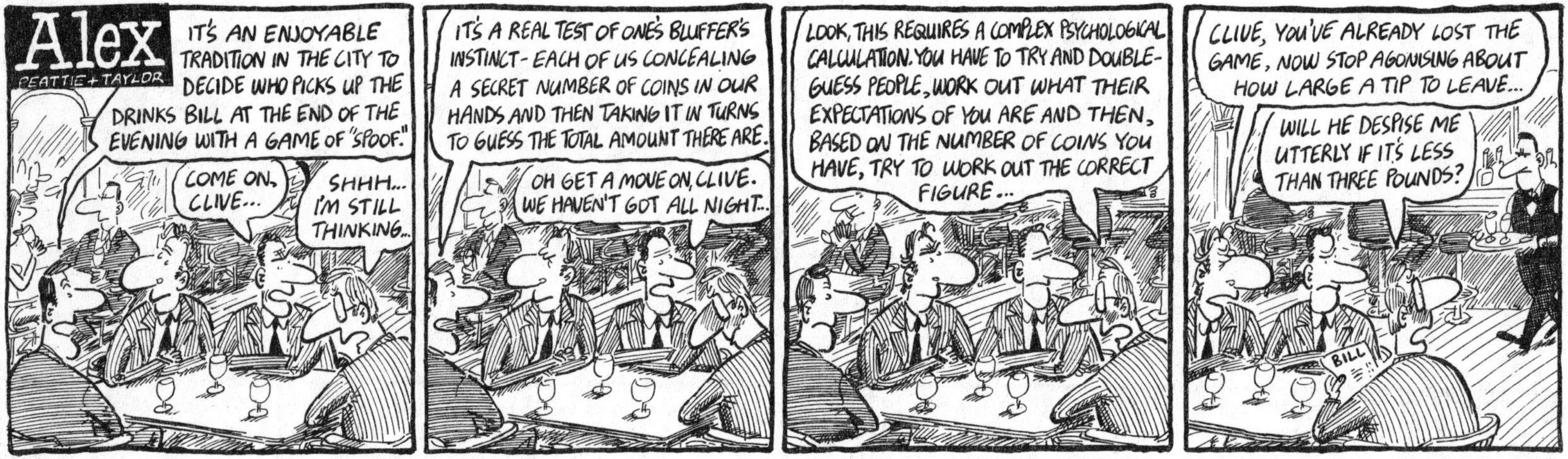
Alex
BEATTIE + TAYLOR
IT'S AN ENJOYABLE TRADITION IN THE CITY TO DECIDE WHO PICKS UP THE DRINKS BILL AT THE END OF THE EVENING WITH A GAME OF "SPOOF."
COME ON, CLIVE...
SHHH... I'M STILL THINKING...
IT'S A REAL TEST OF ONE'S BLUFFER'S INSTINCT - EACH OF US CONCEALING A SECRET NUMBER OF COINS IN OUR HANDS AND THEN TAKING IT IN TURNS TO GUESS THE TOTAL AMOUNT THERE ARE.
OH GET A MOVE ON, CLIVE. WE HAVEN'T GOT ALL NIGHT...
LOOK, THIS REQUIRES A COMPLEX PSYCHOLOGICAL CALCULATION. YOU HAVE TO TRY AND DOUBLE-GUESS PEOPLE, WORK OUT WHAT THEIR EXPECTATIONS OF YOU ARE AND THEN, BASED ON THE NUMBER OF COINS YOU HAVE, TRY TO WORK OUT THE CORRECT FIGURE...
CLIVE, YOU'VE ALREADY LOST THE GAME, NOW STOP AGONISING ABOUT HOW LARGE A TIP TO LEAVE...
WILL HE DESPISE ME UTTERLY IF IT'S LESS THAN THREE POUNDS?
BILL

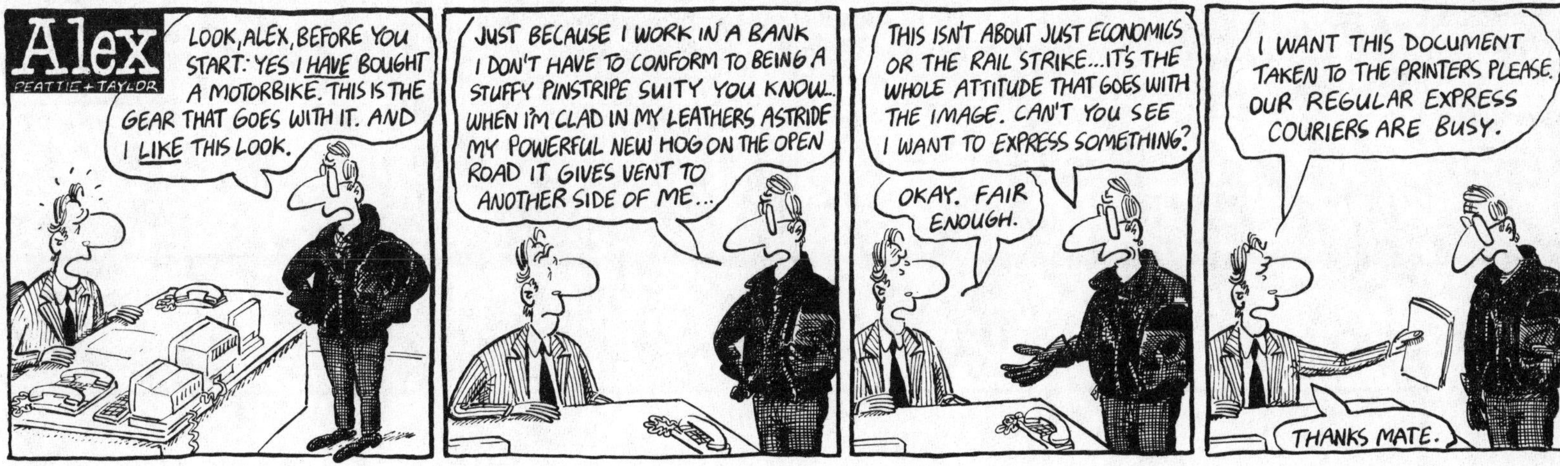
Alex
BEATTIE + TAYLOR
LOOK, ALEX, BEFORE YOU START: YES I HAVE BOUGHT A MOTORBIKE. THIS IS THE GEAR THAT GOES WITH IT. AND I LIKE THIS LOOK.
JUST BECAUSE I WORK IN A BANK I DON'T HAVE TO CONFORM TO BEING A STUFFY PINSTRIPE SUITY YOU KNOW... WHEN I'M CLAD IN MY LEATHERS ASTRIDE MY POWERFUL NEW HOG ON THE OPEN ROAD IT GIVES VENT TO ANOTHER SIDE OF ME...
THIS ISN'T ABOUT JUST ECONOMICS OR THE RAIL STRIKE...IT'S THE WHOLE ATTITUDE THAT GOES WITH THE IMAGE. CAN'T YOU SEE I WANT TO EXPRESS SOMETHING?
OKAY. FAIR ENOUGH.
I WANT THIS DOCUMENT TAKEN TO THE PRINTERS PLEASE. OUR REGULAR EXPRESS COURIERS ARE BUSY.
THANKS MATE.

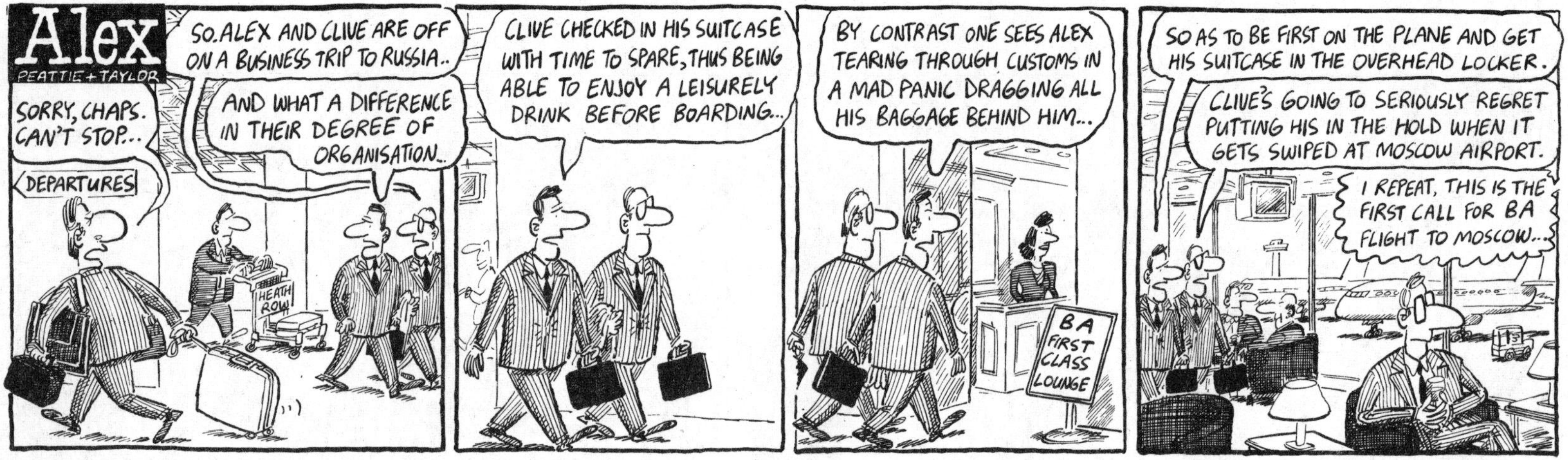
Alex
PEATTIE + TAYLOR
SORRY, CHAPS. CAN'T STOP...
DEPARTURES
SO. ALEX AND CLIVE ARE OFF ON A BUSINESS TRIP TO RUSSIA..
AND WHAT A DIFFERENCE IN THEIR DEGREE OF ORGANISATION..
HEATH ROW
CLIVE CHECKED IN HIS SUITCASE WITH TIME TO SPARE, THUS BEING ABLE TO ENJOY A LEISURELY DRINK BEFORE BOARDING...
BY CONTRAST ONE SEES ALEX TEARING THROUGH CUSTOMS IN A MAD PANIC DRAGGING ALL HIS BAGGAGE BEHIND HIM...
BA FIRST CLASS LOUNGE
SO AS TO BE FIRST ON THE PLANE AND GET HIS SUITCASE IN THE OVERHEAD LOCKER.
CLIVE'S GOING TO SERIOUSLY REGRET PUTTING HIS IN THE HOLD WHEN IT GETS SWIPED AT MOSCOW AIRPORT.
I REPEAT, THIS IS THE FIRST CALL FOR BA FLIGHT TO MOSCOW...

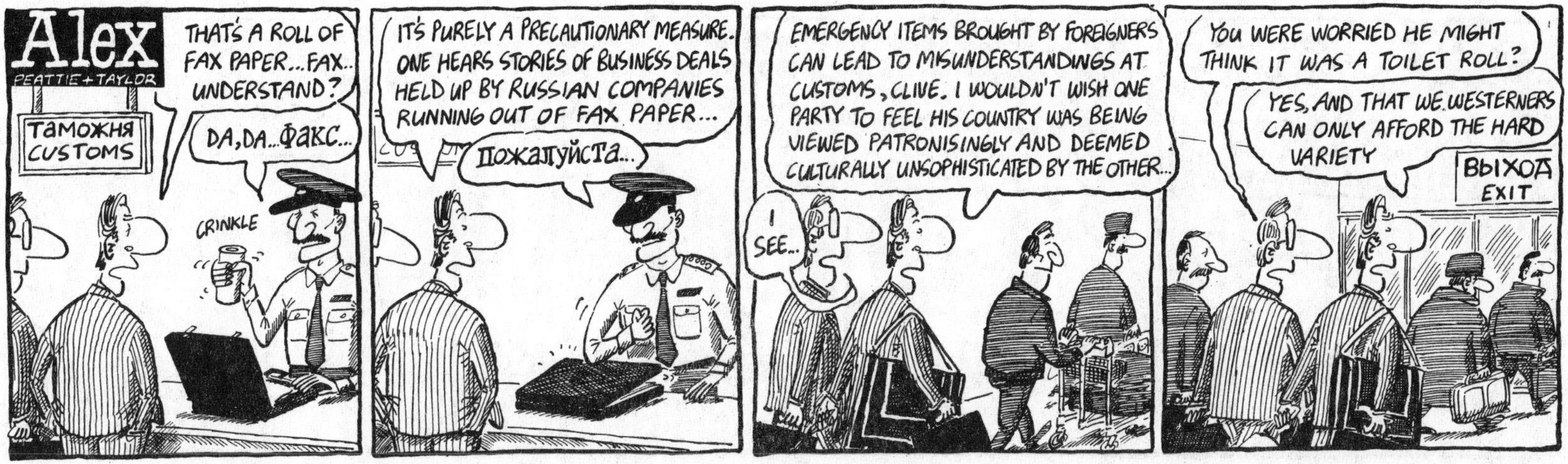
Alex
PEATTIE + TAYLOR
Таможня
CUSTOMS
THAT'S A ROLL OF FAX PAPER... FAX... UNDERSTAND?
DA, DA... Факс...
CRINKLE
IT'S PURELY A PRECAUTIONARY MEASURE. ONE HEARS STORIES OF BUSINESS DEALS HELD UP BY RUSSIAN COMPANIES RUNNING OUT OF FAX PAPER....
Пожалуйста...
EMERGENCY ITEMS BROUGHT BY FOREIGNERS CAN LEAD TO MISUNDERSTANDINGS AT CUSTOMS, CLIVE. I WOULDN'T WISH ONE PARTY TO FEEL HIS COUNTRY WAS BEING VIEWED PATRONISINGLY AND DEEMED CULTURALLY UNSOPHISTICATED BY THE OTHER...
I SEE...
YOU WERE WORRIED HE MIGHT THINK IT WAS A TOILET ROLL?
YES, AND THAT WE WESTERNERS CAN ONLY AFFORD THE HARD VARIETY
ВЫХОД
EXIT

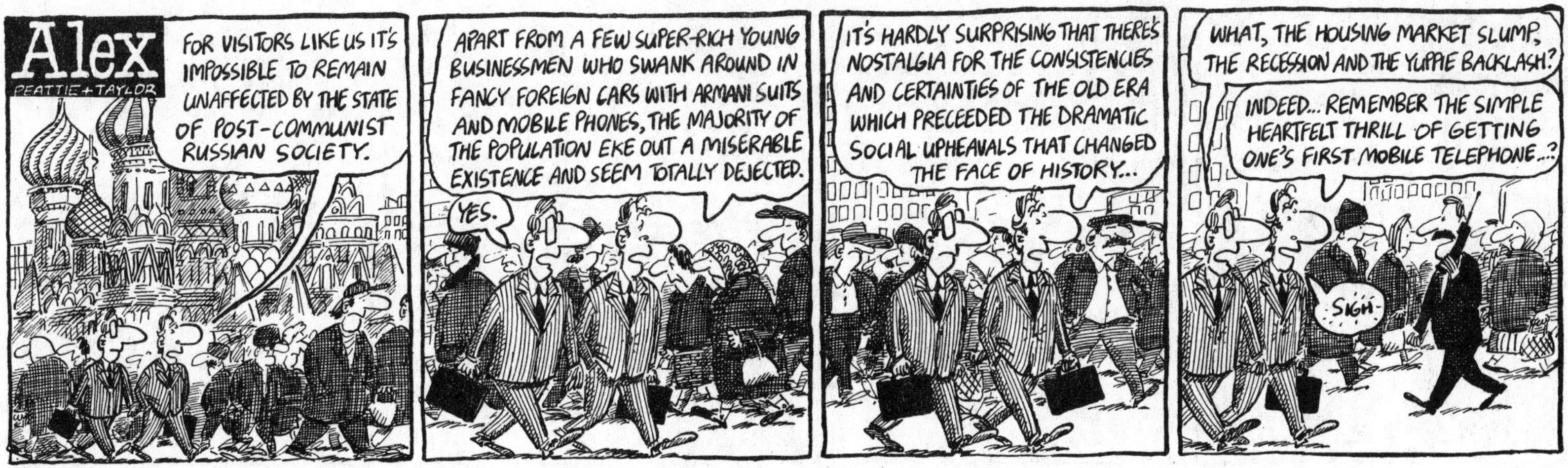
Alex
PEATTIE + TAYLOR
FOR VISITORS LIKE US IT'S IMPOSSIBLE TO REMAIN UNAFFECTED BY THE STATE OF POST-COMMUNIST RUSSIAN SOCIETY.
APART FROM A FEW SUPER-RICH YOUNG BUSINESSMEN WHO SWANK AROUND IN FANCY FOREIGN CARS WITH ARMANI SUITS AND MOBILE PHONES, THE MAJORITY OF THE POPULATION EKE OUT A MISERABLE EXISTENCE AND SEEM TOTALLY DEJECTED.
YES.
IT'S HARDLY SURPRISING THAT THERE'S NOSTALGIA FOR THE CONSISTENCIES AND CERTAINTIES OF THE OLD ERA WHICH PRECEEDED THE DRAMATIC SOCIAL UPHEAVALS THAT CHANGED THE FACE OF HISTORY...
WHAT, THE HOUSING MARKET SLUMP, THE RECESSION AND THE YUPPIE BACKLASH?
INDEED... REMEMBER THE SIMPLE HEARTFELT THRILL OF GETTING ONE'S FIRST MOBILE TELEPHONE...?
SIGH

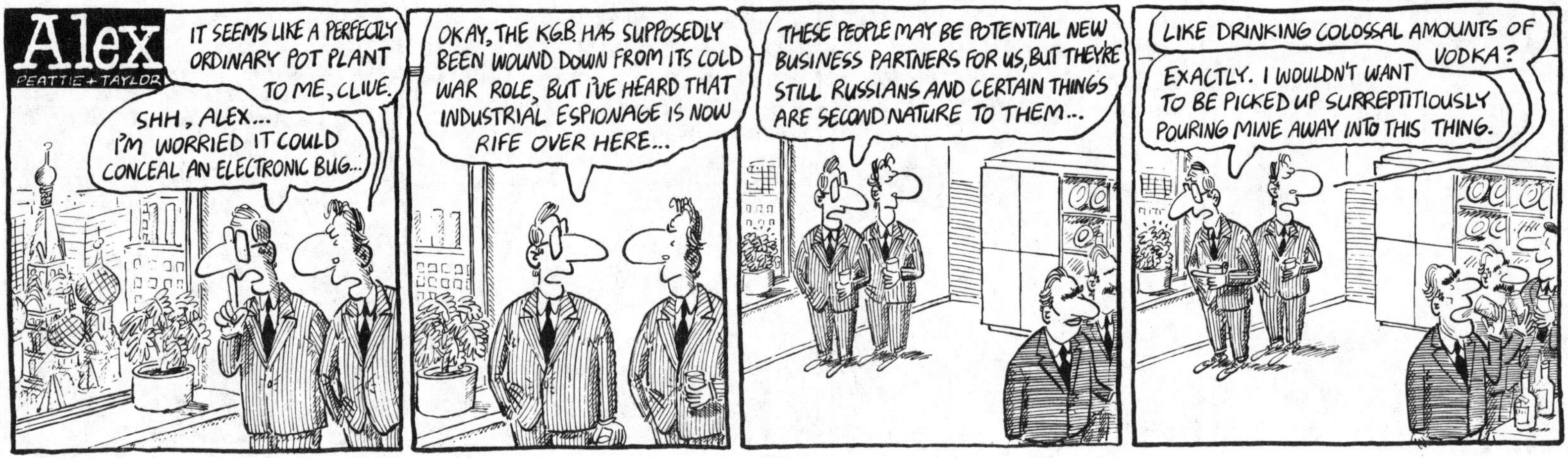
Alex
PEATTIE + TAYLOR
IT SEEMS LIKE A PERFECTLY ORDINARY POT PLANT TO ME, CLIVE.
SHH, ALEX... I'M WORRIED IT COULD CONCEAL AN ELECTRONIC BUG...
OKAY, THE K.G.B. HAS SUPPOSEDLY BEEN WOUND DOWN FROM ITS COLD WAR ROLE, BUT I'VE HEARD THAT INDUSTRIAL ESPIONAGE IS NOW RIFE OVER HERE...
THESE PEOPLE MAY BE POTENTIAL NEW BUSINESS PARTNERS FOR US, BUT THEY'RE STILL RUSSIANS AND CERTAIN THINGS ARE SECOND NATURE TO THEM...
LIKE DRINKING COLOSSAL AMOUNTS OF VODKA?
EXACTLY. I WOULDN'T WANT TO BE PICKED UP SURREPTITIOUSLY POURING MINE AWAY INTO THIS THING.

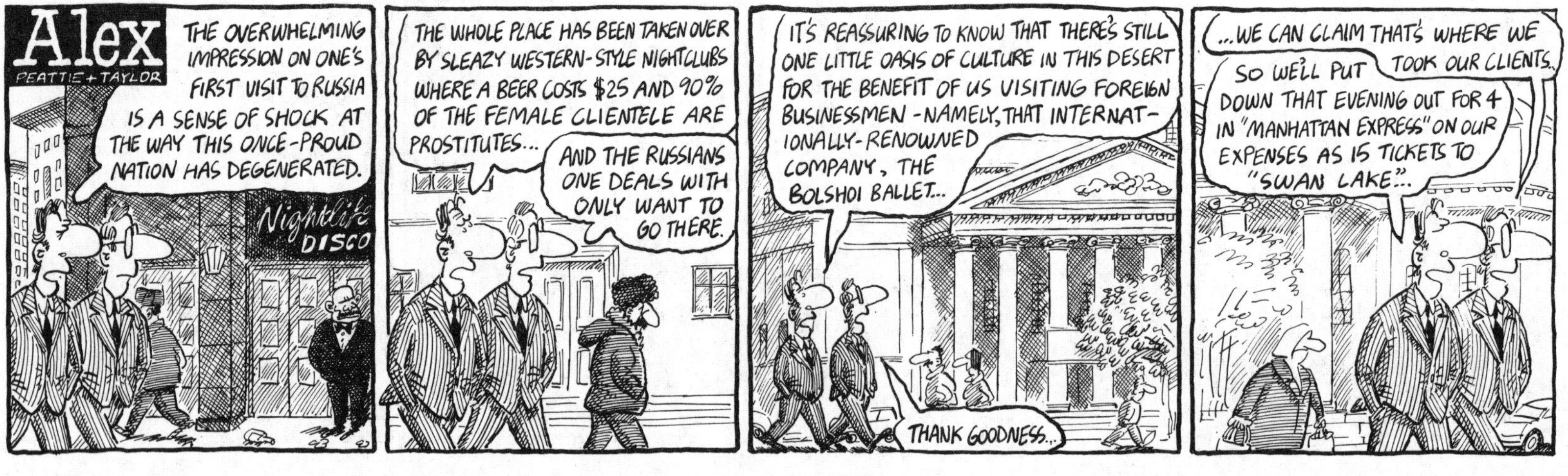
Alex
PEATTIE + TAYLOR
THE OVERWHELMING IMPRESSION ON ONE'S FIRST VISIT TO RUSSIA IS A SENSE OF SHOCK AT THE WAY THIS ONCE-PROUD NATION HAS DEGENERATED.
Nightlife DISCO
THE WHOLE PLACE HAS BEEN TAKEN OVER BY SLEAZY WESTERN-STYLE NIGHTCLUBS WHERE A BEER COSTS $25 AND 90% OF THE FEMALE CLIENTELE ARE PROSTITUTES...
AND THE RUSSIANS ONE DEALS WITH ONLY WANT TO GO THERE.
IT'S REASSURING TO KNOW THAT THERE'S STILL ONE LITTLE OASIS OF CULTURE IN THIS DESERT FOR THE BENEFIT OF US VISITING FOREIGN BUSINESSMEN - NAMELY, THAT INTERNATIONALLY-RENOWNED COMPANY, THE BOLSHOI BALLET...
THANK GOODNESS...
SO WE'LL PUT DOWN THAT EVENING OUT FOR 4 IN "MANHATTAN EXPRESS" ON OUR EXPENSES AS 15 TICKETS TO "SWAN LAKE"...
...WE CAN CLAIM THAT'S WHERE WE TOOK OUR CLIENTS.

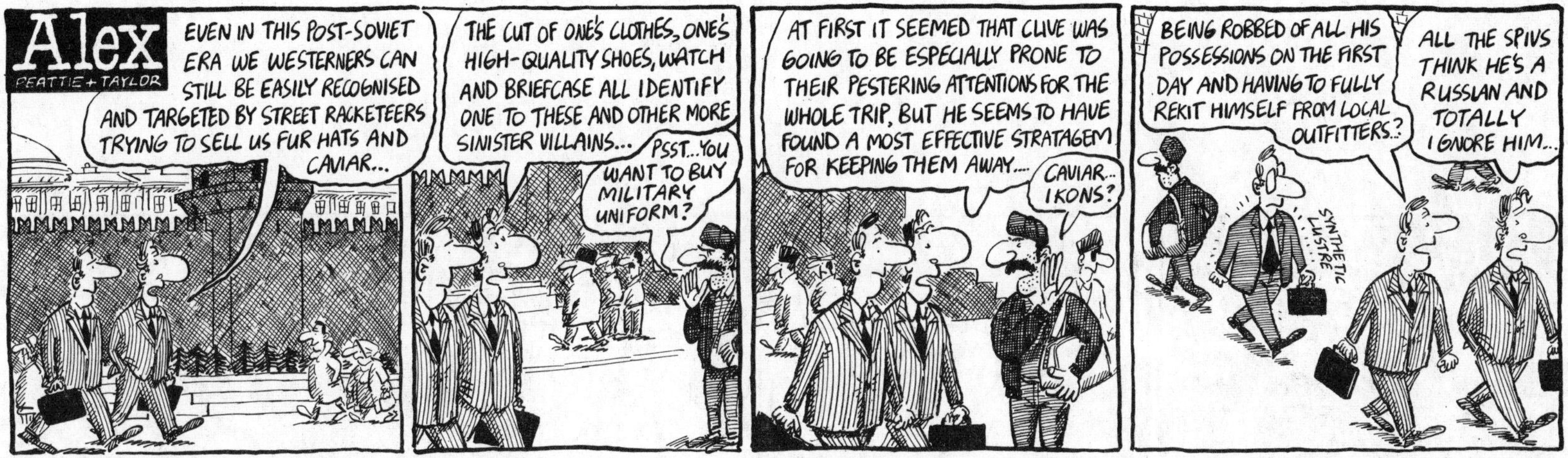
Alex
BEATTIE + TAYLOR
EVEN IN THIS POST-SOVIET ERA WE WESTERNERS CAN STILL BE EASILY RECOGNISED AND TARGETED BY STREET RACKETEERS TRYING TO SELL US FUR HATS AND CAVIAR...
THE CUT OF ONE'S CLOTHES, ONE'S HIGH-QUALITY SHOES, WATCH AND BRIEFCASE ALL IDENTIFY ONE TO THESE AND OTHER MORE SINISTER VILLAINS...
PSST...YOU WANT TO BUY MILITARY UNIFORM?
AT FIRST IT SEEMED THAT CLIVE WAS GOING TO BE ESPECIALLY PRONE TO THEIR PESTERING ATTENTIONS FOR THE WHOLE TRIP, BUT HE SEEMS TO HAVE FOUND A MOST EFFECTIVE STRATAGEM FOR KEEPING THEM AWAY....
CAVIAR... IKONS?
BEING ROBBED OF ALL HIS POSSESSIONS ON THE FIRST DAY AND HAVING TO FULLY REKIT HIMSELF FROM LOCAL OUTFITTERS..?
SYNTHETIC LUSTRE
ALL THE SPIVS THINK HE'S A RUSSIAN AND TOTALLY IGNORE HIM...

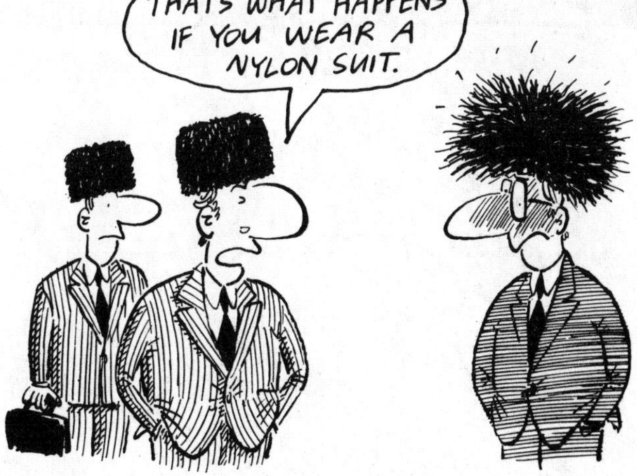
THAT'S WHAT HAPPENS IF YOU WEAR A NYLON SUIT.

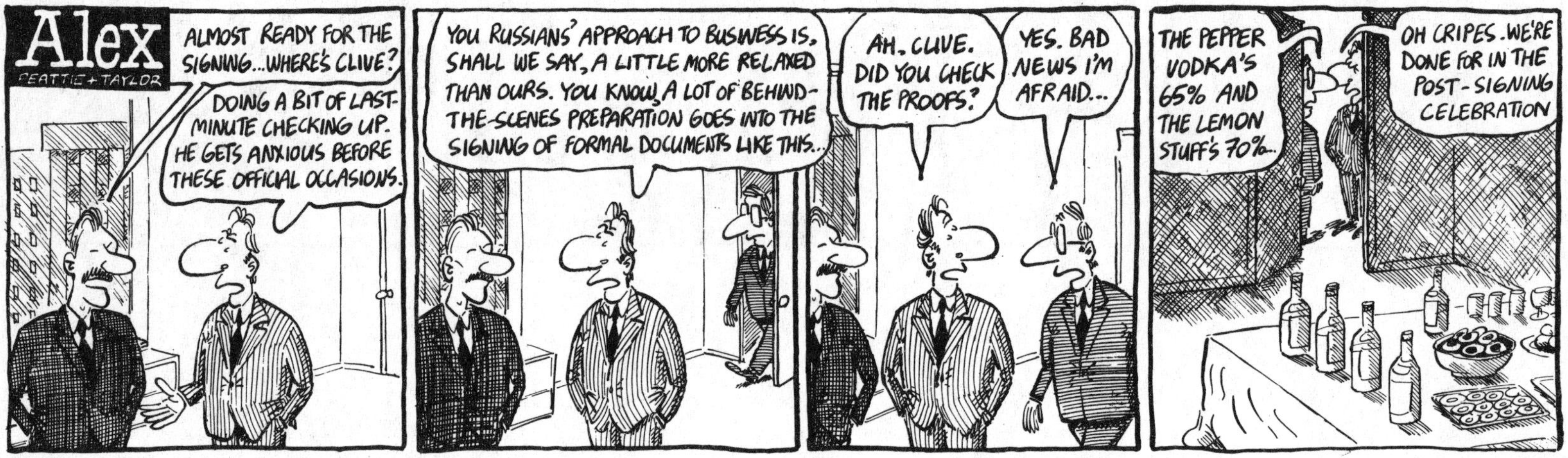
Alex
BEATTIE + TAYLOR
ALMOST READY FOR THE SIGNING...WHERE'S CLIVE?
DOING A BIT OF LAST-MINUTE CHECKING UP. HE GETS ANXIOUS BEFORE THESE OFFICIAL OCCASIONS.
YOU RUSSIANS' APPROACH TO BUSINESS IS, SHALL WE SAY, A LITTLE MORE RELAXED THAN OURS. YOU KNOW, A LOT OF BEHIND-THE-SCENES PREPARATION GOES INTO THE SIGNING OF FORMAL DOCUMENTS LIKE THIS...
AH. CLIVE. DID YOU CHECK THE PROOFS?
YES. BAD NEWS I'M AFRAID...
THE PEPPER VODKA'S 65% AND THE LEMON STUFF'S 70%...
OH CRIPES. WE'RE DONE FOR IN THE POST-SIGNING CELEBRATION

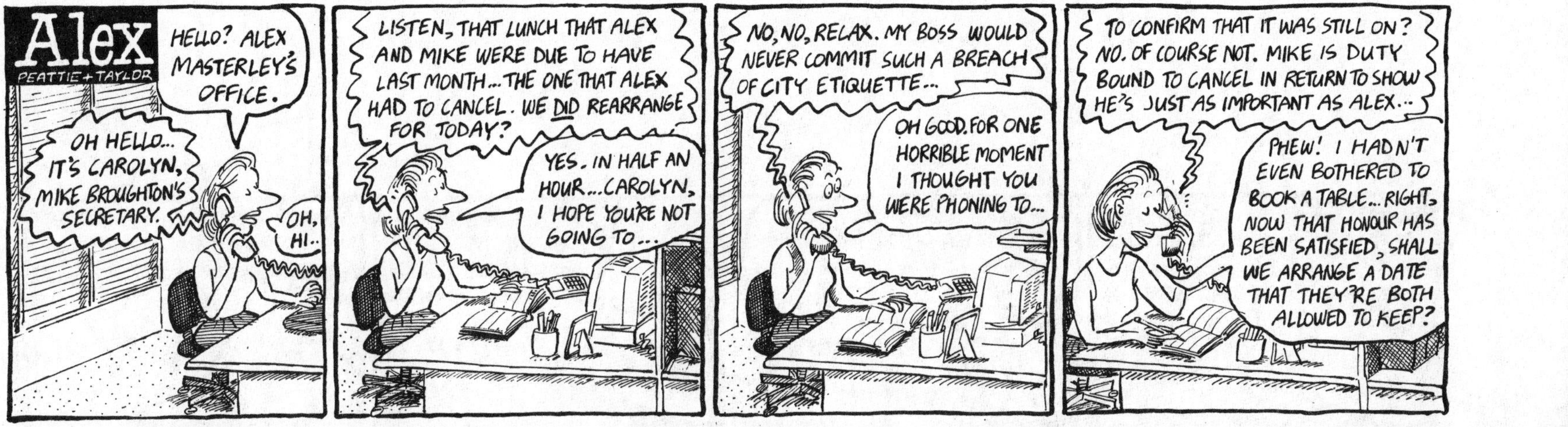
Alex
PEATTIE + TAYLOR
HELLO? ALEX MASTERLEY'S OFFICE.
OH HELLO... IT'S CAROLYN, MIKE BROUGHTON'S SECRETARY.
OH, HI...
LISTEN, THAT LUNCH THAT ALEX AND MIKE WERE DUE TO HAVE LAST MONTH... THE ONE THAT ALEX HAD TO CANCEL. WE DID REARRANGE FOR TODAY?
YES. IN HALF AN HOUR... CAROLYN, I HOPE YOU'RE NOT GOING TO...
NO, NO, RELAX. MY BOSS WOULD NEVER COMMIT SUCH A BREACH OF CITY ETIQUETTE...
OH GOOD. FOR ONE HORRIBLE MOMENT I THOUGHT YOU WERE PHONING TO...
TO CONFIRM THAT IT WAS STILL ON? NO. OF COURSE NOT. MIKE IS DUTY BOUND TO CANCEL IN RETURN TO SHOW HE'S JUST AS IMPORTANT AS ALEX...
PHEW! I HADN'T EVEN BOTHERED TO BOOK A TABLE... RIGHT, NOW THAT HONOUR HAS BEEN SATISFIED, SHALL WE ARRANGE A DATE THAT THEY'RE BOTH ALLOWED TO KEEP?

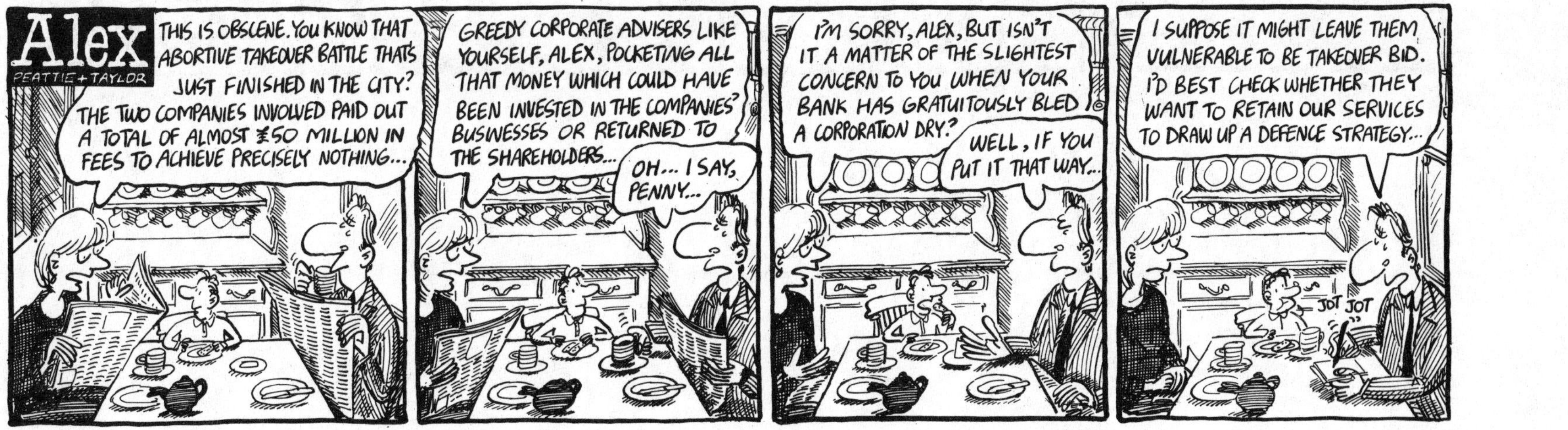
Alex
PEATTIE + TAYLOR
THIS IS OBSCENE. YOU KNOW THAT ABORTIVE TAKEOVER BATTLE THAT'S JUST FINISHED IN THE CITY? THE TWO COMPANIES INVOLVED PAID OUT A TOTAL OF ALMOST ¥50 MILLION IN FEES TO ACHIEVE PRECISELY NOTHING...
GREEDY CORPORATE ADVISERS LIKE YOURSELF, ALEX, POCKETING ALL THAT MONEY WHICH COULD HAVE BEEN INVESTED IN THE COMPANIES' BUSINESSES OR RETURNED TO THE SHAREHOLDERS...
OH... I SAY, PENNY...
I'M SORRY, ALEX, BUT ISN'T IT A MATTER OF THE SLIGHTEST CONCERN TO YOU WHEN YOUR BANK HAS GRATUITOUSLY BLED A CORPORATION DRY?
WELL, IF YOU PUT IT THAT WAY...
I SUPPOSE IT MIGHT LEAVE THEM VULNERABLE TO BE TAKEOVER BID. I'D BEST CHECK WHETHER THEY WANT TO RETAIN OUR SERVICES TO DRAW UP A DEFENCE STRATEGY...
JOT JOT

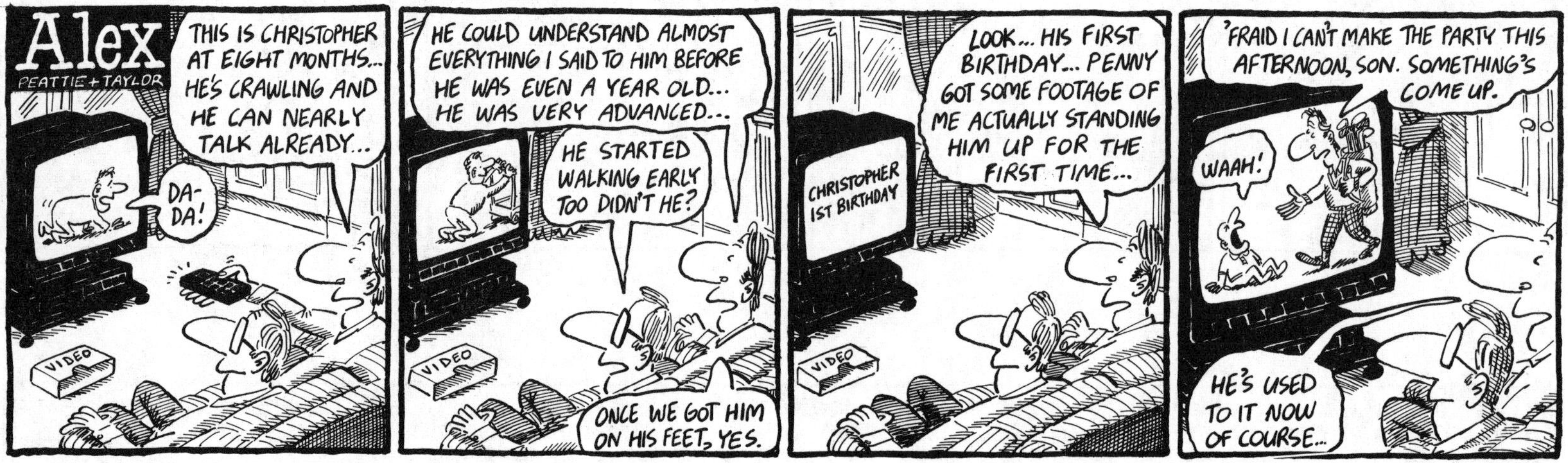

Alex
PEATTIE + TAYLOR
THIS IS CHRISTOPHER AT EIGHT MONTHS... HE'S CRAWLING AND HE CAN NEARLY TALK ALREADY...
DA-DA!
VIDEO
HE COULD UNDERSTAND ALMOST EVERYTHING I SAID TO HIM BEFORE HE WAS EVEN A YEAR OLD... HE WAS VERY ADVANCED...
HE STARTED WALKING EARLY TOO DIDN'T HE?
ONCE WE GOT HIM ON HIS FEET, YES.
VIDEO
LOOK... HIS FIRST BIRTHDAY... PENNY GOT SOME FOOTAGE OF ME ACTUALLY STANDING HIM UP FOR THE FIRST TIME...
CHRISTOPHER 1ST BIRTHDAY
VIDEO
'FRAID I CAN'T MAKE THE PARTY THIS AFTERNOON, SON. SOMETHING'S COME UP.
WAAH!
HE'S USED TO IT NOW OF COURSE...

Alex
PEATTIE + TAYLOR
SO HOW'S IT GOING, STARTING WORK WITH US TODAY?
WELL, IT'S A BIT DIFFERENT. AFTER ALL, I'VE HAD TO TAKE THREE MONTHS' "GARDENING LEAVE".
AND OBVIOUSLY THAT'S BOUND TO HAVE AN EFFECT ON MY PERFORMANCE. YOU KNOW WHAT IT'S LIKE WHEN YOU'VE BEEN OUT OF THE MARKET FOR A WHILE...
NONE OF THE CLIENTS HAVE SPOKEN TO YOU FOR AGES. YOU'VE BEEN OUT OF THE HABIT OF PHONING THEM UP DAILY WITH A FRIENDLY PATTER AND A PIECE OF ADVICE. YOU HAVE TO START ALL OVER WITH THEM FROM SQUARE ONE...
YES... YES...
SO YOU HAVE A BIG HEAD START ON ALL YOUR RIVAL BROKERS?
QUITE. I'M THE ONLY ONE WITHOUT A RECENT RECORD OF PROVEN DUFF RECOMMENDATIONS.

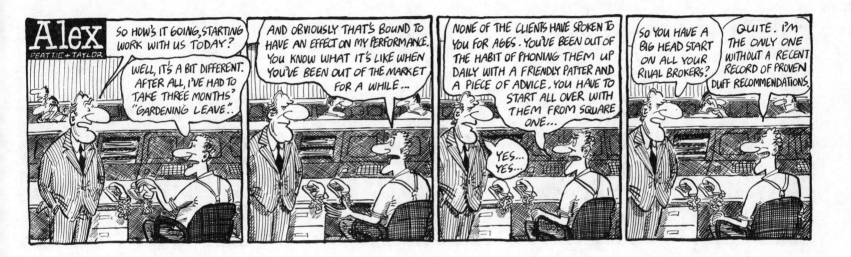

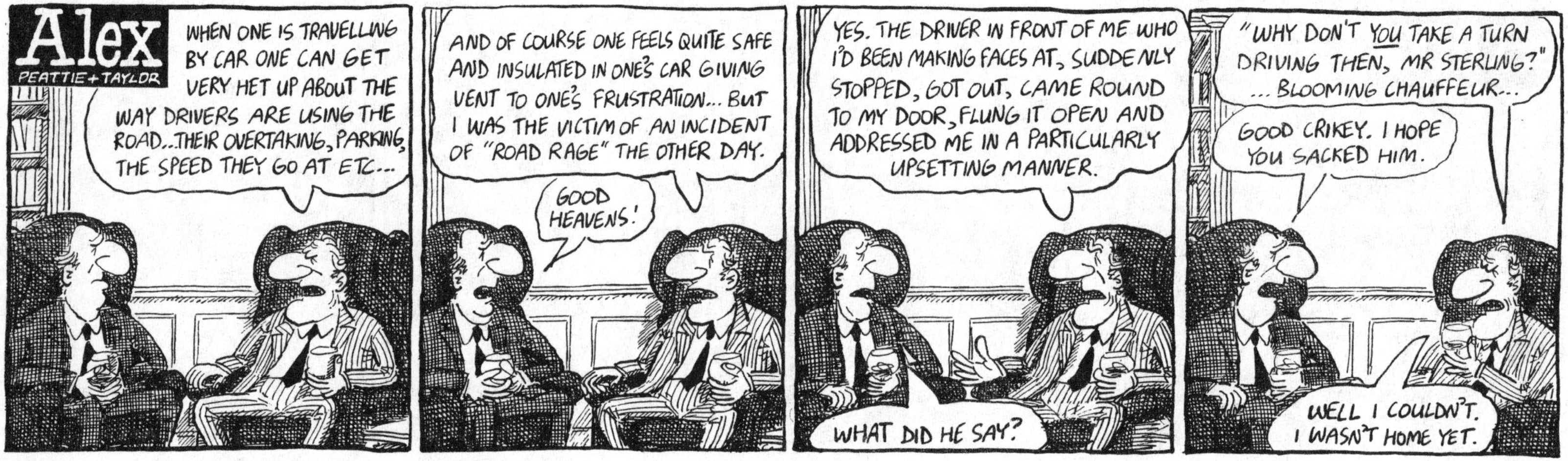
Alex
PEATTIE + TAYLOR
WHEN ONE IS TRAVELLING BY CAR ONE CAN GET VERY HET UP ABOUT THE WAY DRIVERS ARE USING THE ROAD...THEIR OVERTAKING, PARKING, THE SPEED THEY GO AT ETC...
AND OF COURSE ONE FEELS QUITE SAFE AND INSULATED IN ONE'S CAR GIVING VENT TO ONE'S FRUSTRATION... BUT I WAS THE VICTIM OF AN INCIDENT OF "ROAD RAGE" THE OTHER DAY.
GOOD HEAVENS!
YES. THE DRIVER IN FRONT OF ME WHO I'D BEEN MAKING FACES AT, SUDDENLY STOPPED, GOT OUT, CAME ROUND TO MY DOOR, FLUNG IT OPEN AND ADDRESSED ME IN A PARTICULARLY UPSETTING MANNER.
WHAT DID HE SAY?
"WHY DON'T YOU TAKE A TURN DRIVING THEN, MR STERLING?" ... BLOOMING CHAUFFEUR...
GOOD CRIKEY. I HOPE YOU SACKED HIM.
WELL I COULDN'T. I WASN'T HOME YET.

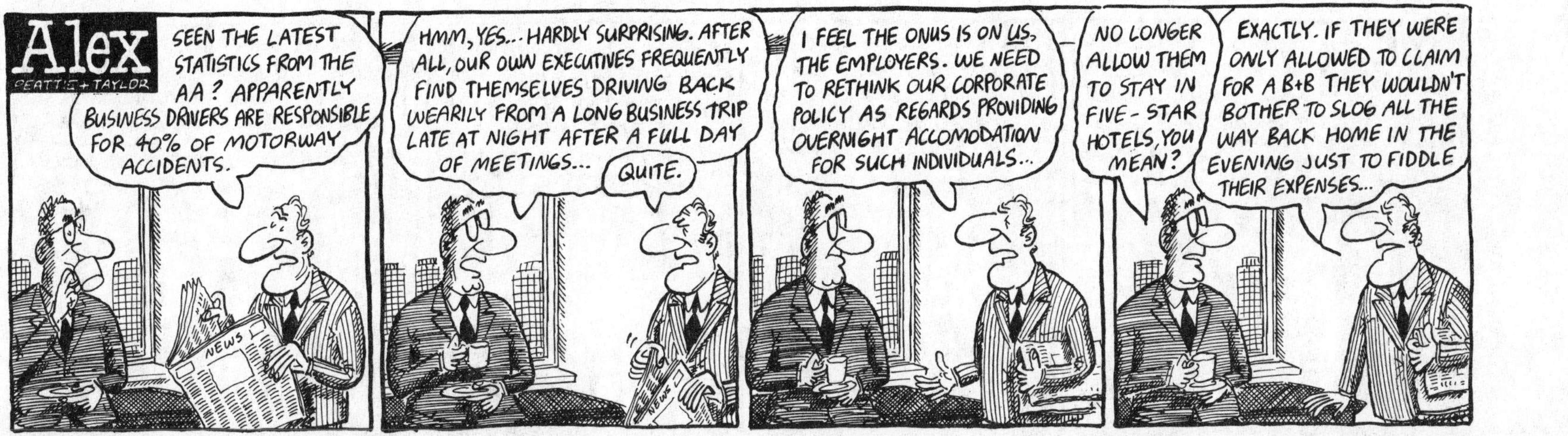
Alex
PEATTIE+TAYLOR
SEEN THE LATEST STATISTICS FROM THE AA? APPARENTLY BUSINESS DRIVERS ARE RESPONSIBLE FOR 40% OF MOTORWAY ACCIDENTS.
NEWS
HMM, YES... HARDLY SURPRISING. AFTER ALL, OUR OWN EXECUTIVES FREQUENTLY FIND THEMSELVES DRIVING BACK WEARILY FROM A LONG BUSINESS TRIP LATE AT NIGHT AFTER A FULL DAY OF MEETINGS...
QUITE.
NEWS
I FEEL THE ONUS IS ON US, THE EMPLOYERS. WE NEED TO RETHINK OUR CORPORATE POLICY AS REGARDS PROVIDING OVERNIGHT ACCOMODATION FOR SUCH INDIVIDUALS...
NO LONGER ALLOW THEM TO STAY IN FIVE-STAR HOTELS, YOU MEAN?
EXACTLY. IF THEY WERE ONLY ALLOWED TO CLAIM FOR A B+B THEY WOULDN'T BOTHER TO SLOG ALL THE WAY BACK HOME IN THE EVENING JUST TO FIDDLE THEIR EXPENSES...

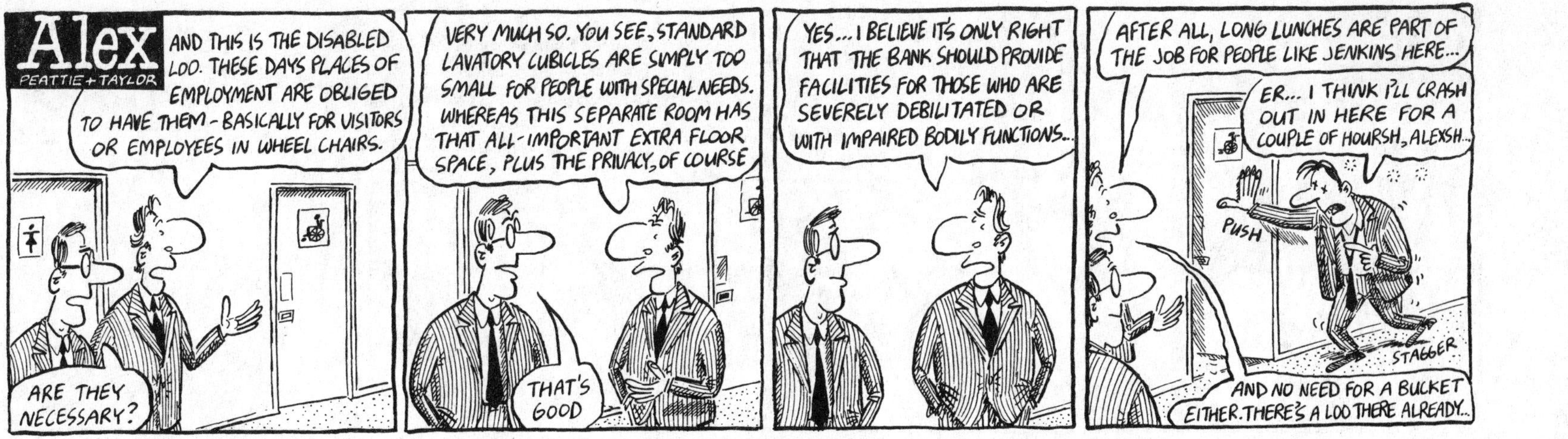
Alex
PEATTIE+TAYLOR
AND THIS IS THE DISABLED LOO. THESE DAYS PLACES OF EMPLOYMENT ARE OBLIGED TO HAVE THEM - BASICALLY FOR VISITORS OR EMPLOYEES IN WHEEL CHAIRS.
ARE THEY NECESSARY?
VERY MUCH SO. YOU SEE, STANDARD LAVATORY CUBICLES ARE SIMPLY TOO SMALL FOR PEOPLE WITH SPECIAL NEEDS. WHEREAS THIS SEPARATE ROOM HAS THAT ALL-IMPORTANT EXTRA FLOOR SPACE, PLUS THE PRIVACY, OF COURSE
THAT'S GOOD
YES... I BELIEVE IT'S ONLY RIGHT THAT THE BANK SHOULD PROVIDE FACILITIES FOR THOSE WHO ARE SEVERELY DEBILITATED OR WITH IMPAIRED BODILY FUNCTIONS...
AFTER ALL, LONG LUNCHES ARE PART OF THE JOB FOR PEOPLE LIKE JENKINS HERE...
ER... I THINK I'LL CRASH OUT IN HERE FOR A COUPLE OF HOURSH, ALEXSH...
PUSH
STAGGER
AND NO NEED FOR A BUCKET EITHER. THERE'S A LOO THERE ALREADY...

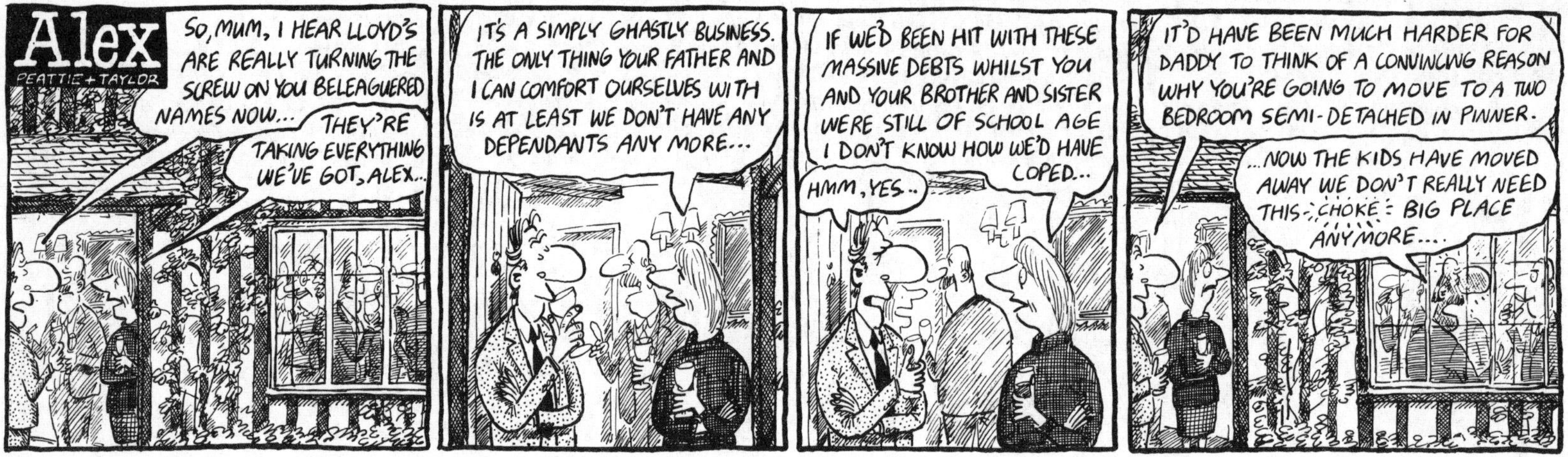
Alex
PEATTIE + TAYLOR
SO, MUM, I HEAR LLOYD'S ARE REALLY TURNING THE SCREW ON YOU BELEAGUERED NAMES NOW...
THEY'RE TAKING EVERYTHING WE'VE GOT, ALEX...
IT'S A SIMPLY GHASTLY BUSINESS. THE ONLY THING YOUR FATHER AND I CAN COMFORT OURSELVES WITH IS AT LEAST WE DON'T HAVE ANY DEPENDANTS ANY MORE...
IF WE'D BEEN HIT WITH THESE MASSIVE DEBTS WHILST YOU AND YOUR BROTHER AND SISTER WERE STILL OF SCHOOL AGE I DON'T KNOW HOW WE'D HAVE COPED...
HMM, YES..
IT'D HAVE BEEN MUCH HARDER FOR DADDY TO THINK OF A CONVINCING REASON WHY YOU'RE GOING TO MOVE TO A TWO BEDROOM SEMI-DETACHED IN PINNER.
...NOW THE KIDS HAVE MOVED AWAY WE DON'T REALLY NEED THIS CHOKE BIG PLACE ANYMORE....

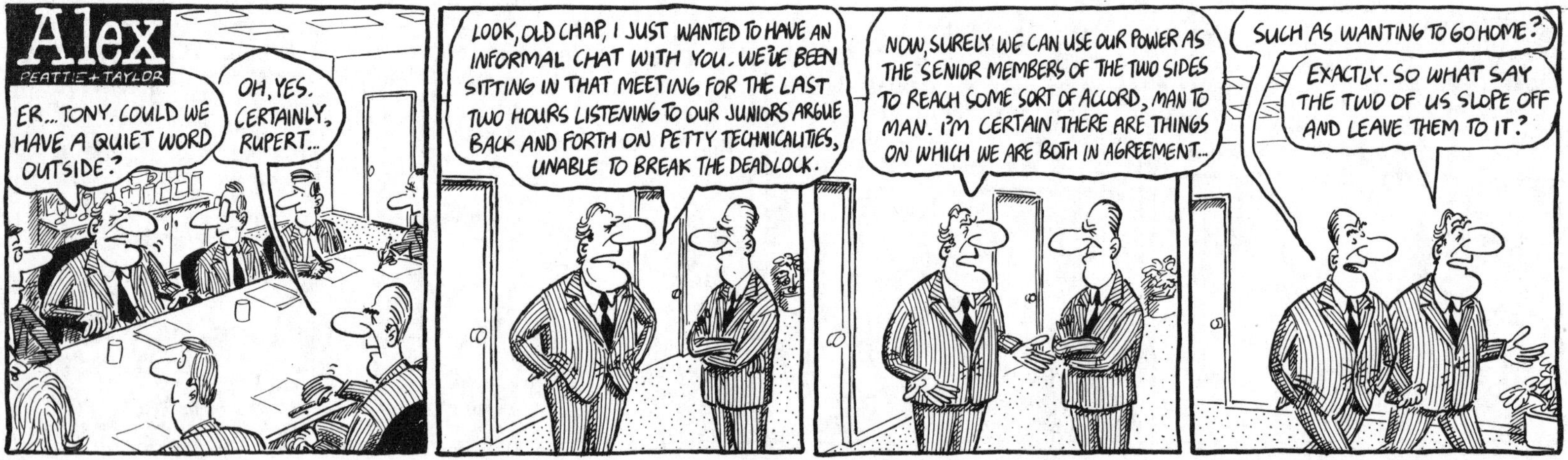
Alex
PEATTIE + TAYLOR
ER... TONY. COULD WE HAVE A QUIET WORD OUTSIDE?
OH, YES. CERTAINLY, RUPERT...
LOOK, OLD CHAP, I JUST WANTED TO HAVE AN INFORMAL CHAT WITH YOU. WE'VE BEEN SITTING IN THAT MEETING FOR THE LAST TWO HOURS LISTENING TO OUR JUNIORS ARGUE BACK AND FORTH ON PETTY TECHNICALITIES, UNABLE TO BREAK THE DEADLOCK.
NOW, SURELY WE CAN USE OUR POWER AS THE SENIOR MEMBERS OF THE TWO SIDES TO REACH SOME SORT OF ACCORD, MAN TO MAN. I'M CERTAIN THERE ARE THINGS ON WHICH WE ARE BOTH IN AGREEMENT...
SUCH AS WANTING TO GO HOME?
EXACTLY. SO WHAT SAY THE TWO OF US SLOPE OFF AND LEAVE THEM TO IT?

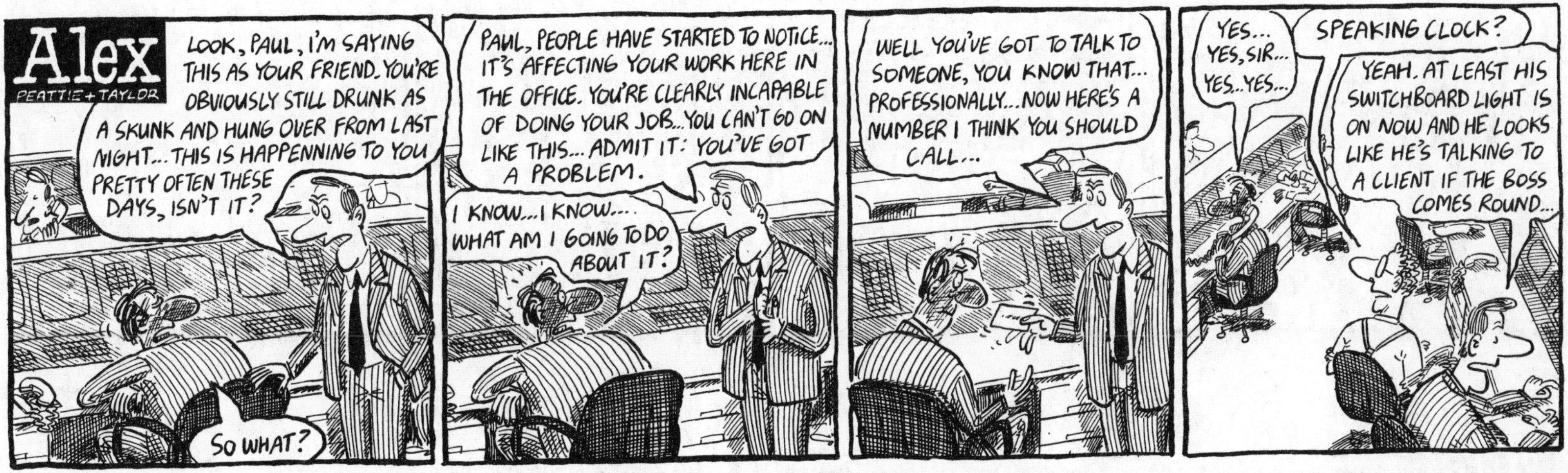
Alex
PEATTIE + TAYLOR
LOOK, PAUL, I'M SAYING THIS AS YOUR FRIEND. YOU'RE OBVIOUSLY STILL DRUNK AS A SKUNK AND HUNG OVER FROM LAST NIGHT... THIS IS HAPPENNING TO YOU PRETTY OFTEN THESE DAYS, ISN'T IT?
SO WHAT?
PAUL, PEOPLE HAVE STARTED TO NOTICE... IT'S AFFECTING YOUR WORK HERE IN THE OFFICE. YOU'RE CLEARLY INCAPABLE OF DOING YOUR JOB... YOU CAN'T GO ON LIKE THIS... ADMIT IT: YOU'VE GOT A PROBLEM.
I KNOW... I KNOW.... WHAT AM I GOING TO DO ABOUT IT?
WELL YOU'VE GOT TO TALK TO SOMEONE, YOU KNOW THAT... PROFESSIONALLY... NOW HERE'S A NUMBER I THINK YOU SHOULD CALL...
YES... YES, SIR... YES... YES...
SPEAKING CLOCK?
YEAH. AT LEAST HIS SWITCHBOARD LIGHT IS ON NOW AND HE LOOKS LIKE HE'S TALKING TO A CLIENT IF THE BOSS COMES ROUND...

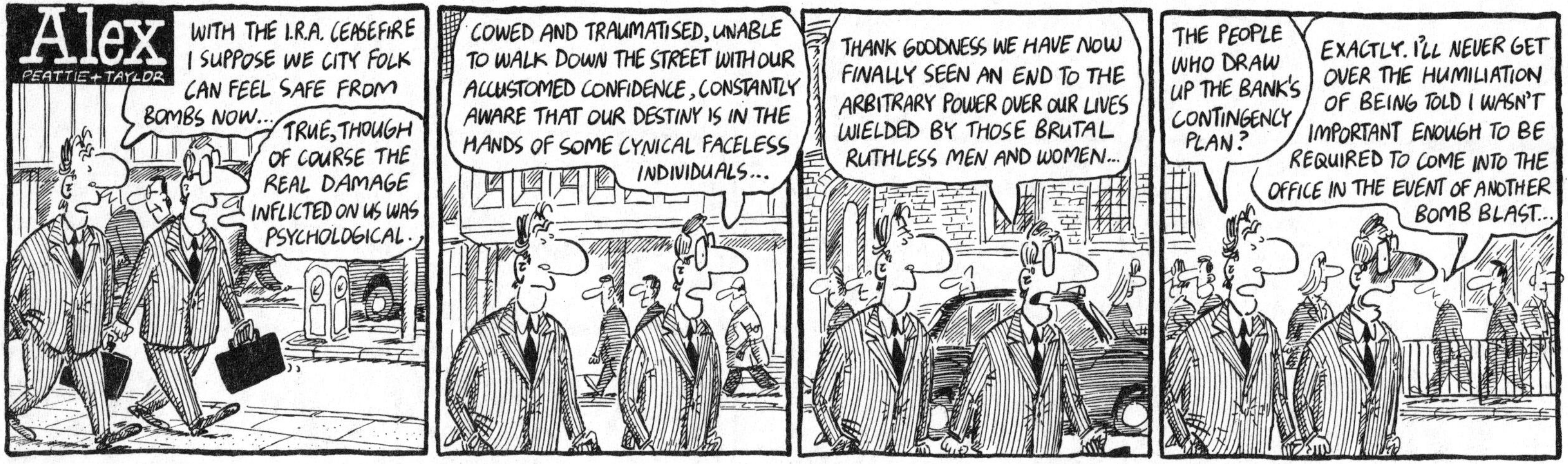
Alex
PEATTIE + TAYLOR
WITH THE I.R.A. CEASEFIRE I SUPPOSE WE CITY FOLK CAN FEEL SAFE FROM BOMBS NOW...
TRUE, THOUGH OF COURSE THE REAL DAMAGE INFLICTED ON US WAS PSYCHOLOGICAL.
COWED AND TRAUMATISED, UNABLE TO WALK DOWN THE STREET WITH OUR ACCUSTOMED CONFIDENCE, CONSTANTLY AWARE THAT OUR DESTINY IS IN THE HANDS OF SOME CYNICAL FACELESS INDIVIDUALS...
THANK GOODNESS WE HAVE NOW FINALLY SEEN AN END TO THE ARBITRARY POWER OVER OUR LIVES WIELDED BY THOSE BRUTAL RUTHLESS MEN AND WOMEN...
THE PEOPLE WHO DRAW UP THE BANK'S CONTINGENCY PLAN?
EXACTLY. I'LL NEVER GET OVER THE HUMILIATION OF BEING TOLD I WASN'T IMPORTANT ENOUGH TO BE REQUIRED TO COME INTO THE OFFICE IN THE EVENT OF ANOTHER BOMB BLAST...

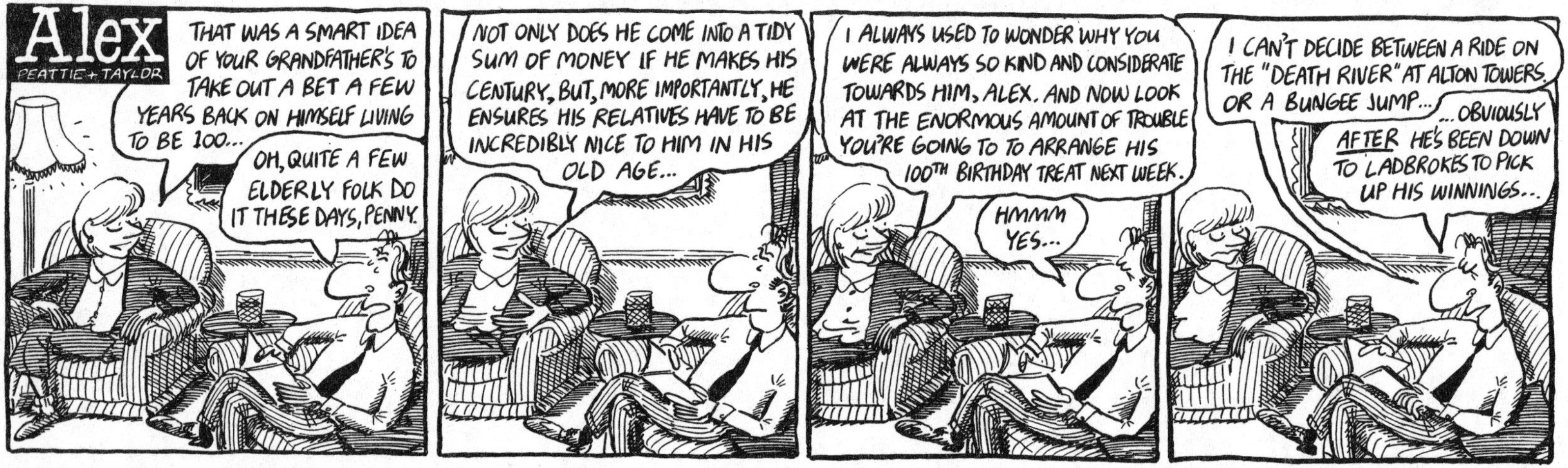
Alex
PEATTIE + TAYLOR
THAT WAS A SMART IDEA OF YOUR GRANDFATHER'S TO TAKE OUT A BET A FEW YEARS BACK ON HIMSELF LIVING TO BE 100...
OH, QUITE A FEW ELDERLY FOLK DO IT THESE DAYS, PENNY.
NOT ONLY DOES HE COME INTO A TIDY SUM OF MONEY IF HE MAKES HIS CENTURY, BUT, MORE IMPORTANTLY, HE ENSURES HIS RELATIVES HAVE TO BE INCREDIBLY NICE TO HIM IN HIS OLD AGE...
I ALWAYS USED TO WONDER WHY YOU WERE ALWAYS SO KIND AND CONSIDERATE TOWARDS HIM, ALEX. AND NOW LOOK AT THE ENORMOUS AMOUNT OF TROUBLE YOU'RE GOING TO TO ARRANGE HIS 100TH BIRTHDAY TREAT NEXT WEEK.
HMMM YES...
I CAN'T DECIDE BETWEEN A RIDE ON THE "DEATH RIVER" AT ALTON TOWERS OR A BUNGEE JUMP...
...OBVIOUSLY AFTER HE'S BEEN DOWN TO LADBROKES TO PICK UP HIS WINNINGS...

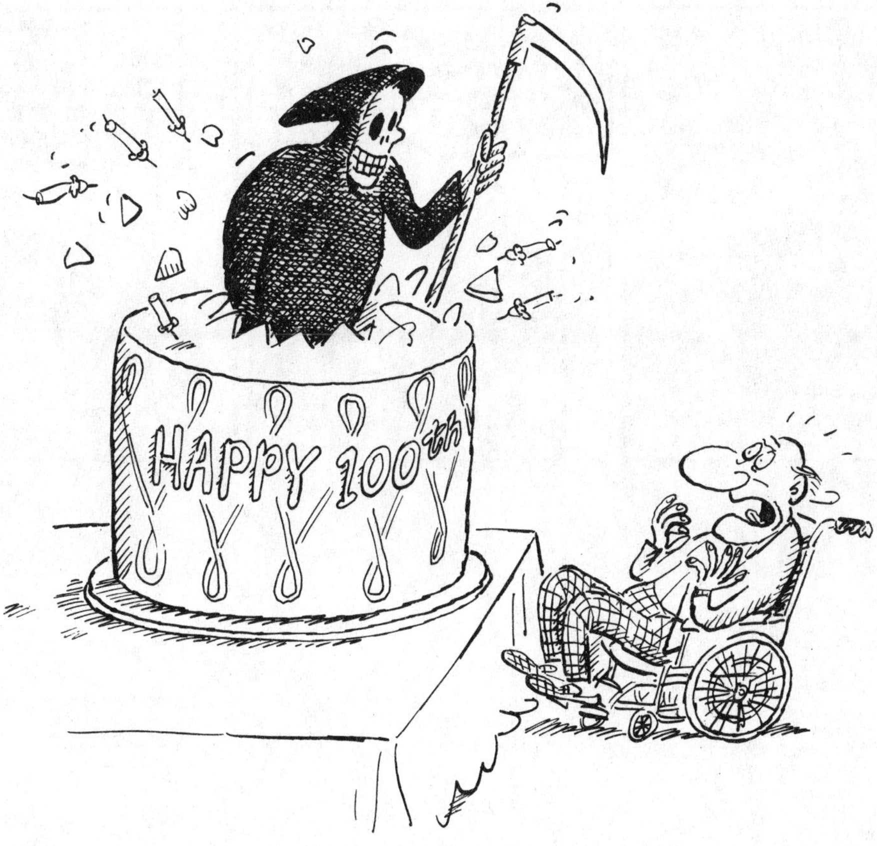
HAPPY 100th

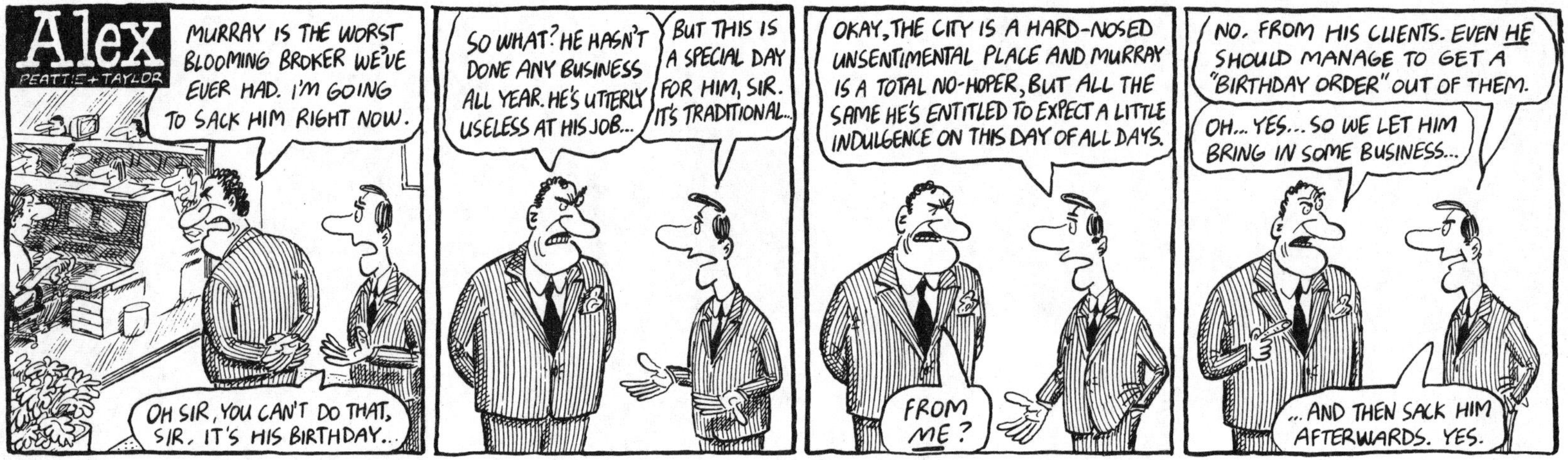
Alex
PEATTIE + TAYLOR
MURRAY IS THE WORST BLOOMING BROKER WE'VE EVER HAD. I'M GOING TO SACK HIM RIGHT NOW.
OH SIR, YOU CAN'T DO THAT, SIR. IT'S HIS BIRTHDAY...
SO WHAT? HE HASN'T DONE ANY BUSINESS ALL YEAR. HE'S UTTERLY USELESS AT HIS JOB...
BUT THIS IS A SPECIAL DAY FOR HIM, SIR. IT'S TRADITIONAL...
OKAY, THE CITY IS A HARD-NOSED UNSENTIMENTAL PLACE AND MURRAY IS A TOTAL NO-HOPER, BUT ALL THE SAME HE'S ENTITLED TO EXPECT A LITTLE INDULGENCE ON THIS DAY OF ALL DAYS.
FROM ME?
NO. FROM HIS CLIENTS. EVEN HE SHOULD MANAGE TO GET A "BIRTHDAY ORDER" OUT OF THEM.
OH... YES... SO WE LET HIM BRING IN SOME BUSINESS...
...AND THEN SACK HIM AFTERWARDS. YES.

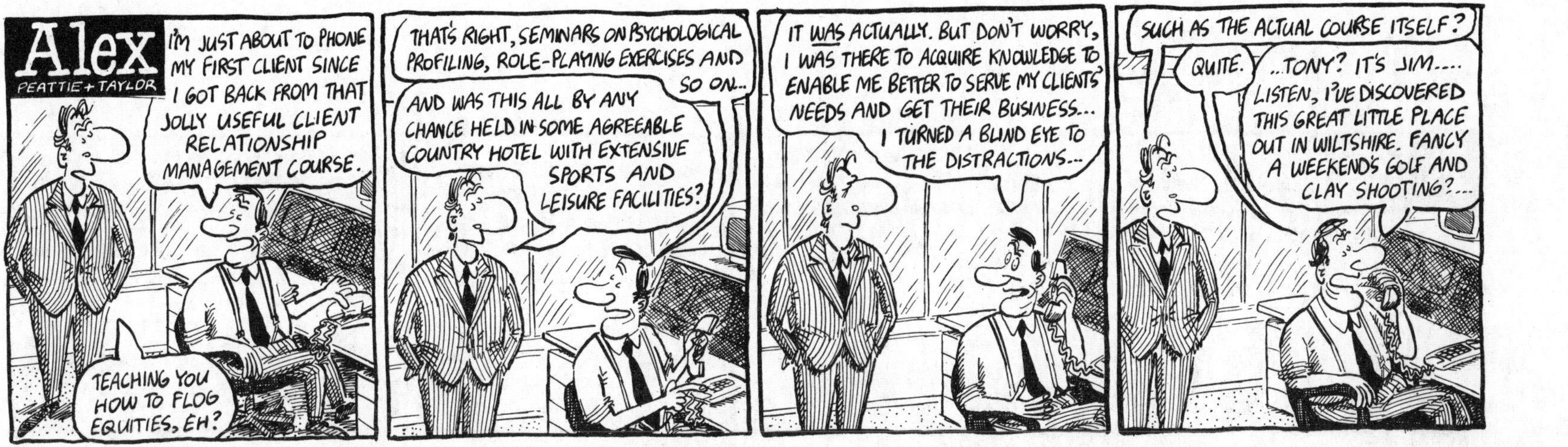
Alex
PEATTIE + TAYLOR
I'M JUST ABOUT TO PHONE MY FIRST CLIENT SINCE I GOT BACK FROM THAT JOLLY USEFUL CLIENT RELATIONSHIP MANAGEMENT COURSE.
TEACHING YOU HOW TO FLOG EQUITIES, EH?
THAT'S RIGHT, SEMINARS ON PSYCHOLOGICAL PROFILING, ROLE-PLAYING EXERCISES AND SO ON...
AND WAS THIS ALL BY ANY CHANCE HELD IN SOME AGREEABLE COUNTRY HOTEL WITH EXTENSIVE SPORTS AND LEISURE FACILITIES?
IT WAS ACTUALLY. BUT DON'T WORRY, I WAS THERE TO ACQUIRE KNOWLEDGE TO ENABLE ME BETTER TO SERVE MY CLIENTS' NEEDS AND GET THEIR BUSINESS... I TURNED A BLIND EYE TO THE DISTRACTIONS...
SUCH AS THE ACTUAL COURSE ITSELF?
QUITE.
...TONY? IT'S JIM.... LISTEN, I'VE DISCOVERED THIS GREAT LITTLE PLACE OUT IN WILTSHIRE. FANCY A WEEKEND'S GOLF AND CLAY SHOOTING?...

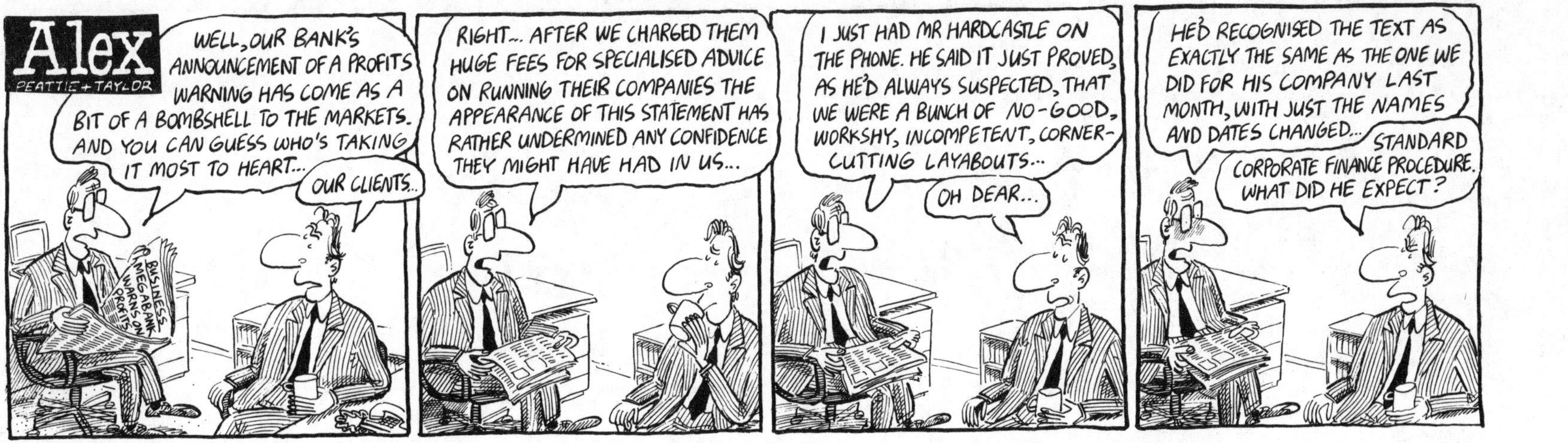
Alex
PEATTIE + TAYLOR
WELL, OUR BANK'S ANNOUNCEMENT OF A PROFITS WARNING HAS COME AS A BIT OF A BOMBSHELL TO THE MARKETS. AND YOU CAN GUESS WHO'S TAKING IT MOST TO HEART...
OUR CLIENTS...
BUSINESS MEGABANK WARNS ON PROFITS
RIGHT... AFTER WE CHARGED THEM HUGE FEES FOR SPECIALISED ADVICE ON RUNNING THEIR COMPANIES THE APPEARANCE OF THIS STATEMENT HAS RATHER UNDERMINED ANY CONFIDENCE THEY MIGHT HAVE HAD IN US...
I JUST HAD MR HARDCASTLE ON THE PHONE. HE SAID IT JUST PROVED, AS HE'D ALWAYS SUSPECTED, THAT WE WERE A BUNCH OF NO-GOOD, WORKSHY, INCOMPETENT, CORNER-CUTTING LAYABOUTS...
OH DEAR...
HE'D RECOGNISED THE TEXT AS EXACTLY THE SAME AS THE ONE WE DID FOR HIS COMPANY LAST MONTH, WITH JUST THE NAMES AND DATES CHANGED...
STANDARD CORPORATE FINANCE PROCEDURE. WHAT DID HE EXPECT?

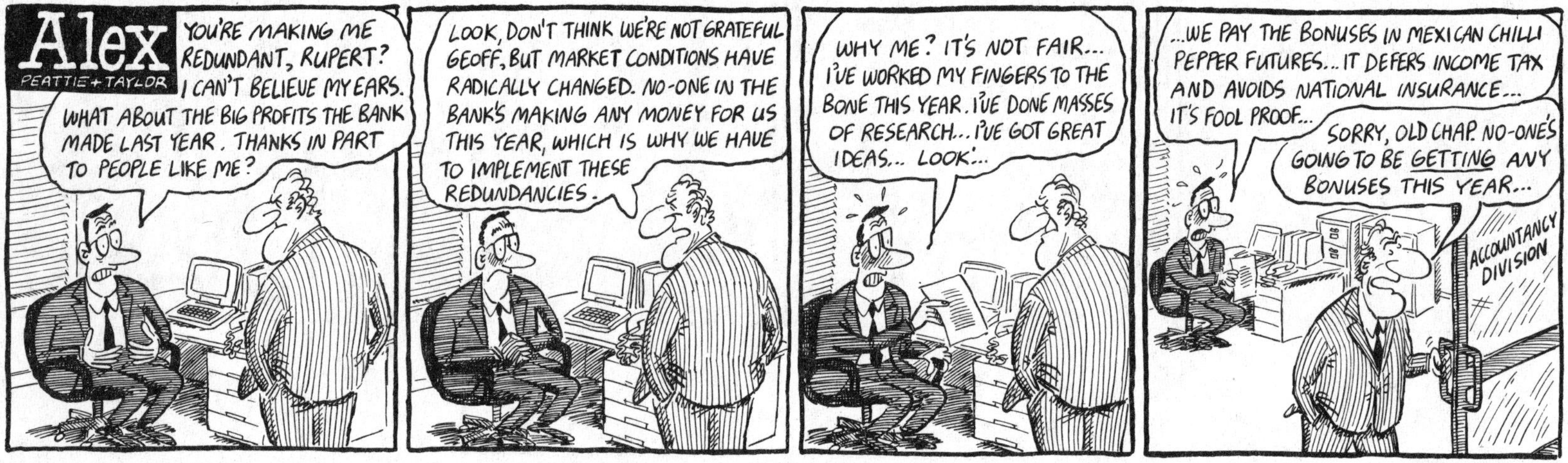
Alex
PEATTIE + TAYLOR
YOU'RE MAKING ME REDUNDANT, RUPERT? I CAN'T BELIEVE MY EARS.
WHAT ABOUT THE BIG PROFITS THE BANK MADE LAST YEAR. THANKS IN PART TO PEOPLE LIKE ME?
LOOK, DON'T THINK WE'RE NOT GRATEFUL GEOFF, BUT MARKET CONDITIONS HAVE RADICALLY CHANGED. NO-ONE IN THE BANK'S MAKING ANY MONEY FOR US THIS YEAR, WHICH IS WHY WE HAVE TO IMPLEMENT THESE REDUNDANCIES.
WHY ME? IT'S NOT FAIR... I'VE WORKED MY FINGERS TO THE BONE THIS YEAR. I'VE DONE MASSES OF RESEARCH... I'VE GOT GREAT IDEAS... LOOK!...
...WE PAY THE BONUSES IN MEXICAN CHILLI PEPPER FUTURES... IT DEFERS INCOME TAX AND AVOIDS NATIONAL INSURANCE... IT'S FOOL PROOF...
SORRY, OLD CHAP. NO-ONE'S GOING TO BE GETTING ANY BONUSES THIS YEAR...
ACCOUNTANCY DIVISION

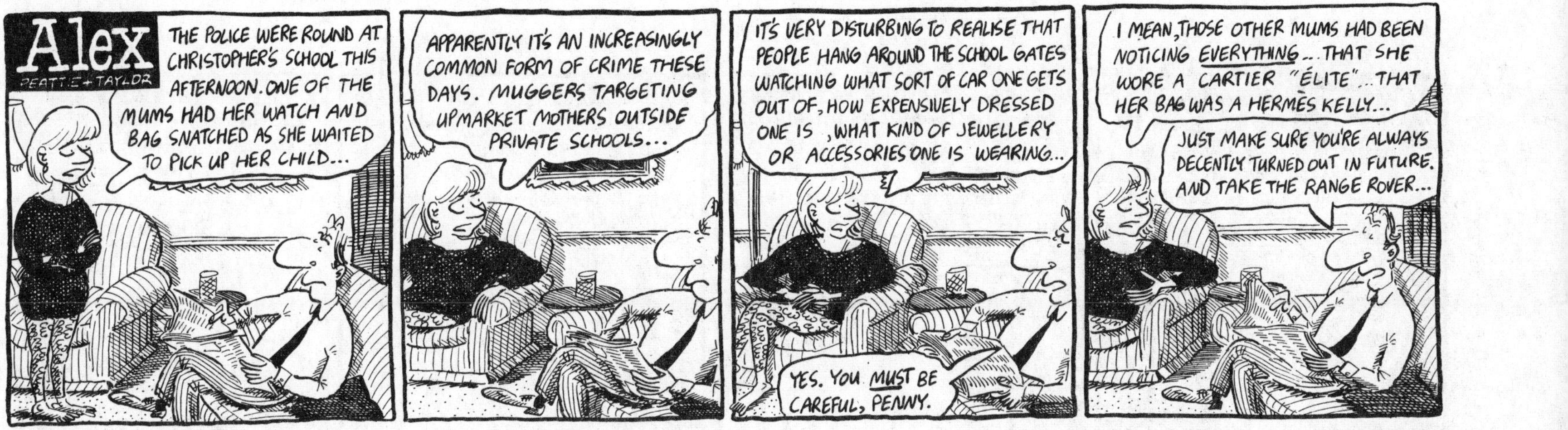
Alex
BEATTIE + TAYLOR
THE POLICE WERE ROUND AT CHRISTOPHER'S SCHOOL THIS AFTERNOON. ONE OF THE MUMS HAD HER WATCH AND BAG SNATCHED AS SHE WAITED TO PICK UP HER CHILD...
APPARENTLY IT'S AN INCREASINGLY COMMON FORM OF CRIME THESE DAYS. MUGGERS TARGETING UPMARKET MOTHERS OUTSIDE PRIVATE SCHOOLS...
IT'S VERY DISTURBING TO REALISE THAT PEOPLE HANG AROUND THE SCHOOL GATES WATCHING WHAT SORT OF CAR ONE GETS OUT OF, HOW EXPENSIVELY DRESSED ONE IS, WHAT KIND OF JEWELLERY OR ACCESSORIES ONE IS WEARING...
YES. YOU MUST BE CAREFUL, PENNY.
I MEAN, THOSE OTHER MUMS HAD BEEN NOTICING EVERYTHING... THAT SHE WORE A CARTIER "ÉLITE"... THAT HER BAG WAS A HERMÈS KELLY...
JUST MAKE SURE YOU'RE ALWAYS DECENTLY TURNED OUT IN FUTURE. AND TAKE THE RANGE ROVER...

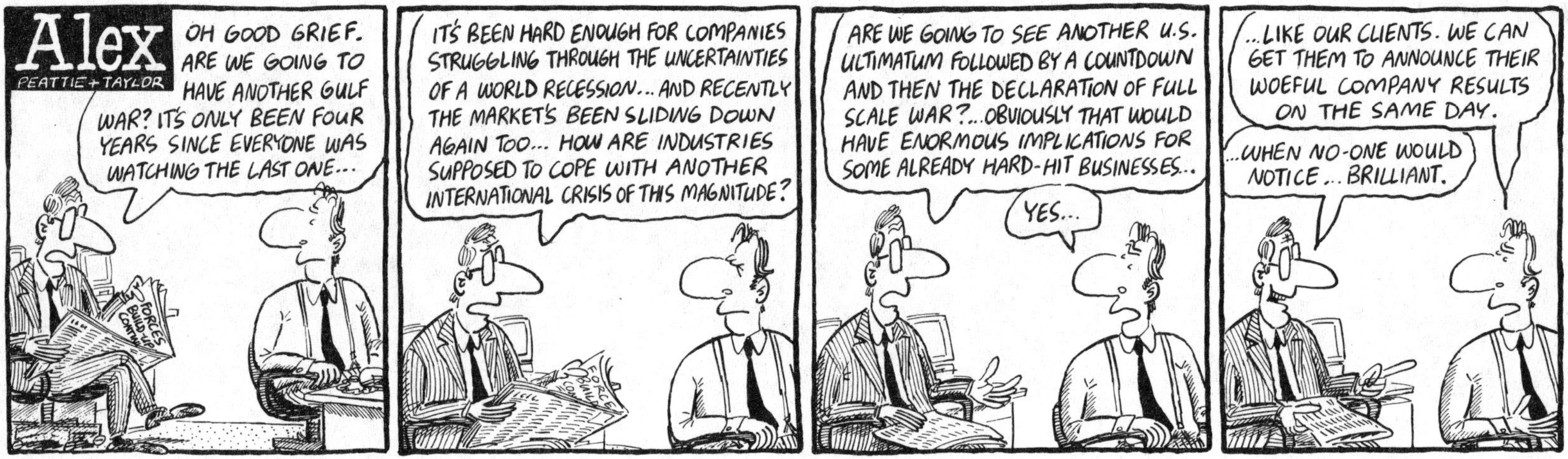
Alex
PEATTIE + TAYLOR
OH GOOD GRIEF. ARE WE GOING TO HAVE ANOTHER GULF WAR? IT'S ONLY BEEN FOUR YEARS SINCE EVERYONE WAS WATCHING THE LAST ONE...
IT'S BEEN HARD ENOUGH FOR COMPANIES STRUGGLING THROUGH THE UNCERTAINTIES OF A WORLD RECESSION... AND RECENTLY THE MARKET'S BEEN SLIDING DOWN AGAIN TOO... HOW ARE INDUSTRIES SUPPOSED TO COPE WITH ANOTHER INTERNATIONAL CRISIS OF THIS MAGNITUDE?
ARE WE GOING TO SEE ANOTHER U.S. ULTIMATUM FOLLOWED BY A COUNTDOWN AND THEN THE DECLARATION OF FULL SCALE WAR?... OBVIOUSLY THAT WOULD HAVE ENORMOUS IMPLICATIONS FOR SOME ALREADY HARD-HIT BUSINESSES...
YES...
...LIKE OUR CLIENTS. WE CAN GET THEM TO ANNOUNCE THEIR WOEFUL COMPANY RESULTS ON THE SAME DAY.
...WHEN NO-ONE WOULD NOTICE... BRILLIANT.

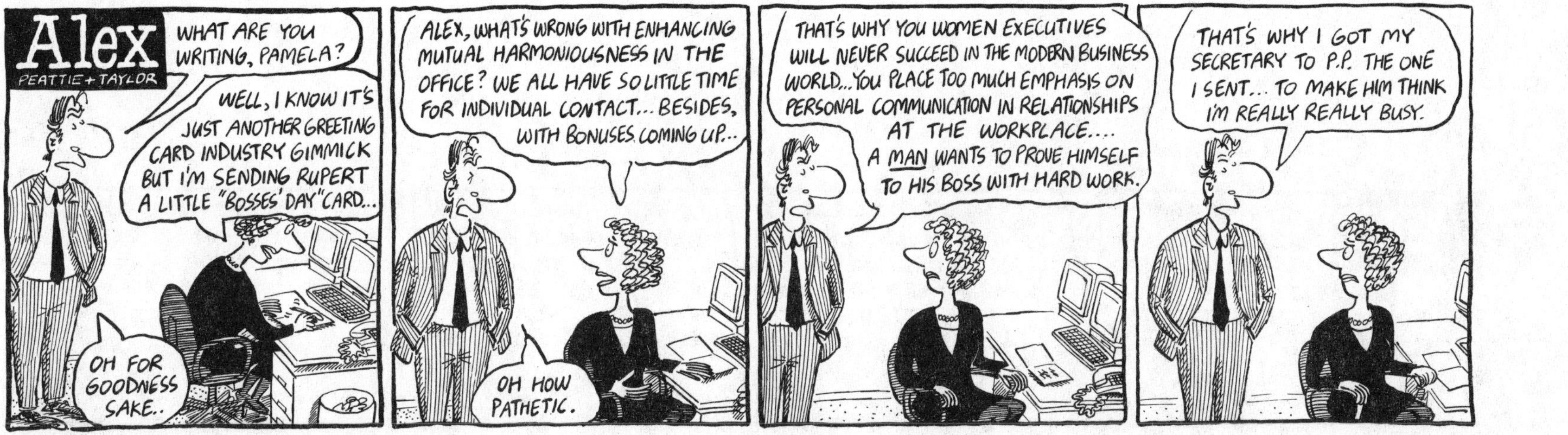
Alex
PEATTIE + TAYLOR
WHAT ARE YOU WRITING, PAMELA?
WELL, I KNOW IT'S JUST ANOTHER GREETING CARD INDUSTRY GIMMICK BUT I'M SENDING RUPERT A LITTLE "BOSSES' DAY" CARD...
OH FOR GOODNESS SAKE..
ALEX, WHAT'S WRONG WITH ENHANCING MUTUAL HARMONIOUSNESS IN THE OFFICE? WE ALL HAVE SO LITTLE TIME FOR INDIVIDUAL CONTACT... BESIDES, WITH BONUSES COMING UP...
OH HOW PATHETIC.
THAT'S WHY YOU WOMEN EXECUTIVES WILL NEVER SUCCEED IN THE MODERN BUSINESS WORLD... YOU PLACE TOO MUCH EMPHASIS ON PERSONAL COMMUNICATION IN RELATIONSHIPS AT THE WORKPLACE....
A MAN WANTS TO PROVE HIMSELF TO HIS BOSS WITH HARD WORK.
THAT'S WHY I GOT MY SECRETARY TO P.P. THE ONE I SENT... TO MAKE HIM THINK I'M REALLY REALLY BUSY.

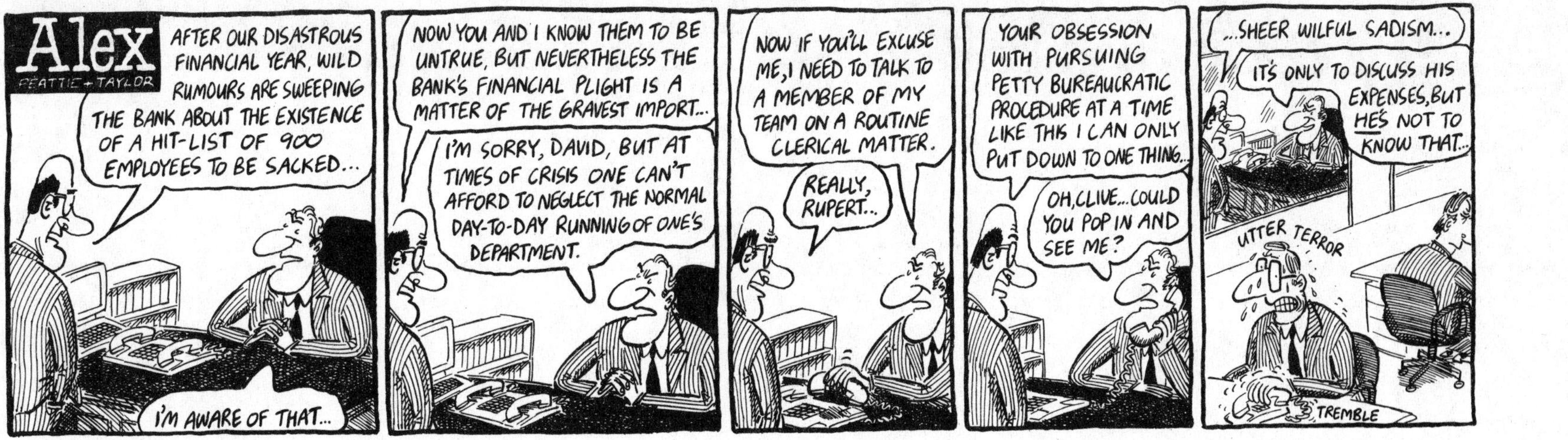
Alex
PEATTIE + TAYLOR
AFTER OUR DISASTROUS FINANCIAL YEAR, WILD RUMOURS ARE SWEEPING THE BANK ABOUT THE EXISTENCE OF A HIT-LIST OF 900 EMPLOYEES TO BE SACKED...
I'M AWARE OF THAT...
NOW YOU AND I KNOW THEM TO BE UNTRUE, BUT NEVERTHELESS THE BANK'S FINANCIAL PLIGHT IS A MATTER OF THE GRAVEST IMPORT...
I'M SORRY, DAVID, BUT AT TIMES OF CRISIS ONE CAN'T AFFORD TO NEGLECT THE NORMAL DAY-TO-DAY RUNNING OF ONE'S DEPARTMENT.
NOW IF YOU'LL EXCUSE ME, I NEED TO TALK TO A MEMBER OF MY TEAM ON A ROUTINE CLERICAL MATTER.
REALLY, RUPERT...
YOUR OBSESSION WITH PURSUING PETTY BUREAUCRATIC PROCEDURE AT A TIME LIKE THIS I CAN ONLY PUT DOWN TO ONE THING...
OH, CLIVE... COULD YOU POP IN AND SEE ME?
...SHEER WILFUL SADISM...
IT'S ONLY TO DISCUSS HIS EXPENSES, BUT HE'S NOT TO KNOW THAT...
UTTER TERROR
TREMBLE

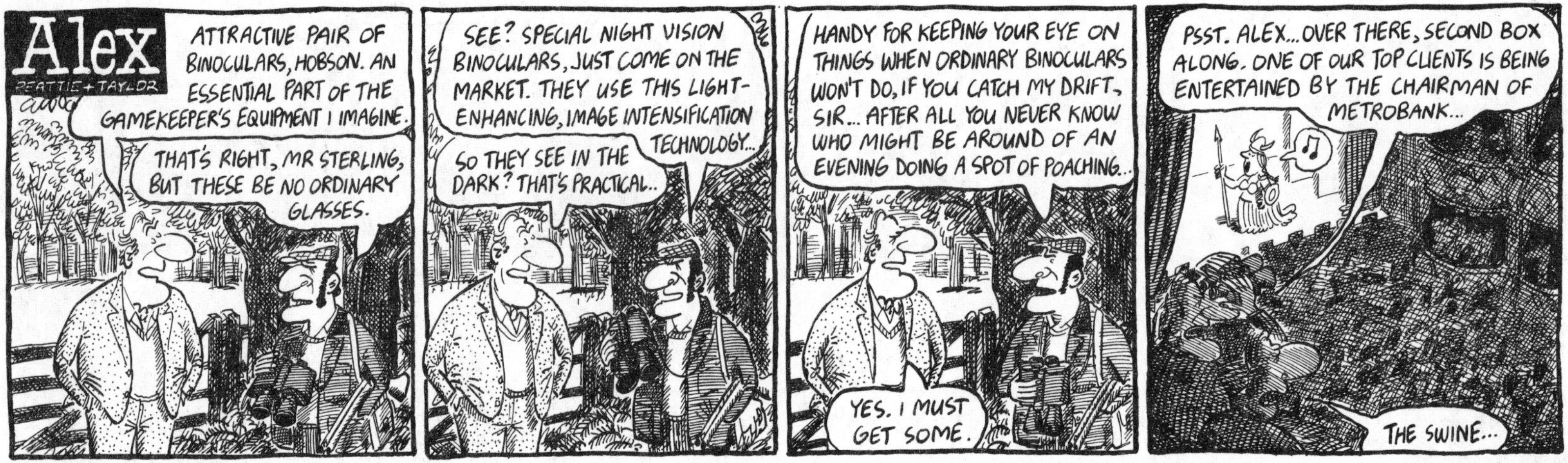
Alex
BEATTIE + TAYLOR
ATTRACTIVE PAIR OF BINOCULARS, HOBSON. AN ESSENTIAL PART OF THE GAMEKEEPER'S EQUIPMENT I IMAGINE.
THAT'S RIGHT, MR STERLING, BUT THESE BE NO ORDINARY GLASSES.
SEE? SPECIAL NIGHT VISION BINOCULARS, JUST COME ON THE MARKET. THEY USE THIS LIGHT-ENHANCING, IMAGE INTENSIFICATION TECHNOLOGY...
SO THEY SEE IN THE DARK? THAT'S PRACTICAL..
HANDY FOR KEEPING YOUR EYE ON THINGS WHEN ORDINARY BINOCULARS WON'T DO, IF YOU CATCH MY DRIFT, SIR... AFTER ALL YOU NEVER KNOW WHO MIGHT BE AROUND OF AN EVENING DOING A SPOT OF POACHING...
YES. I MUST GET SOME.
PSST. ALEX... OVER THERE, SECOND BOX ALONG. ONE OF OUR TOP CLIENTS IS BEING ENTERTAINED BY THE CHAIRMAN OF METROBANK...
THE SWINE...

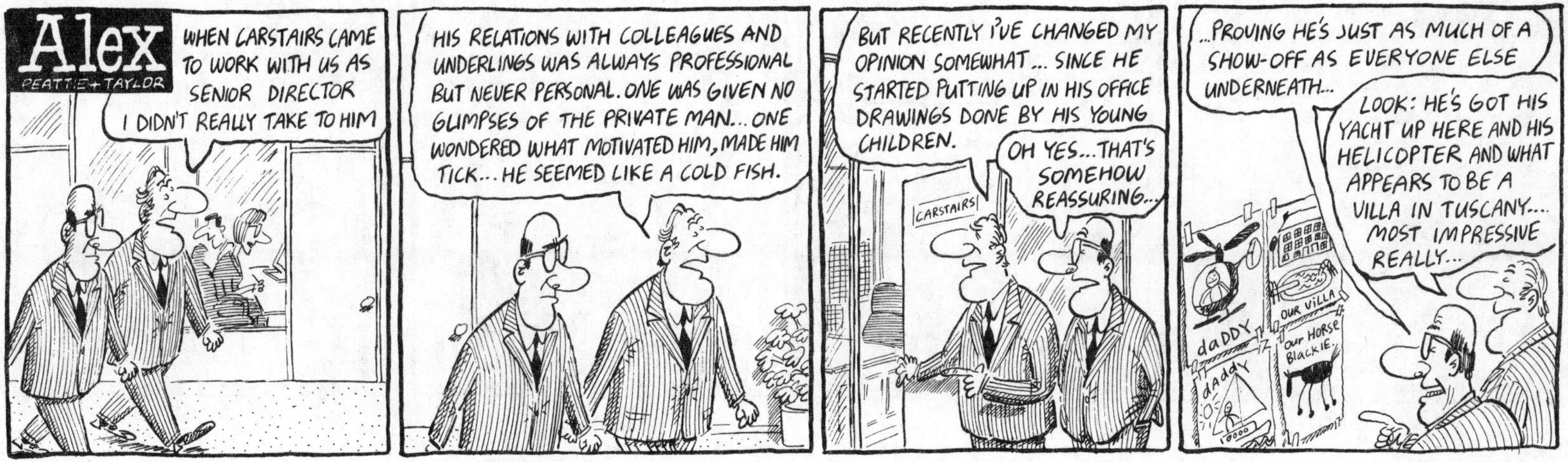
Alex
PEATTIE + TAYLOR
WHEN CARSTAIRS CAME TO WORK WITH US AS SENIOR DIRECTOR I DIDN'T REALLY TAKE TO HIM
HIS RELATIONS WITH COLLEAGUES AND UNDERLINGS WAS ALWAYS PROFESSIONAL BUT NEVER PERSONAL. ONE WAS GIVEN NO GLIMPSES OF THE PRIVATE MAN... ONE WONDERED WHAT MOTIVATED HIM, MADE HIM TICK... HE SEEMED LIKE A COLD FISH.
BUT RECENTLY I'VE CHANGED MY OPINION SOMEWHAT... SINCE HE STARTED PUTTING UP IN HIS OFFICE DRAWINGS DONE BY HIS YOUNG CHILDREN.
CARSTAIRS
OH YES... THAT'S SOMEHOW REASSURING...
...PROVING HE'S JUST AS MUCH OF A SHOW-OFF AS EVERYONE ELSE UNDERNEATH...
LOOK: HE'S GOT HIS YACHT UP HERE AND HIS HELICOPTER AND WHAT APPEARS TO BE A VILLA IN TUSCANY.... MOST IMPRESSIVE REALLY...
daDDY
daddy
OUR VILLA
Our Horse Blackie.

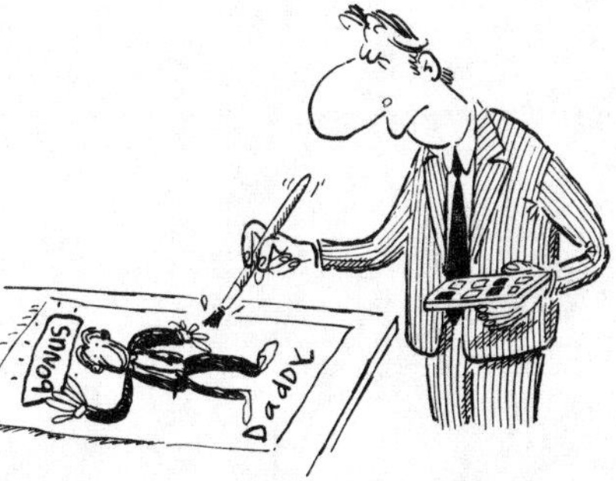
BONUS
DaDDY

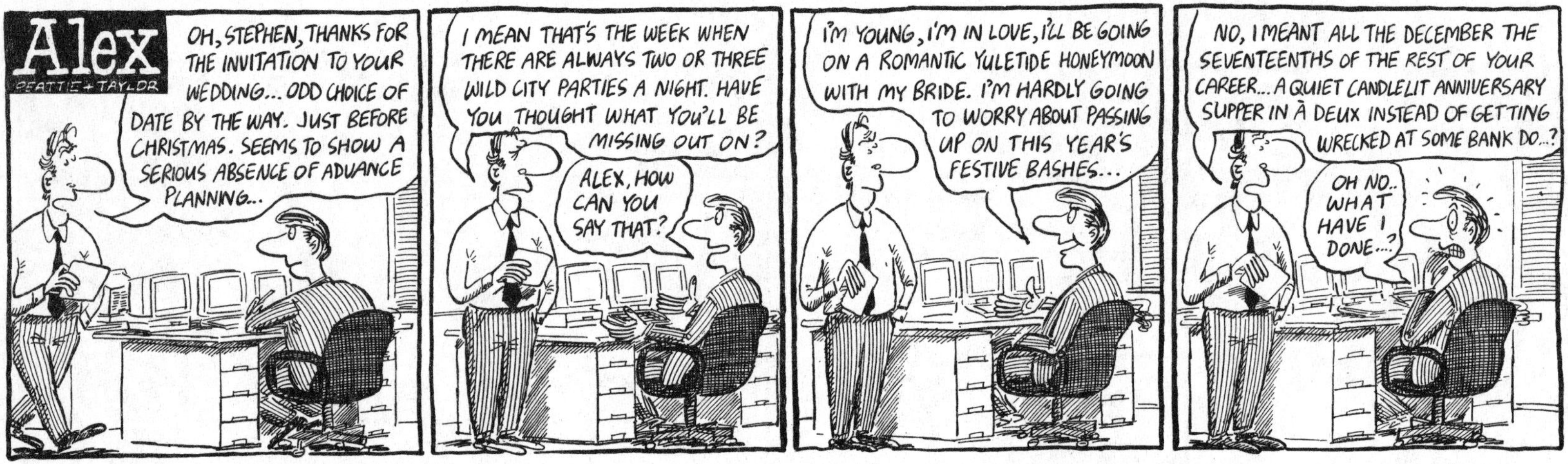
Alex
BEATTIE + TAYLOR
OH, STEPHEN, THANKS FOR THE INVITATION TO YOUR WEDDING... ODD CHOICE OF DATE BY THE WAY. JUST BEFORE CHRISTMAS. SEEMS TO SHOW A SERIOUS ABSENCE OF ADVANCE PLANNING...
I MEAN THAT'S THE WEEK WHEN THERE ARE ALWAYS TWO OR THREE WILD CITY PARTIES A NIGHT. HAVE YOU THOUGHT WHAT YOU'LL BE MISSING OUT ON?
ALEX, HOW CAN YOU SAY THAT?
I'M YOUNG, I'M IN LOVE, I'LL BE GOING ON A ROMANTIC YULETIDE HONEYMOON WITH MY BRIDE. I'M HARDLY GOING TO WORRY ABOUT PASSING UP ON THIS YEAR'S FESTIVE BASHES...
NO, I MEANT ALL THE DECEMBER THE SEVENTEENTHS OF THE REST OF YOUR CAREER... A QUIET CANDLELIT ANNIVERSARY SUPPER IN À DEUX INSTEAD OF GETTING WRECKED AT SOME BANK DO...?
OH NO.. WHAT HAVE I DONE...?

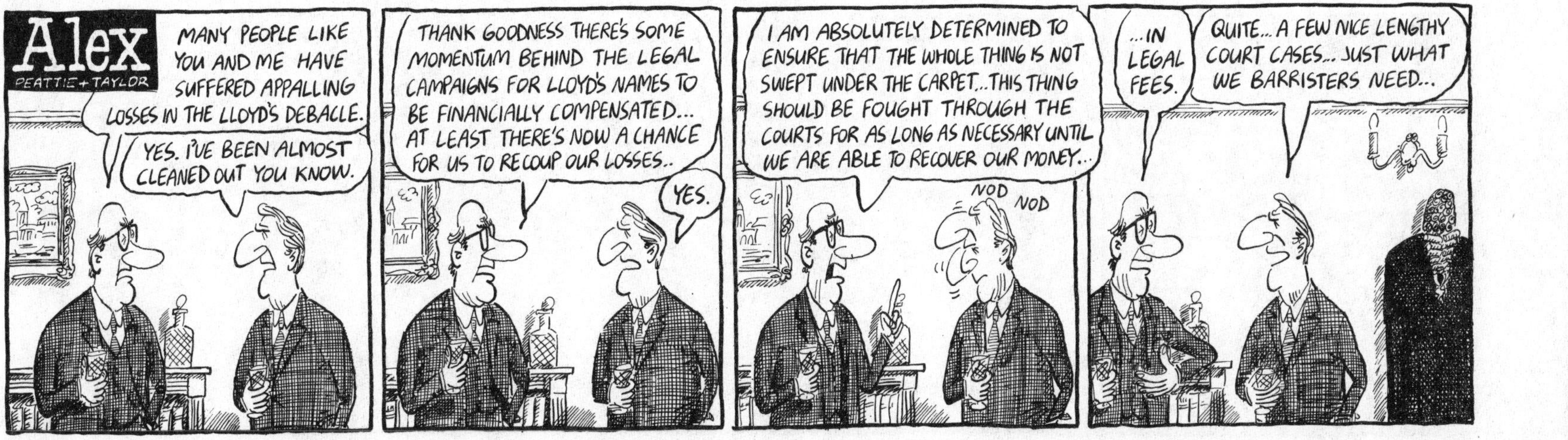
Alex
PEATTIE + TAYLOR
MANY PEOPLE LIKE YOU AND ME HAVE SUFFERED APPALLING LOSSES IN THE LLOYD'S DEBACLE.
YES. I'VE BEEN ALMOST CLEANED OUT YOU KNOW.
THANK GOODNESS THERE'S SOME MOMENTUM BEHIND THE LEGAL CAMPAIGNS FOR LLOYD'S NAMES TO BE FINANCIALLY COMPENSATED... AT LEAST THERE'S NOW A CHANCE FOR US TO RECOUP OUR LOSSES..
YES.
I AM ABSOLUTELY DETERMINED TO ENSURE THAT THE WHOLE THING IS NOT SWEPT UNDER THE CARPET... THIS THING SHOULD BE FOUGHT THROUGH THE COURTS FOR AS LONG AS NECESSARY UNTIL WE ARE ABLE TO RECOVER OUR MONEY...
NOD NOD
...IN LEGAL FEES.
QUITE... A FEW NICE LENGTHY COURT CASES... JUST WHAT WE BARRISTERS NEED...

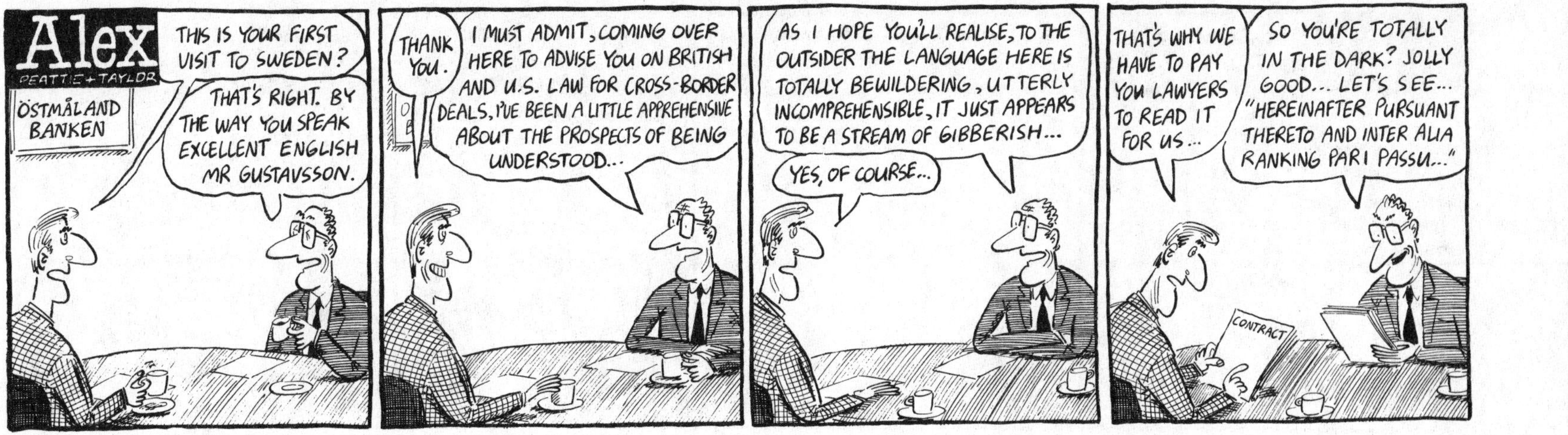
Alex
PEATTIE + TAYLOR
ÖSTMÅLAND BANKEN
THIS IS YOUR FIRST VISIT TO SWEDEN?
THAT'S RIGHT. BY THE WAY YOU SPEAK EXCELLENT ENGLISH MR GUSTAVSSON.
THANK YOU.
I MUST ADMIT, COMING OVER HERE TO ADVISE YOU ON BRITISH AND U.S. LAW FOR CROSS-BORDER DEALS, I'VE BEEN A LITTLE APPREHENSIVE ABOUT THE PROSPECTS OF BEING UNDERSTOOD...
AS I HOPE YOU'LL REALISE, TO THE OUTSIDER THE LANGUAGE HERE IS TOTALLY BEWILDERING, UTTERLY INCOMPREHENSIBLE, IT JUST APPEARS TO BE A STREAM OF GIBBERISH...
YES, OF COURSE...
THAT'S WHY WE HAVE TO PAY YOU LAWYERS TO READ IT FOR US...
SO YOU'RE TOTALLY IN THE DARK? JOLLY GOOD... LET'S SEE... "HEREINAFTER PURSUANT THERETO AND INTER ALIA RANKING PARI PASSU..."
CONTRACT

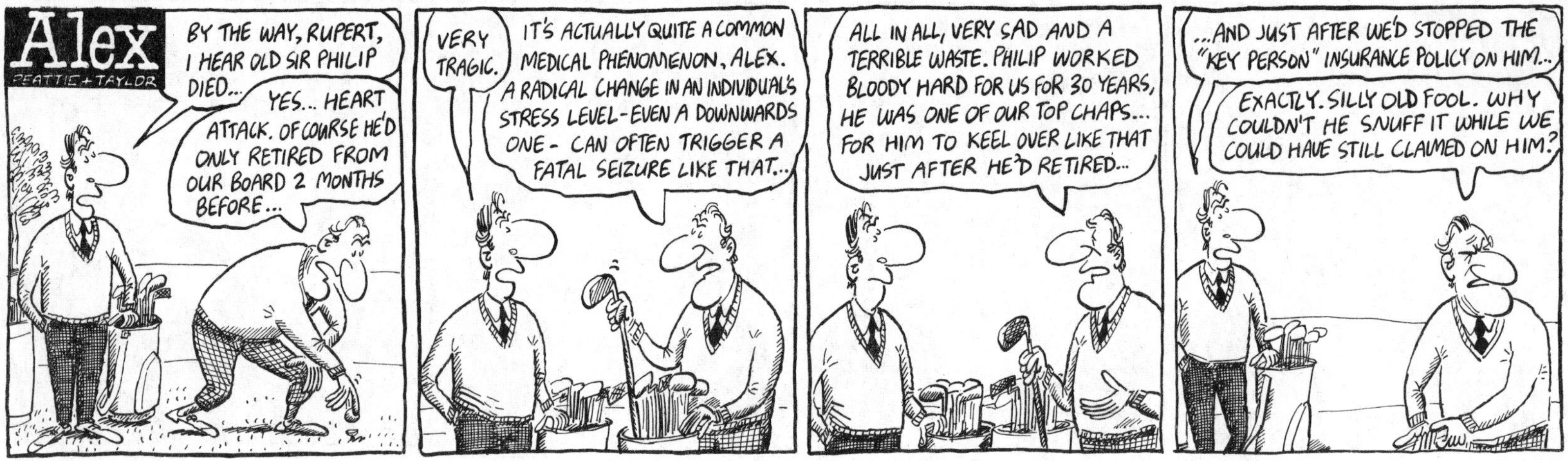
Alex
PEATTIE + TAYLOR
BY THE WAY, RUPERT, I HEAR OLD SIR PHILIP DIED...
YES... HEART ATTACK. OF COURSE HE'D ONLY RETIRED FROM OUR BOARD 2 MONTHS BEFORE...
VERY TRAGIC.
IT'S ACTUALLY QUITE A COMMON MEDICAL PHENOMENON, ALEX. A RADICAL CHANGE IN AN INDIVIDUAL'S STRESS LEVEL - EVEN A DOWNWARDS ONE - CAN OFTEN TRIGGER A FATAL SEIZURE LIKE THAT...
ALL IN ALL, VERY SAD AND A TERRIBLE WASTE. PHILIP WORKED BLOODY HARD FOR US FOR 30 YEARS, HE WAS ONE OF OUR TOP CHAPS... FOR HIM TO KEEL OVER LIKE THAT JUST AFTER HE'D RETIRED...
...AND JUST AFTER WE'D STOPPED THE "KEY PERSON" INSURANCE POLICY ON HIM...
EXACTLY. SILLY OLD FOOL. WHY COULDN'T HE SNUFF IT WHILE WE COULD HAVE STILL CLAIMED ON HIM?

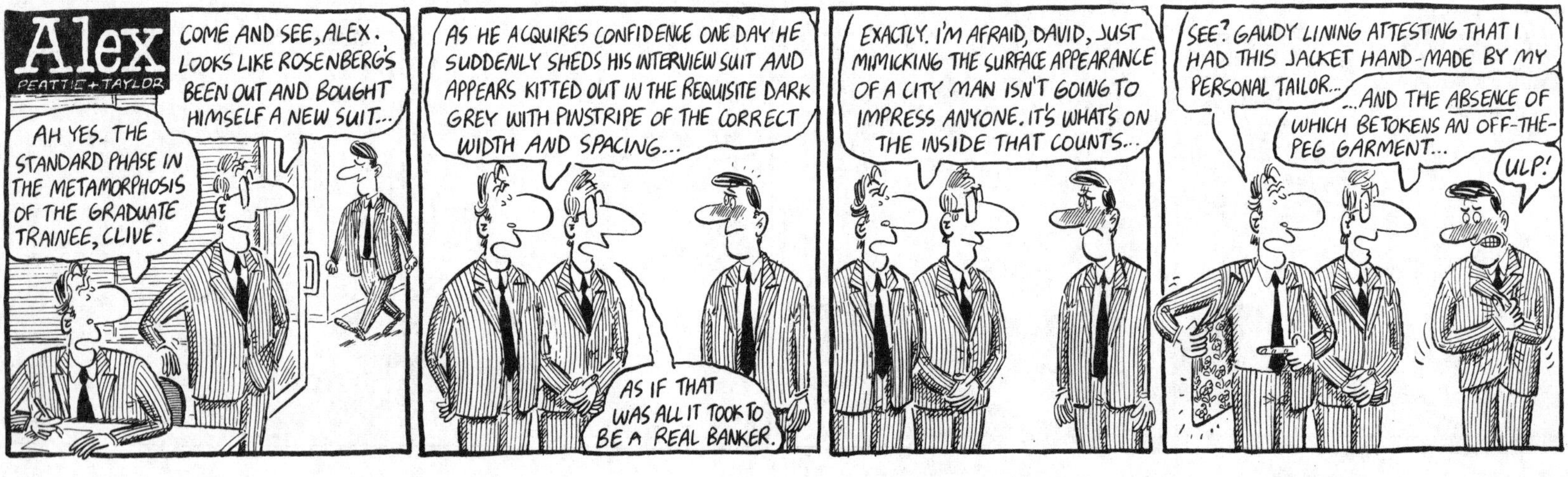
Alex
PEATTIE + TAYLOR
COME AND SEE, ALEX. LOOKS LIKE ROSENBERG'S BEEN OUT AND BOUGHT HIMSELF A NEW SUIT...
AH YES. THE STANDARD PHASE IN THE METAMORPHOSIS OF THE GRADUATE TRAINEE, CLIVE.
AS HE ACQUIRES CONFIDENCE ONE DAY HE SUDDENLY SHEDS HIS INTERVIEW SUIT AND APPEARS KITTED OUT IN THE REQUISITE DARK GREY WITH PINSTRIPE OF THE CORRECT WIDTH AND SPACING...
AS IF THAT WAS ALL IT TOOK TO BE A REAL BANKER.
EXACTLY. I'M AFRAID, DAVID, JUST MIMICKING THE SURFACE APPEARANCE OF A CITY MAN ISN'T GOING TO IMPRESS ANYONE. IT'S WHAT'S ON THE INSIDE THAT COUNTS...
SEE? GAUDY LINING ATTESTING THAT I HAD THIS JACKET HAND-MADE BY MY PERSONAL TAILOR...
...AND THE ABSENCE OF WHICH BETOKENS AN OFF-THE-PEG GARMENT...
ULP!

GLARE
GLARE

BRAKE

Alex
PEATTIE + TAYLOR

GENTLEMEN, AS YOU KNOW THERE'S BEEN A BIT OF A BROUHAHA OVER OUR HEAD OF CURRENCY BROKING LEAVING...

AFTER WHAT'S BEEN A BAD YEAR FOR THE CITY THE SUDDEN DISAPPEARANCE OF HIGH LEVEL PERSONNEL FROM A COMPANY IS TOO EASILY OPEN TO MISINTERPRETATION...

SO IF CLIENTS PHONE UP WANTING TO KNOW WHAT'S HAPPENED TO HIM I WANT EVERYONE HERE TO BE VERY CAREFUL ABOUT WHAT PHRASE OR CHOICE OF WORDS THEY EMPLOY TO DESCRIBE HIS DEPARTURE.

RIGHT YOU ARE, GUV.

BASICALLY I'D LIKE FOR ALL OF US TO USE TACT. OKAY?

NOD NOD NOD

GOT YOU..

HE GOT "TACKED" THIS MORNING...

HE'S BEEN "TIN TACKED", MATE...

HE GOT THE OLD "TIN TACK"...

HELL! BLOODY RHYMING SLANG.

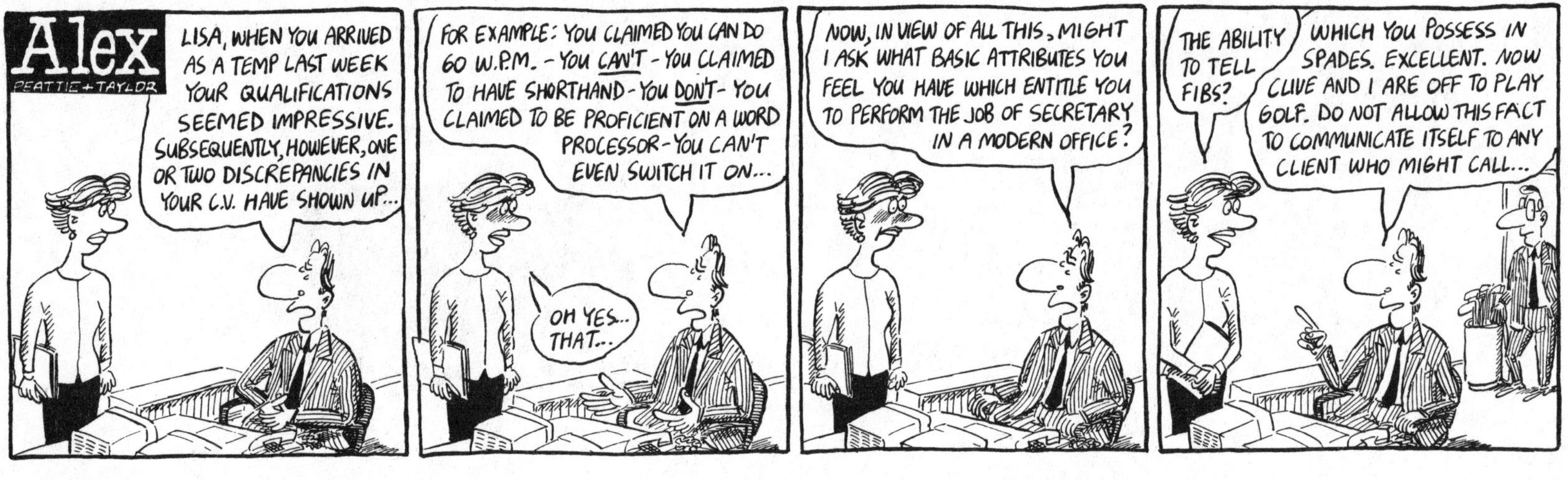
Alex
PEATTIE + TAYLOR
LISA, WHEN YOU ARRIVED AS A TEMP LAST WEEK YOUR QUALIFICATIONS SEEMED IMPRESSIVE. SUBSEQUENTLY, HOWEVER, ONE OR TWO DISCREPANCIES IN YOUR C.V. HAVE SHOWN UP...
FOR EXAMPLE: YOU CLAIMED YOU CAN DO 60 W.P.M. - YOU CAN'T - YOU CLAIMED TO HAVE SHORTHAND - YOU DON'T - YOU CLAIMED TO BE PROFICIENT ON A WORD PROCESSOR - YOU CAN'T EVEN SWITCH IT ON...
OH YES... THAT...
NOW, IN VIEW OF ALL THIS, MIGHT I ASK WHAT BASIC ATTRIBUTES YOU FEEL YOU HAVE WHICH ENTITLE YOU TO PERFORM THE JOB OF SECRETARY IN A MODERN OFFICE?
THE ABILITY TO TELL FIBS?
WHICH YOU POSSESS IN SPADES. EXCELLENT. NOW CLIVE AND I ARE OFF TO PLAY GOLF. DO NOT ALLOW THIS FACT TO COMMUNICATE ITSELF TO ANY CLIENT WHO MIGHT CALL...

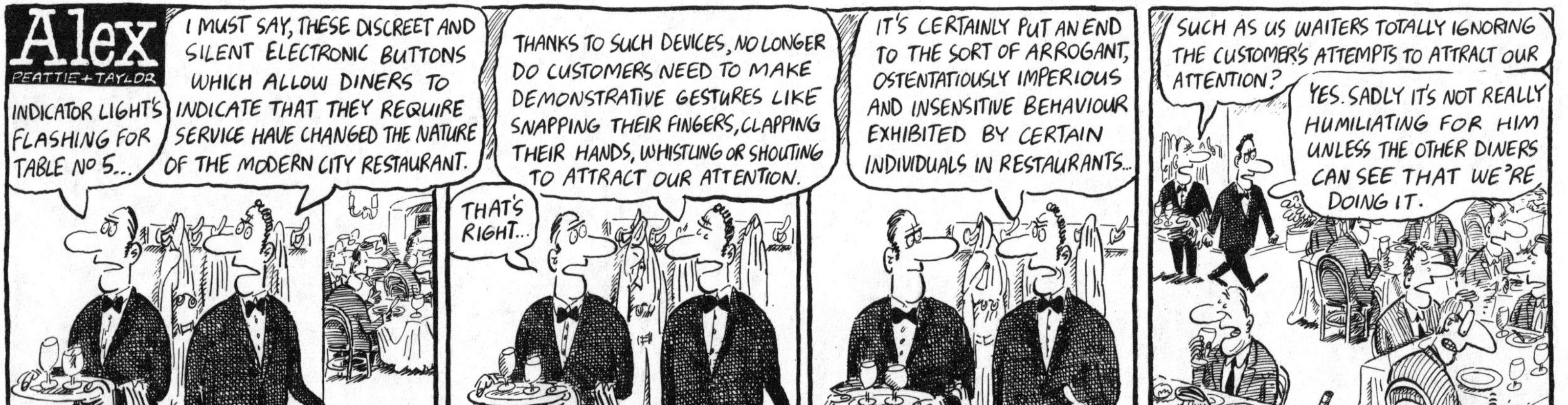
Alex
PEATTIE + TAYLOR
INDICATOR LIGHT'S FLASHING FOR TABLE No 5...
I MUST SAY, THESE DISCREET AND SILENT ELECTRONIC BUTTONS WHICH ALLOW DINERS TO INDICATE THAT THEY REQUIRE SERVICE HAVE CHANGED THE NATURE OF THE MODERN CITY RESTAURANT.
THANKS TO SUCH DEVICES, NO LONGER DO CUSTOMERS NEED TO MAKE DEMONSTRATIVE GESTURES LIKE SNAPPING THEIR FINGERS, CLAPPING THEIR HANDS, WHISTLING OR SHOUTING TO ATTRACT OUR ATTENTION.
THAT'S RIGHT...
IT'S CERTAINLY PUT AN END TO THE SORT OF ARROGANT, OSTENTATIOUSLY IMPERIOUS AND INSENSITIVE BEHAVIOUR EXHIBITED BY CERTAIN INDIVIDUALS IN RESTAURANTS...
SUCH AS US WAITERS TOTALLY IGNORING THE CUSTOMER'S ATTEMPTS TO ATTRACT OUR ATTENTION?
YES. SADLY IT'S NOT REALLY HUMILIATING FOR HIM UNLESS THE OTHER DINERS CAN SEE THAT WE'RE DOING IT.

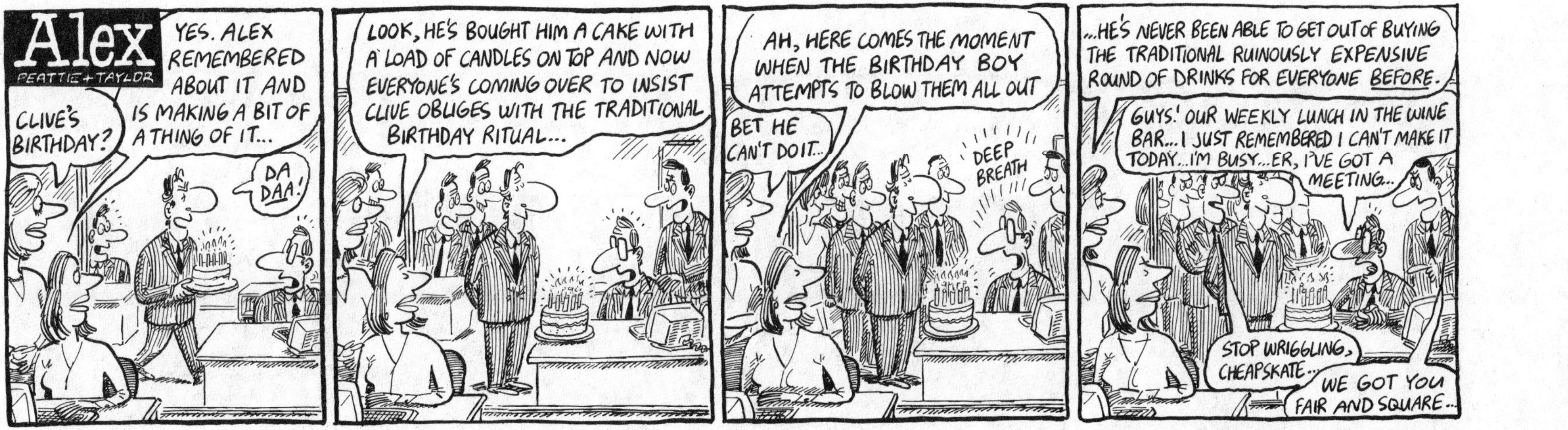
Alex
PEATTIE + TAYLOR
CLIVE'S BIRTHDAY?
YES. ALEX REMEMBERED ABOUT IT AND IS MAKING A BIT OF A THING OF IT...
DA DAA!
LOOK, HE'S BOUGHT HIM A CAKE WITH A LOAD OF CANDLES ON TOP AND NOW EVERYONE'S COMING OVER TO INSIST CLIVE OBLIGES WITH THE TRADITIONAL BIRTHDAY RITUAL...
AH, HERE COMES THE MOMENT WHEN THE BIRTHDAY BOY ATTEMPTS TO BLOW THEM ALL OUT
BET HE CAN'T DO IT...
DEEP BREATH
...HE'S NEVER BEEN ABLE TO GET OUT OF BUYING THE TRADITIONAL RUINOUSLY EXPENSIVE ROUND OF DRINKS FOR EVERYONE BEFORE.
GUYS! OUR WEEKLY LUNCH IN THE WINE BAR... I JUST REMEMBERED I CAN'T MAKE IT TODAY... I'M BUSY... ER, I'VE GOT A MEETING...
STOP WRIGGLING, CHEAPSKATE...
WE GOT YOU FAIR AND SQUARE...

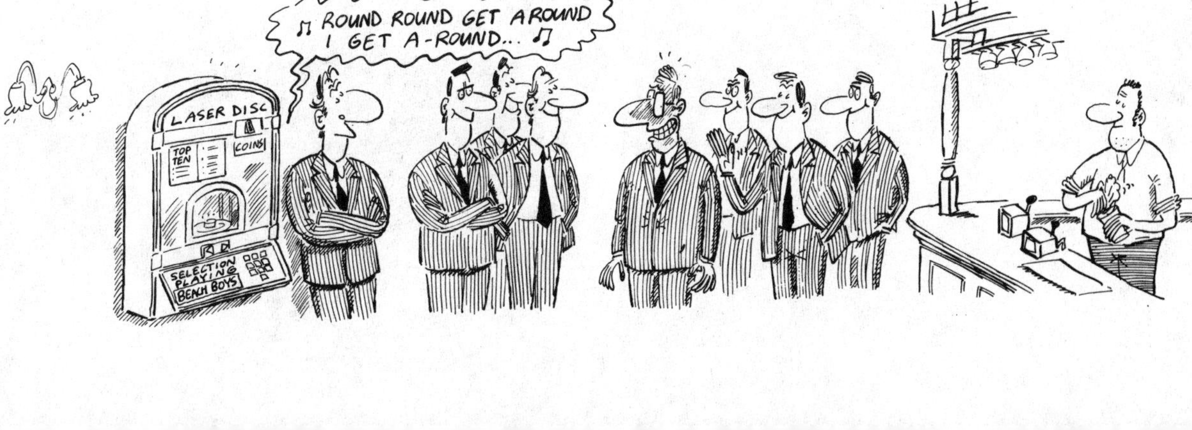
♫ ROUND ROUND GET AROUND I GET A-ROUND... ♫
LASER DISC
TOP TEN
COINS
SELECTION PLAYING
BEACH BOYS

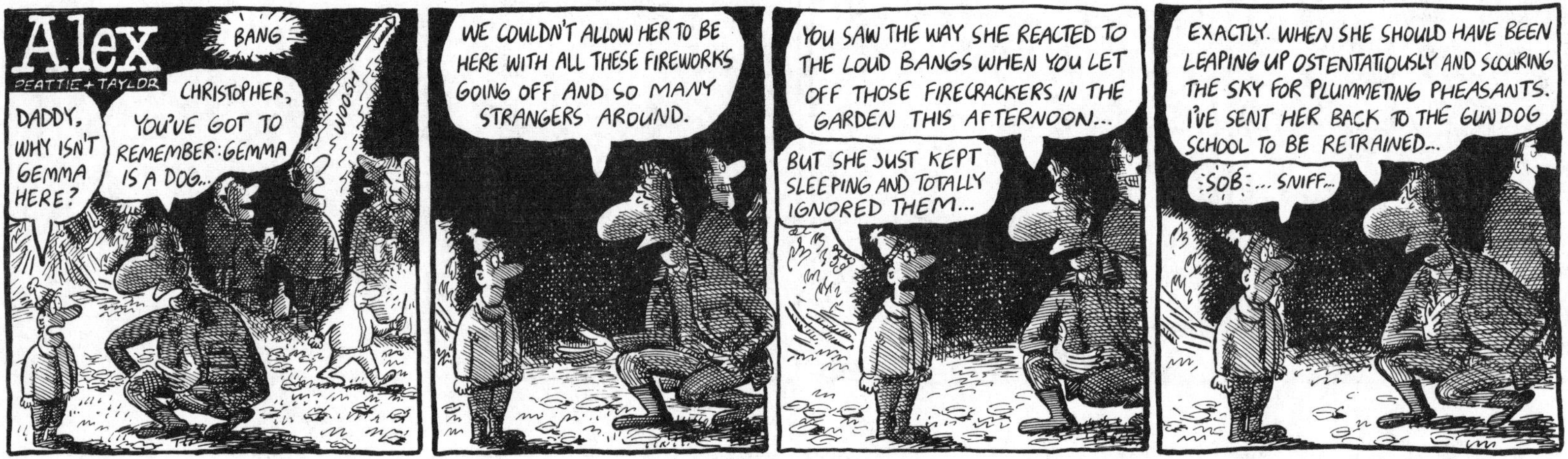
Alex
BEATTIE + TAYLOR
BANG
WOOSH
DADDY, WHY ISN'T GEMMA HERE?
CHRISTOPHER, YOU'VE GOT TO REMEMBER: GEMMA IS A DOG...
WE COULDN'T ALLOW HER TO BE HERE WITH ALL THESE FIREWORKS GOING OFF AND SO MANY STRANGERS AROUND.
YOU SAW THE WAY SHE REACTED TO THE LOUD BANGS WHEN YOU LET OFF THOSE FIRECRACKERS IN THE GARDEN THIS AFTERNOON...
BUT SHE JUST KEPT SLEEPING AND TOTALLY IGNORED THEM...
EXACTLY. WHEN SHE SHOULD HAVE BEEN LEAPING UP OSTENTATIOUSLY AND SCOURING THE SKY FOR PLUMMETING PHEASANTS. I'VE SENT HER BACK TO THE GUN DOG SCHOOL TO BE RETRAINED...
SOB ... SNIFF...

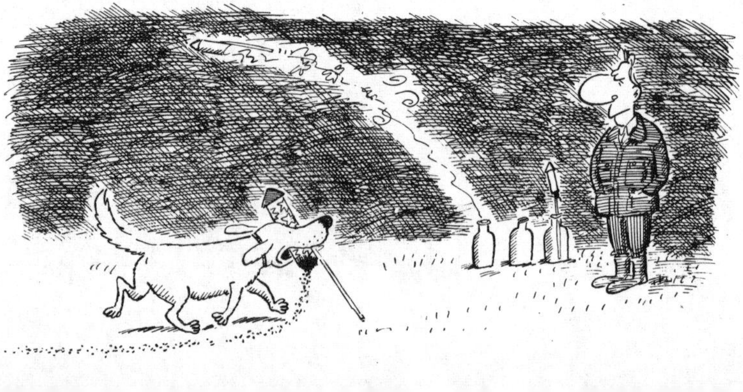

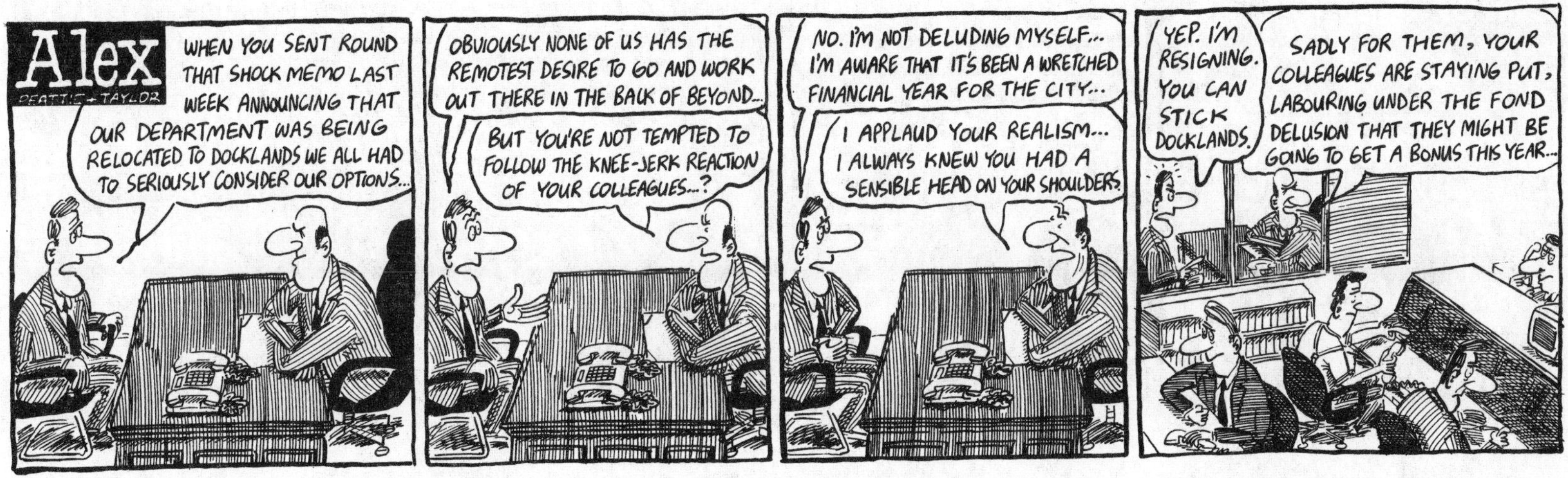
Alex
BEATTIE + TAYLOR
WHEN YOU SENT ROUND THAT SHOCK MEMO LAST WEEK ANNOUNCING THAT OUR DEPARTMENT WAS BEING RELOCATED TO DOCKLANDS WE ALL HAD TO SERIOUSLY CONSIDER OUR OPTIONS...
OBVIOUSLY NONE OF US HAS THE REMOTEST DESIRE TO GO AND WORK OUT THERE IN THE BACK OF BEYOND...
BUT YOU'RE NOT TEMPTED TO FOLLOW THE KNEE-JERK REACTION OF YOUR COLLEAGUES...?
NO. I'M NOT DELUDING MYSELF... I'M AWARE THAT IT'S BEEN A WRETCHED FINANCIAL YEAR FOR THE CITY...
I APPLAUD YOUR REALISM... I ALWAYS KNEW YOU HAD A SENSIBLE HEAD ON YOUR SHOULDERS.
YEP. I'M RESIGNING. YOU CAN STICK DOCKLANDS.
SADLY FOR THEM, YOUR COLLEAGUES ARE STAYING PUT, LABOURING UNDER THE FOND DELUSION THAT THEY MIGHT BE GOING TO GET A BONUS THIS YEAR...

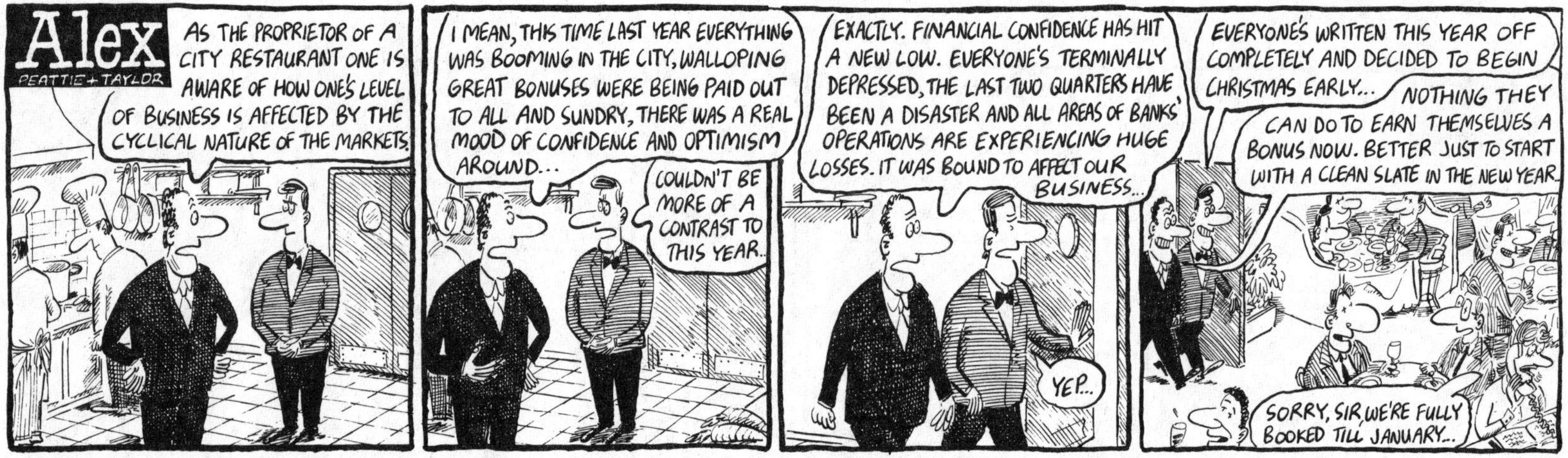
Alex
PEATTIE + TAYLOR
AS THE PROPRIETOR OF A CITY RESTAURANT ONE IS AWARE OF HOW ONE'S LEVEL OF BUSINESS IS AFFECTED BY THE CYCLICAL NATURE OF THE MARKETS.
I MEAN, THIS TIME LAST YEAR EVERYTHING WAS BOOMING IN THE CITY, WALLOPING GREAT BONUSES WERE BEING PAID OUT TO ALL AND SUNDRY, THERE WAS A REAL MOOD OF CONFIDENCE AND OPTIMISM AROUND...
COULDN'T BE MORE OF A CONTRAST TO THIS YEAR...
EXACTLY. FINANCIAL CONFIDENCE HAS HIT A NEW LOW. EVERYONE'S TERMINALLY DEPRESSED, THE LAST TWO QUARTERS HAVE BEEN A DISASTER AND ALL AREAS OF BANKS' OPERATIONS ARE EXPERIENCING HUGE LOSSES. IT WAS BOUND TO AFFECT OUR BUSINESS...
YEP...
EVERYONE'S WRITTEN THIS YEAR OFF COMPLETELY AND DECIDED TO BEGIN CHRISTMAS EARLY...
NOTHING THEY CAN DO TO EARN THEMSELVES A BONUS NOW. BETTER JUST TO START WITH A CLEAN SLATE IN THE NEW YEAR.
SORRY, SIR, WE'RE FULLY BOOKED TILL JANUARY...

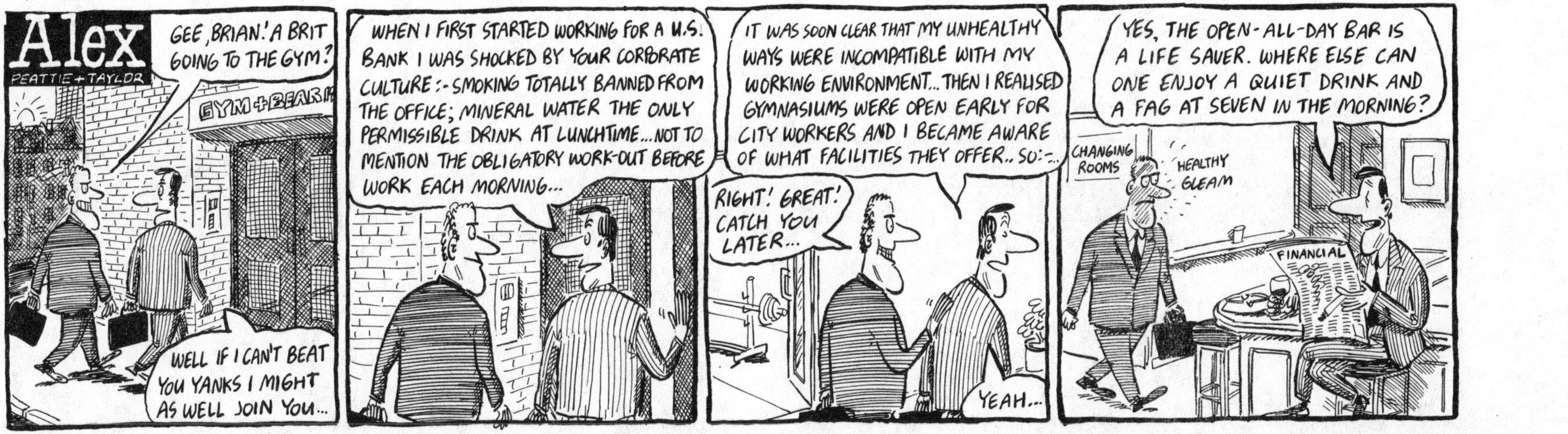
Alex
PEATTIE + TAYLOR
GEE, BRIAN! A BRIT GOING TO THE GYM?
GYM + BEAR
WELL IF I CAN'T BEAT YOU YANKS I MIGHT AS WELL JOIN YOU...
WHEN I FIRST STARTED WORKING FOR A U.S. BANK I WAS SHOCKED BY YOUR CORPORATE CULTURE:- SMOKING TOTALLY BANNED FROM THE OFFICE; MINERAL WATER THE ONLY PERMISSIBLE DRINK AT LUNCHTIME... NOT TO MENTION THE OBLIGATORY WORK-OUT BEFORE WORK EACH MORNING...
IT WAS SOON CLEAR THAT MY UNHEALTHY WAYS WERE INCOMPATIBLE WITH MY WORKING ENVIRONMENT... THEN I REALISED GYMNASIUMS WERE OPEN EARLY FOR CITY WORKERS AND I BECAME AWARE OF WHAT FACILITIES THEY OFFER.. SO:-..
RIGHT! GREAT! CATCH YOU LATER...
YEAH...
YES, THE OPEN-ALL-DAY BAR IS A LIFE SAVER. WHERE ELSE CAN ONE ENJOY A QUIET DRINK AND A FAG AT SEVEN IN THE MORNING?
CHANGING ROOMS
HEALTHY GLEAM
FINANCIAL

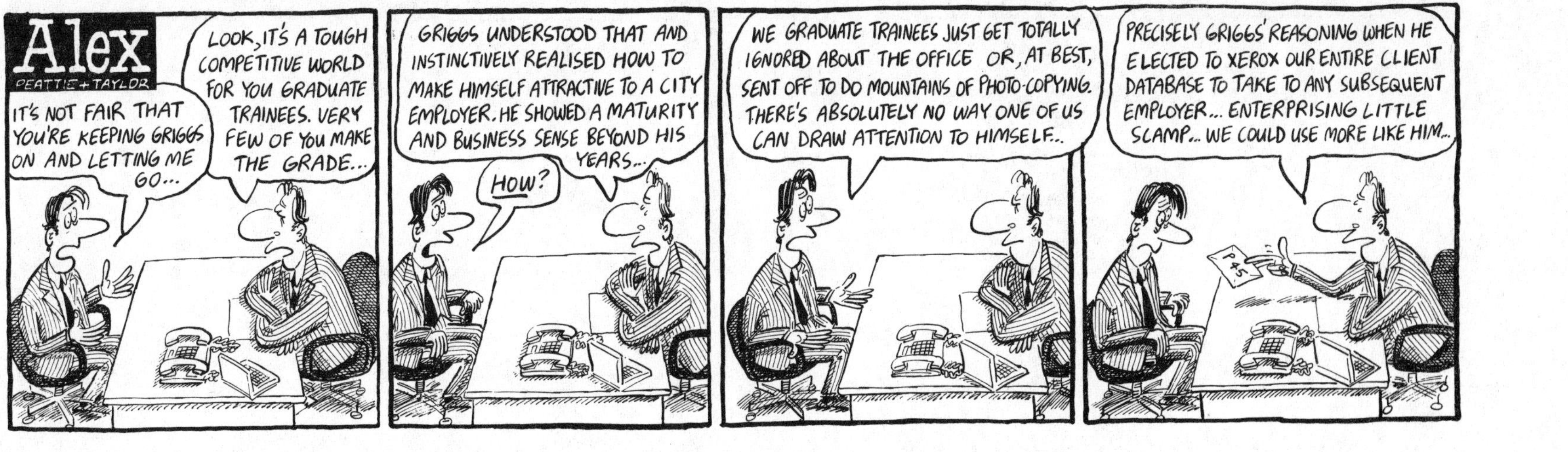
Alex
PEATTIE + TAYLOR
IT'S NOT FAIR THAT YOU'RE KEEPING GRIGGS ON AND LETTING ME GO...
LOOK, IT'S A TOUGH COMPETITIVE WORLD FOR YOU GRADUATE TRAINEES. VERY FEW OF YOU MAKE THE GRADE...
GRIGGS UNDERSTOOD THAT AND INSTINCTIVELY REALISED HOW TO MAKE HIMSELF ATTRACTIVE TO A CITY EMPLOYER. HE SHOWED A MATURITY AND BUSINESS SENSE BEYOND HIS YEARS...
HOW?
WE GRADUATE TRAINEES JUST GET TOTALLY IGNORED ABOUT THE OFFICE OR, AT BEST, SENT OFF TO DO MOUNTAINS OF PHOTO-COPYING. THERE'S ABSOLUTELY NO WAY ONE OF US CAN DRAW ATTENTION TO HIMSELF...
PRECISELY GRIGGS' REASONING WHEN HE ELECTED TO XEROX OUR ENTIRE CLIENT DATABASE TO TAKE TO ANY SUBSEQUENT EMPLOYER... ENTERPRISING LITTLE SCAMP... WE COULD USE MORE LIKE HIM...
P45

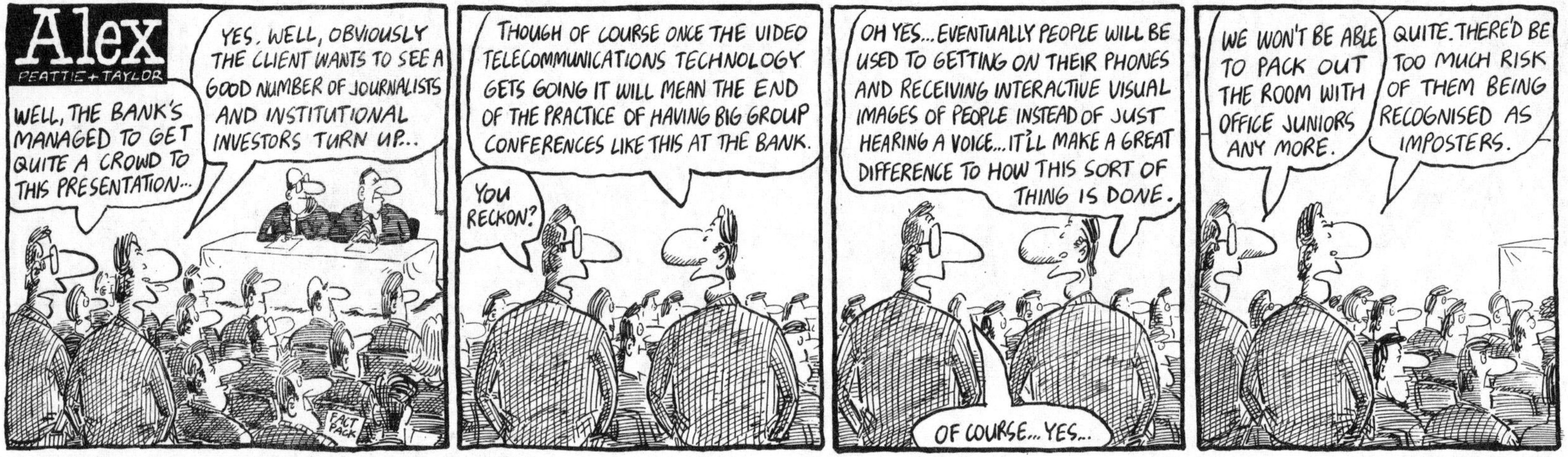
Alex
PEATTIE + TAYLOR
WELL, THE BANK'S MANAGED TO GET QUITE A CROWD TO THIS PRESENTATION...
YES. WELL, OBVIOUSLY THE CLIENT WANTS TO SEE A GOOD NUMBER OF JOURNALISTS AND INSTITUTIONAL INVESTORS TURN UP...
FACT PACK
THOUGH OF COURSE ONCE THE VIDEO TELECOMMUNICATIONS TECHNOLOGY GETS GOING IT WILL MEAN THE END OF THE PRACTICE OF HAVING BIG GROUP CONFERENCES LIKE THIS AT THE BANK.
YOU RECKON?
OH YES... EVENTUALLY PEOPLE WILL BE USED TO GETTING ON THEIR PHONES AND RECEIVING INTERACTIVE VISUAL IMAGES OF PEOPLE INSTEAD OF JUST HEARING A VOICE... IT'LL MAKE A GREAT DIFFERENCE TO HOW THIS SORT OF THING IS DONE.
OF COURSE... YES...
WE WON'T BE ABLE TO PACK OUT THE ROOM WITH OFFICE JUNIORS ANY MORE.
QUITE. THERE'D BE TOO MUCH RISK OF THEM BEING RECOGNISED AS IMPOSTERS.

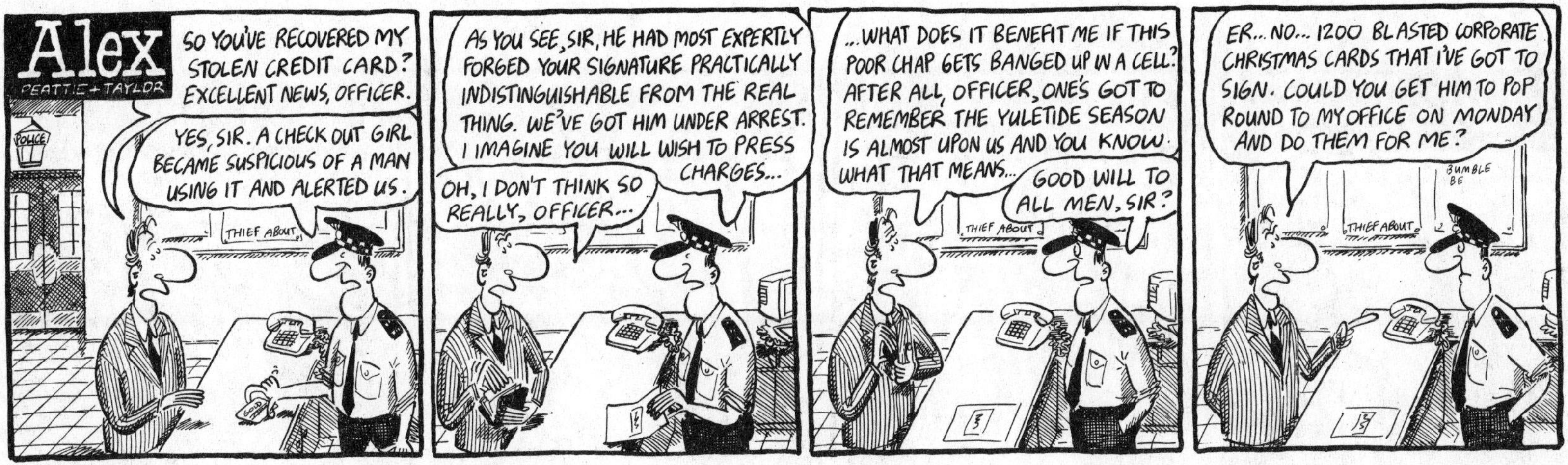
Alex
PEATTIE + TAYLOR
POLICE
SO YOU'VE RECOVERED MY STOLEN CREDIT CARD? EXCELLENT NEWS, OFFICER.
YES, SIR. A CHECK OUT GIRL BECAME SUSPICIOUS OF A MAN USING IT AND ALERTED US.
THIEF ABOUT
AS YOU SEE, SIR, HE HAD MOST EXPERTLY FORGED YOUR SIGNATURE PRACTICALLY INDISTINGUISHABLE FROM THE REAL THING. WE'VE GOT HIM UNDER ARREST. I IMAGINE YOU WILL WISH TO PRESS CHARGES...
OH, I DON'T THINK SO REALLY, OFFICER...
...WHAT DOES IT BENEFIT ME IF THIS POOR CHAP GETS BANGED UP IN A CELL? AFTER ALL, OFFICER, ONE'S GOT TO REMEMBER THE YULETIDE SEASON IS ALMOST UPON US AND YOU KNOW WHAT THAT MEANS...
GOOD WILL TO ALL MEN, SIR?
THIEF ABOUT
ER... NO... 1200 BLASTED CORPORATE CHRISTMAS CARDS THAT I'VE GOT TO SIGN. COULD YOU GET HIM TO POP ROUND TO MY OFFICE ON MONDAY AND DO THEM FOR ME?
BUMBLE BE
THIEF ABOUT

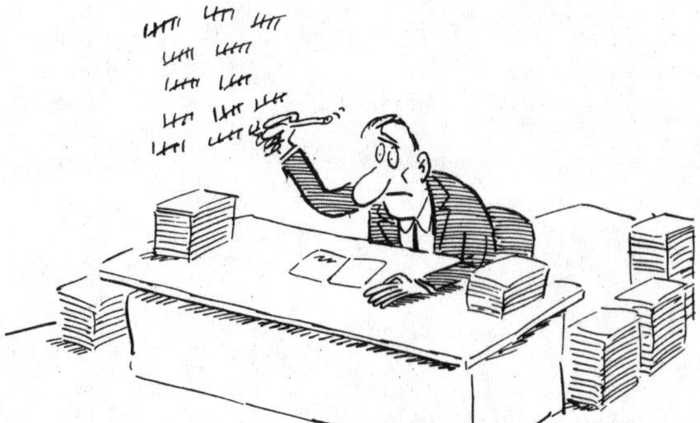

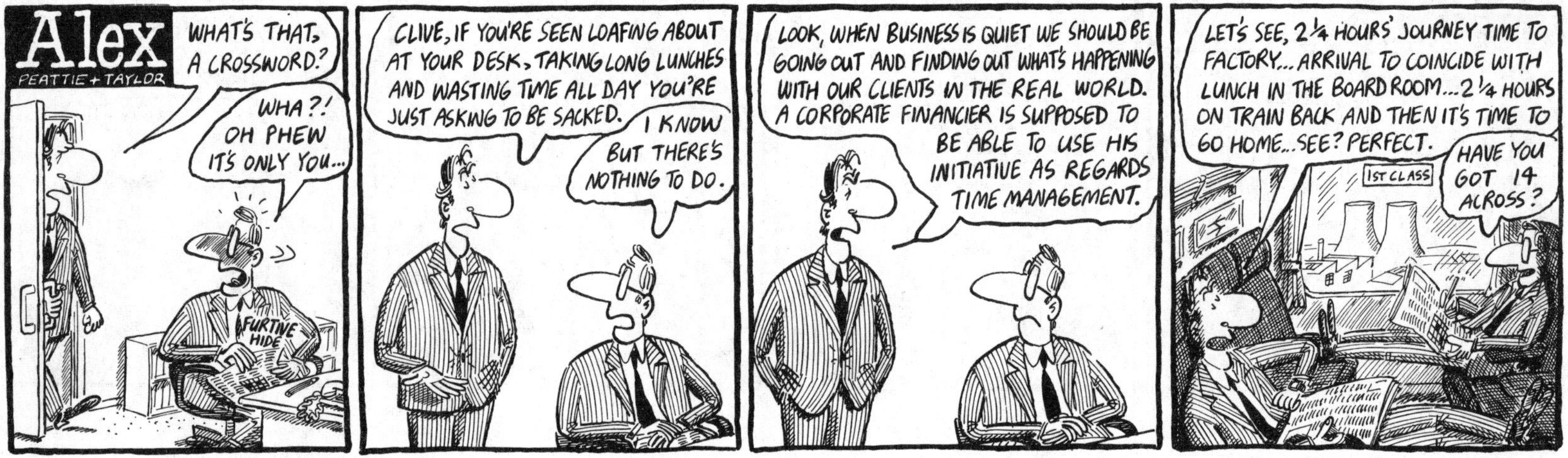
Alex
PEATTIE + TAYLOR
WHAT'S THAT, A CROSSWORD?
WHA?! OH PHEW IT'S ONLY YOU...
FURTIVE HIDE
CLIVE, IF YOU'RE SEEN LOAFING ABOUT AT YOUR DESK, TAKING LONG LUNCHES AND WASTING TIME ALL DAY YOU'RE JUST ASKING TO BE SACKED.
I KNOW BUT THERE'S NOTHING TO DO.
LOOK, WHEN BUSINESS IS QUIET WE SHOULD BE GOING OUT AND FINDING OUT WHAT'S HAPPENING WITH OUR CLIENTS IN THE REAL WORLD. A CORPORATE FINANCIER IS SUPPOSED TO BE ABLE TO USE HIS INITIATIVE AS REGARDS TIME MANAGEMENT.
LET'S SEE, 2¼ HOURS' JOURNEY TIME TO FACTORY... ARRIVAL TO COINCIDE WITH LUNCH IN THE BOARD ROOM... 2¼ HOURS ON TRAIN BACK AND THEN IT'S TIME TO GO HOME... SEE? PERFECT.
1ST CLASS
HAVE YOU GOT 14 ACROSS?

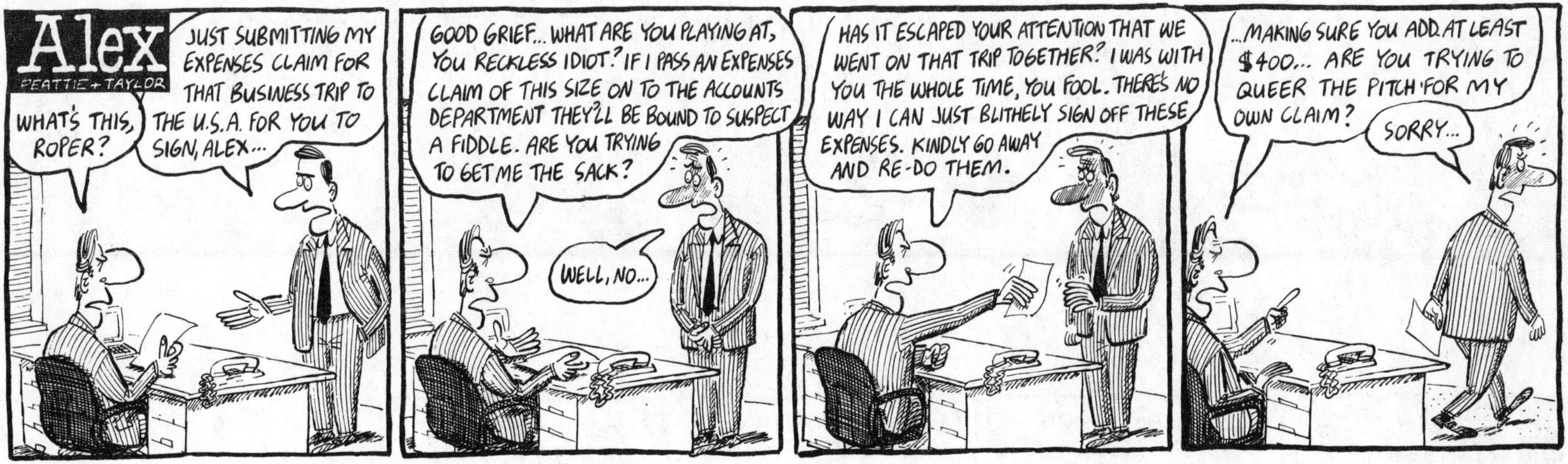
Alex
PEATTIE + TAYLOR
WHAT'S THIS, ROPER?
JUST SUBMITTING MY EXPENSES CLAIM FOR THAT BUSINESS TRIP TO THE U.S.A. FOR YOU TO SIGN, ALEX...
GOOD GRIEF... WHAT ARE YOU PLAYING AT, YOU RECKLESS IDIOT? IF I PASS AN EXPENSES CLAIM OF THIS SIZE ON TO THE ACCOUNTS DEPARTMENT THEY'LL BE BOUND TO SUSPECT A FIDDLE. ARE YOU TRYING TO GET ME THE SACK?
WELL, NO...
HAS IT ESCAPED YOUR ATTENTION THAT WE WENT ON THAT TRIP TOGETHER? I WAS WITH YOU THE WHOLE TIME, YOU FOOL. THERE'S NO WAY I CAN JUST BLITHELY SIGN OFF THESE EXPENSES. KINDLY GO AWAY AND RE-DO THEM.
...MAKING SURE YOU ADD AT LEAST $400... ARE YOU TRYING TO QUEER THE PITCH FOR MY OWN CLAIM?
SORRY...

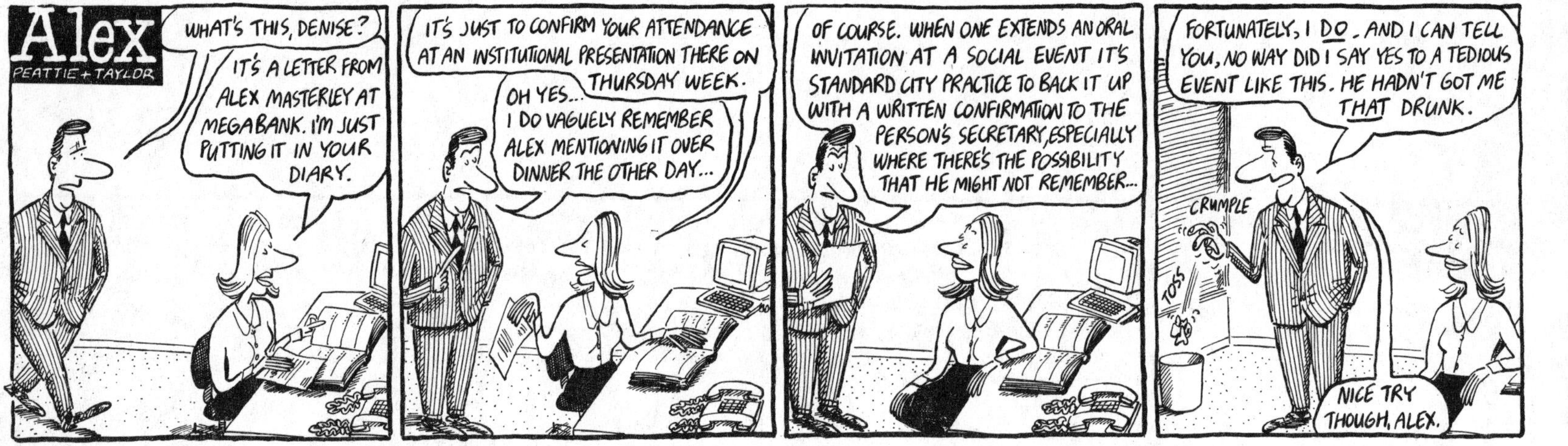
Alex
PEATTIE + TAYLOR
WHAT'S THIS, DENISE?
IT'S A LETTER FROM ALEX MASTERLEY AT MEGABANK. I'M JUST PUTTING IT IN YOUR DIARY.
IT'S JUST TO CONFIRM YOUR ATTENDANCE AT AN INSTITUTIONAL PRESENTATION THERE ON THURSDAY WEEK.
OH YES... I DO VAGUELY REMEMBER ALEX MENTIONING IT OVER DINNER THE OTHER DAY...
OF COURSE. WHEN ONE EXTENDS AN ORAL INVITATION AT A SOCIAL EVENT IT'S STANDARD CITY PRACTICE TO BACK IT UP WITH A WRITTEN CONFIRMATION TO THE PERSON'S SECRETARY, ESPECIALLY WHERE THERE'S THE POSSIBILITY THAT HE MIGHT NOT REMEMBER...
FORTUNATELY, I DO. AND I CAN TELL YOU, NO WAY DID I SAY YES TO A TEDIOUS EVENT LIKE THIS. HE HADN'T GOT ME THAT DRUNK.
CRUMPLE
TOSS
NICE TRY THOUGH, ALEX.

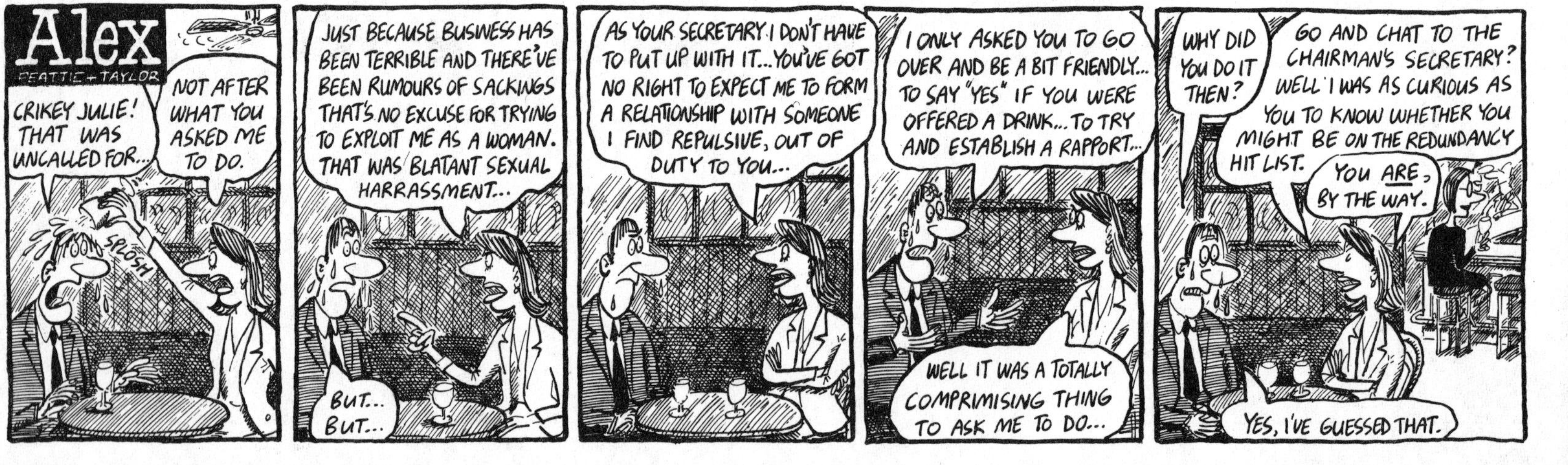
Alex
PEATTIE + TAYLOR
CRIKEY JULIE! THAT WAS UNCALLED FOR...
NOT AFTER WHAT YOU ASKED ME TO DO.
SPLOSH
JUST BECAUSE BUSINESS HAS BEEN TERRIBLE AND THERE'VE BEEN RUMOURS OF SACKINGS THAT'S NO EXCUSE FOR TRYING TO EXPLOIT ME AS A WOMAN. THAT WAS BLATANT SEXUAL HARRASSMENT...
BUT... BUT...
AS YOUR SECRETARY I DON'T HAVE TO PUT UP WITH IT... YOU'VE GOT NO RIGHT TO EXPECT ME TO FORM A RELATIONSHIP WITH SOMEONE I FIND REPULSIVE, OUT OF DUTY TO YOU...
I ONLY ASKED YOU TO GO OVER AND BE A BIT FRIENDLY... TO SAY "YES" IF YOU WERE OFFERED A DRINK... TO TRY AND ESTABLISH A RAPPORT...
WELL IT WAS A TOTALLY COMPRIMISING THING TO ASK ME TO DO...
WHY DID YOU DO IT THEN?
GO AND CHAT TO THE CHAIRMAN'S SECRETARY? WELL I WAS AS CURIOUS AS YOU TO KNOW WHETHER YOU MIGHT BE ON THE REDUNDANCY HIT LIST.
YOU ARE, BY THE WAY.
YES, I'VE GUESSED THAT.

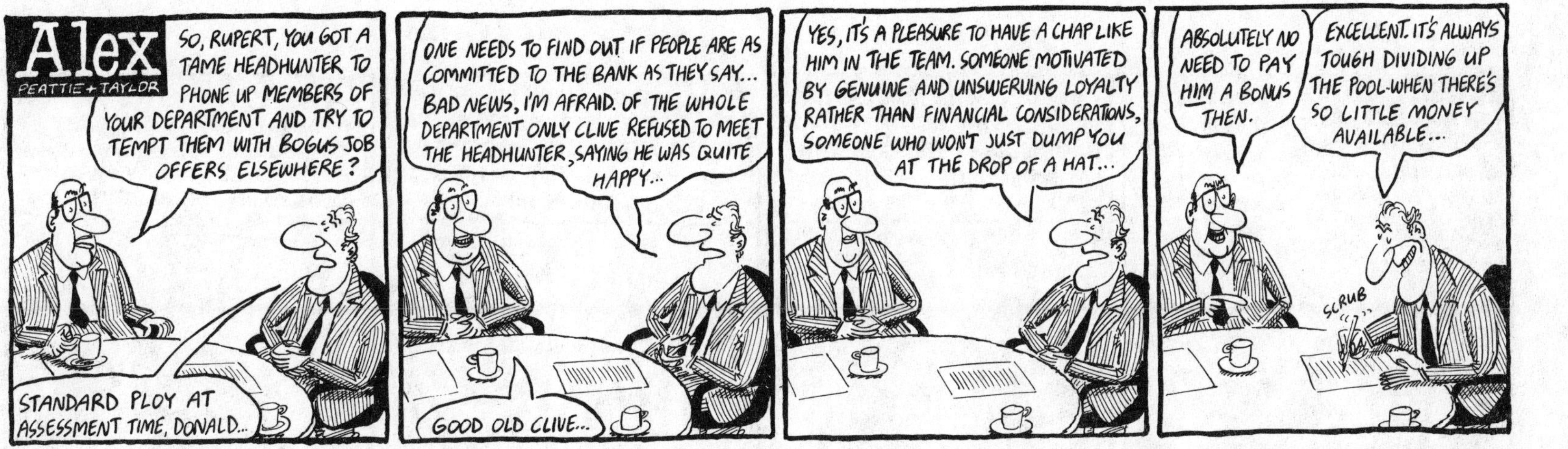
Alex
PEATTIE + TAYLOR
SO, RUPERT, YOU GOT A TAME HEADHUNTER TO PHONE UP MEMBERS OF YOUR DEPARTMENT AND TRY TO TEMPT THEM WITH BOGUS JOB OFFERS ELSEWHERE?
STANDARD PLOY AT ASSESSMENT TIME, DONALD...
ONE NEEDS TO FIND OUT IF PEOPLE ARE AS COMMITTED TO THE BANK AS THEY SAY... BAD NEWS, I'M AFRAID. OF THE WHOLE DEPARTMENT ONLY CLIVE REFUSED TO MEET THE HEADHUNTER, SAYING HE WAS QUITE HAPPY...
GOOD OLD CLIVE...
YES, IT'S A PLEASURE TO HAVE A CHAP LIKE HIM IN THE TEAM. SOMEONE MOTIVATED BY GENUINE AND UNSWERVING LOYALTY RATHER THAN FINANCIAL CONSIDERATIONS, SOMEONE WHO WON'T JUST DUMP YOU AT THE DROP OF A HAT...
ABSOLUTELY NO NEED TO PAY HIM A BONUS THEN.
EXCELLENT. IT'S ALWAYS TOUGH DIVIDING UP THE POOL-WHEN THERE'S SO LITTLE MONEY AVAILABLE...
SCRUB

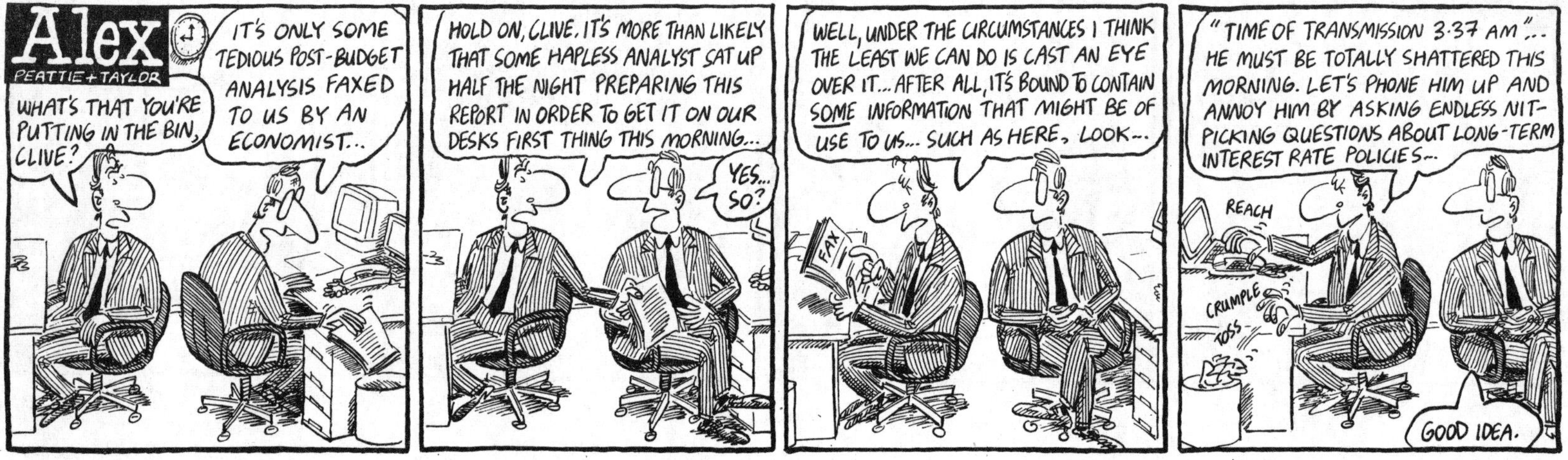
Alex
PEATTIE + TAYLOR
WHAT'S THAT YOU'RE PUTTING IN THE BIN, CLIVE?
IT'S ONLY SOME TEDIOUS POST-BUDGET ANALYSIS FAXED TO US BY AN ECONOMIST...
HOLD ON, CLIVE. IT'S MORE THAN LIKELY THAT SOME HAPLESS ANALYST SAT UP HALF THE NIGHT PREPARING THIS REPORT IN ORDER TO GET IT ON OUR DESKS FIRST THING THIS MORNING...
YES... SO?
WELL, UNDER THE CIRCUMSTANCES I THINK THE LEAST WE CAN DO IS CAST AN EYE OVER IT... AFTER ALL, IT'S BOUND TO CONTAIN SOME INFORMATION THAT MIGHT BE OF USE TO US... SUCH AS HERE, LOOK...
FAX
"TIME OF TRANSMISSION 3·37 AM"... HE MUST BE TOTALLY SHATTERED THIS MORNING. LET'S PHONE HIM UP AND ANNOY HIM BY ASKING ENDLESS NIT-PICKING QUESTIONS ABOUT LONG-TERM INTEREST RATE POLICIES...
REACH
CRUMPLE
TOSS
GOOD IDEA.

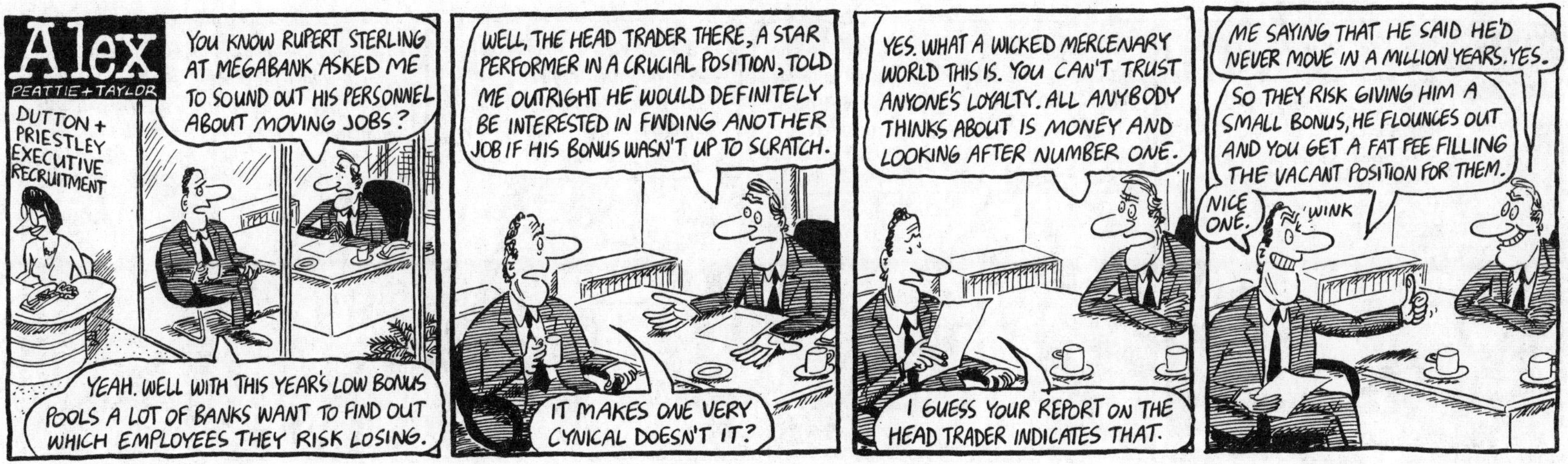
Alex
PEATTIE + TAYLOR
DUTTON + PRIESTLEY EXECUTIVE RECRUITMENT
YOU KNOW RUPERT STERLING AT MEGABANK ASKED ME TO SOUND OUT HIS PERSONNEL ABOUT MOVING JOBS?
YEAH. WELL WITH THIS YEAR'S LOW BONUS POOLS A LOT OF BANKS WANT TO FIND OUT WHICH EMPLOYEES THEY RISK LOSING.
WELL, THE HEAD TRADER THERE, A STAR PERFORMER IN A CRUCIAL POSITION, TOLD ME OUTRIGHT HE WOULD DEFINITELY BE INTERESTED IN FINDING ANOTHER JOB IF HIS BONUS WASN'T UP TO SCRATCH.
IT MAKES ONE VERY CYNICAL DOESN'T IT?
YES. WHAT A WICKED MERCENARY WORLD THIS IS. YOU CAN'T TRUST ANYONE'S LOYALTY. ALL ANYBODY THINKS ABOUT IS MONEY AND LOOKING AFTER NUMBER ONE.
I GUESS YOUR REPORT ON THE HEAD TRADER INDICATES THAT.
ME SAYING THAT HE SAID HE'D NEVER MOVE IN A MILLION YEARS. YES.
SO THEY RISK GIVING HIM A SMALL BONUS, HE FLOUNCES OUT AND YOU GET A FAT FEE FILLING THE VACANT POSITION FOR THEM.
NICE ONE.
WINK

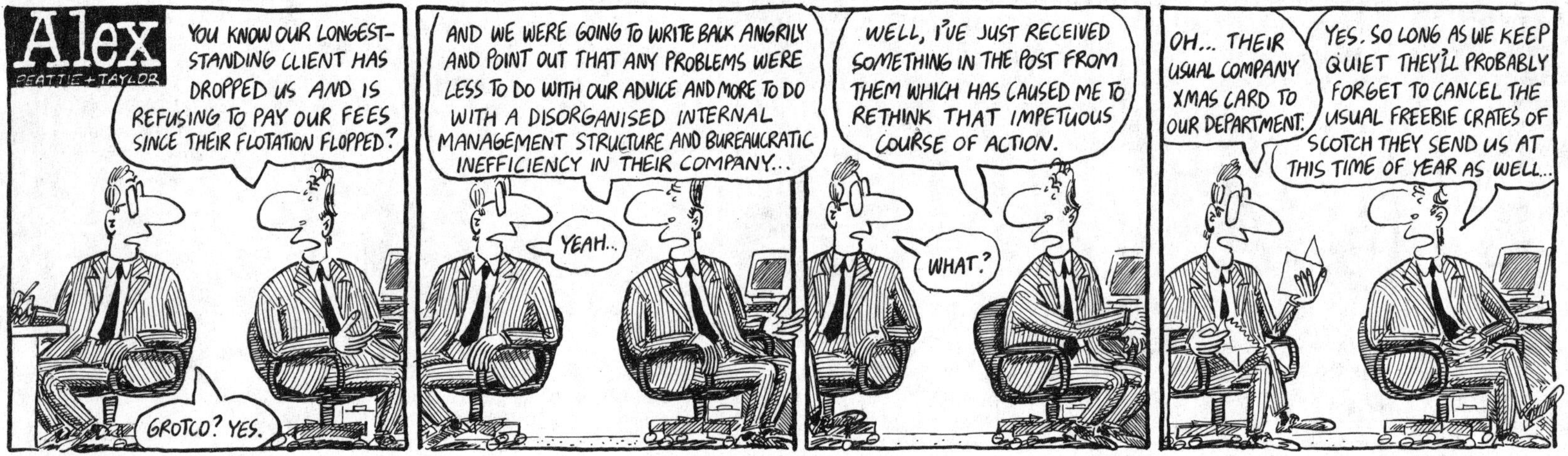
Alex
BEATTIE + TAYLOR
YOU KNOW OUR LONGEST-STANDING CLIENT HAS DROPPED US AND IS REFUSING TO PAY OUR FEES SINCE THEIR FLOTATION FLOPPED?
GROTCO? YES.
AND WE WERE GOING TO WRITE BACK ANGRILY AND POINT OUT THAT ANY PROBLEMS WERE LESS TO DO WITH OUR ADVICE AND MORE TO DO WITH A DISORGANISED INTERNAL MANAGEMENT STRUCTURE AND BUREAUCRATIC INEFFICIENCY IN THEIR COMPANY...
YEAH..
WELL, I'VE JUST RECEIVED SOMETHING IN THE POST FROM THEM WHICH HAS CAUSED ME TO RETHINK THAT IMPETUOUS COURSE OF ACTION.
WHAT?
OH... THEIR USUAL COMPANY XMAS CARD TO OUR DEPARTMENT.
YES. SO LONG AS WE KEEP QUIET THEY'LL PROBABLY FORGET TO CANCEL THE USUAL FREEBIE CRATES OF SCOTCH THEY SEND US AT THIS TIME OF YEAR AS WELL...

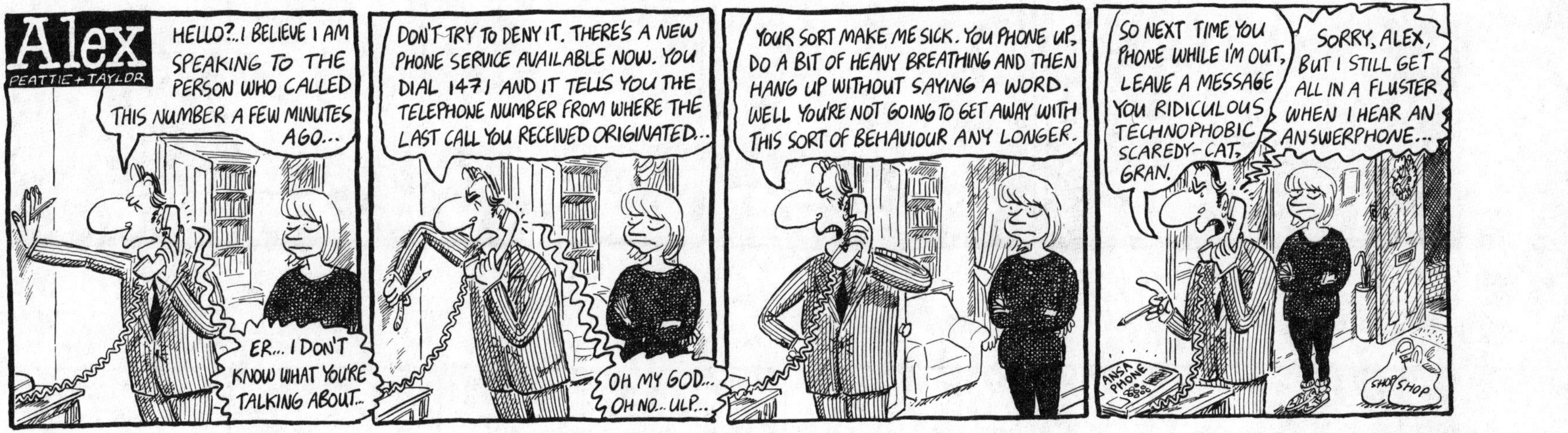
Alex
PEATTIE + TAYLOR
HELLO?.. I BELIEVE I AM SPEAKING TO THE PERSON WHO CALLED THIS NUMBER A FEW MINUTES AGO...
ER... I DON'T KNOW WHAT YOU'RE TALKING ABOUT...
DON'T TRY TO DENY IT. THERE'S A NEW PHONE SERVICE AVAILABLE NOW. YOU DIAL 1471 AND IT TELLS YOU THE TELEPHONE NUMBER FROM WHERE THE LAST CALL YOU RECEIVED ORIGINATED...
OH MY GOD... OH NO... ULP...
YOUR SORT MAKE ME SICK. YOU PHONE UP, DO A BIT OF HEAVY BREATHING AND THEN HANG UP WITHOUT SAYING A WORD. WELL YOU'RE NOT GOING TO GET AWAY WITH THIS SORT OF BEHAVIOUR ANY LONGER.
SO NEXT TIME YOU PHONE WHILE I'M OUT, LEAVE A MESSAGE YOU RIDICULOUS TECHNOPHOBIC SCAREDY-CAT, GRAN.
SORRY, ALEX, BUT I STILL GET ALL IN A FLUSTER WHEN I HEAR AN ANSWERPHONE...
ANSA PHONE
SHOP
SHOP

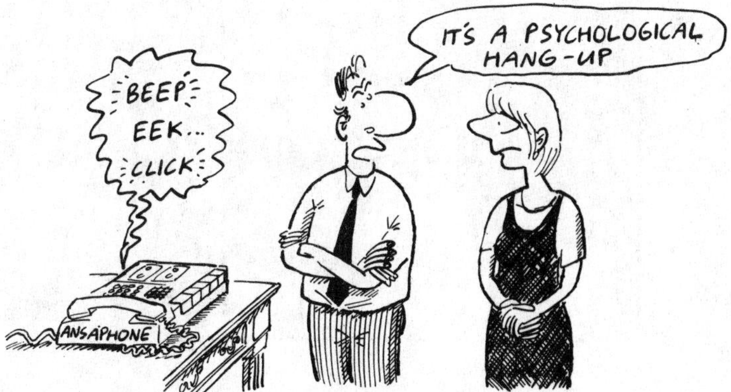
BEEP
EEK...
CLICK
IT'S A PSYCHOLOGICAL HANG-UP
ANSAPHONE

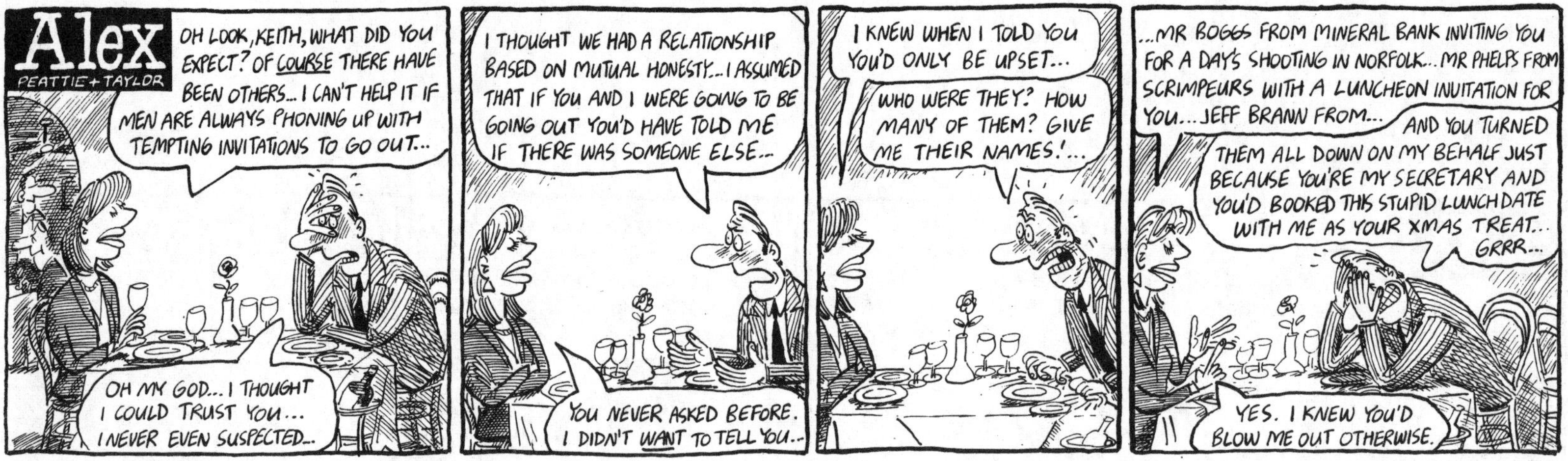
Alex
PEATTIE + TAYLOR
OH LOOK, KEITH, WHAT DID YOU EXPECT? OF COURSE THERE HAVE BEEN OTHERS... I CAN'T HELP IT IF MEN ARE ALWAYS PHONING UP WITH TEMPTING INVITATIONS TO GO OUT...
OH MY GOD... I THOUGHT I COULD TRUST YOU... I NEVER EVEN SUSPECTED...
I THOUGHT WE HAD A RELATIONSHIP BASED ON MUTUAL HONESTY... I ASSUMED THAT IF YOU AND I WERE GOING TO BE GOING OUT YOU'D HAVE TOLD ME IF THERE WAS SOMEONE ELSE...
YOU NEVER ASKED BEFORE. I DIDN'T WANT TO TELL YOU...
I KNEW WHEN I TOLD YOU YOU'D ONLY BE UPSET...
WHO WERE THEY? HOW MANY OF THEM? GIVE ME THEIR NAMES!...
...MR BOGGS FROM MINERAL BANK INVITING YOU FOR A DAY'S SHOOTING IN NORFOLK... MR PHELPS FROM SCRIMPEURS WITH A LUNCHEON INVITATION FOR YOU... JEFF BRANN FROM...
AND YOU TURNED THEM ALL DOWN ON MY BEHALF JUST BECAUSE YOU'RE MY SECRETARY AND YOU'D BOOKED THIS STUPID LUNCHDATE WITH ME AS YOUR XMAS TREAT... GRRR...
YES. I KNEW YOU'D BLOW ME OUT OTHERWISE.

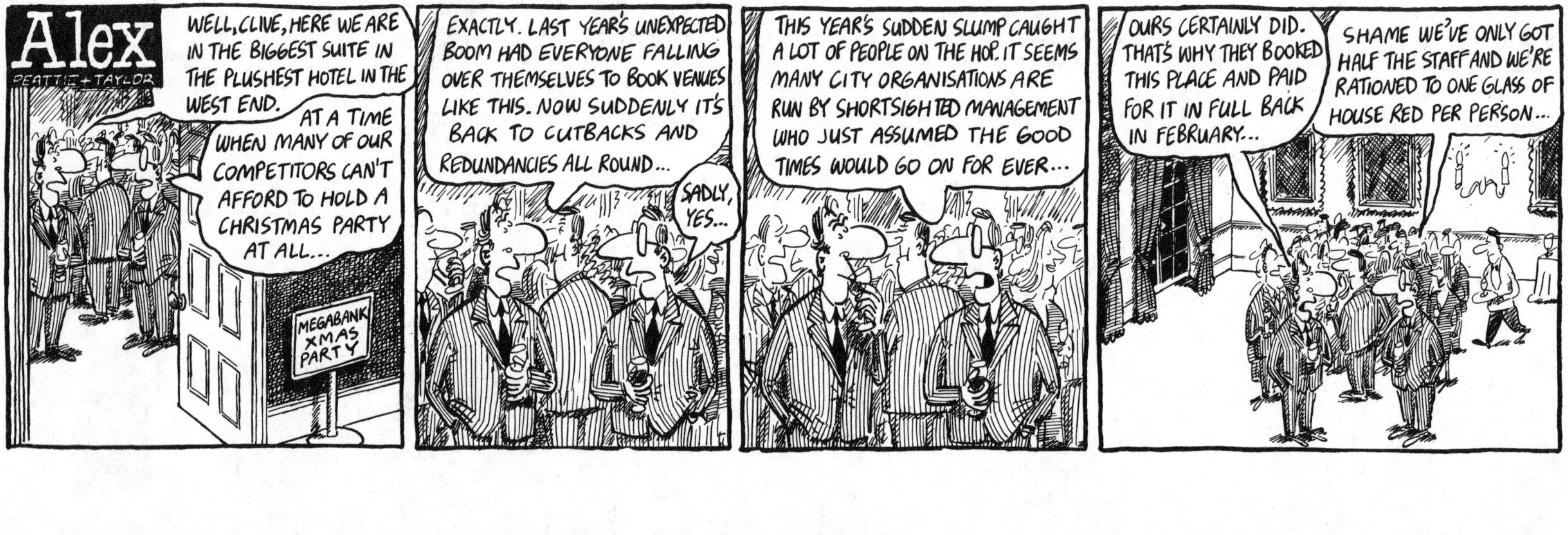
Alex
PEATTIE + TAYLOR
WELL, CLIVE, HERE WE ARE IN THE BIGGEST SUITE IN THE PLUSHEST HOTEL IN THE WEST END.
AT A TIME WHEN MANY OF OUR COMPETITORS CAN'T AFFORD TO HOLD A CHRISTMAS PARTY AT ALL...
MEGABANK XMAS PARTY
EXACTLY. LAST YEAR'S UNEXPECTED BOOM HAD EVERYONE FALLING OVER THEMSELVES TO BOOK VENUES LIKE THIS. NOW SUDDENLY IT'S BACK TO CUTBACKS AND REDUNDANCIES ALL ROUND...
SADLY, YES...
THIS YEAR'S SUDDEN SLUMP CAUGHT A LOT OF PEOPLE ON THE HOP. IT SEEMS MANY CITY ORGANISATIONS ARE RUN BY SHORTSIGHTED MANAGEMENT WHO JUST ASSUMED THE GOOD TIMES WOULD GO ON FOR EVER...
OURS CERTAINLY DID. THAT'S WHY THEY BOOKED THIS PLACE AND PAID FOR IT IN FULL BACK IN FEBRUARY...
SHAME WE'VE ONLY GOT HALF THE STAFF AND WE'RE RATIONED TO ONE GLASS OF HOUSE RED PER PERSON...

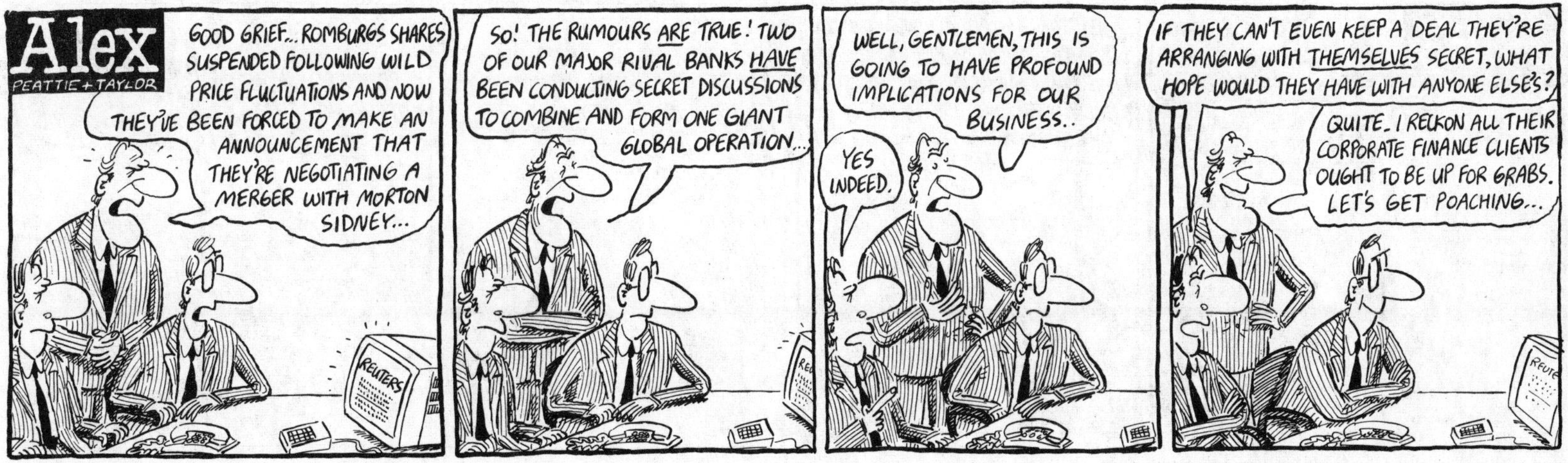
Alex
PEATTIE + TAYLOR
GOOD GRIEF... ROMBURGS SHARES SUSPENDED FOLLOWING WILD PRICE FLUCTUATIONS AND NOW THEY'VE BEEN FORCED TO MAKE AN ANNOUNCEMENT THAT THEY'RE NEGOTIATING A MERGER WITH MORTON SIDNEY...
REUTERS
SO! THE RUMOURS ARE TRUE! TWO OF OUR MAJOR RIVAL BANKS HAVE BEEN CONDUCTING SECRET DISCUSSIONS TO COMBINE AND FORM ONE GIANT GLOBAL OPERATION...
WELL, GENTLEMEN, THIS IS GOING TO HAVE PROFOUND IMPLICATIONS FOR OUR BUSINESS..
YES INDEED.
IF THEY CAN'T EVEN KEEP A DEAL THEY'RE ARRANGING WITH THEMSELVES SECRET, WHAT HOPE WOULD THEY HAVE WITH ANYONE ELSE'S?
QUITE. I RECKON ALL THEIR CORPORATE FINANCE CLIENTS OUGHT TO BE UP FOR GRABS. LET'S GET POACHING...

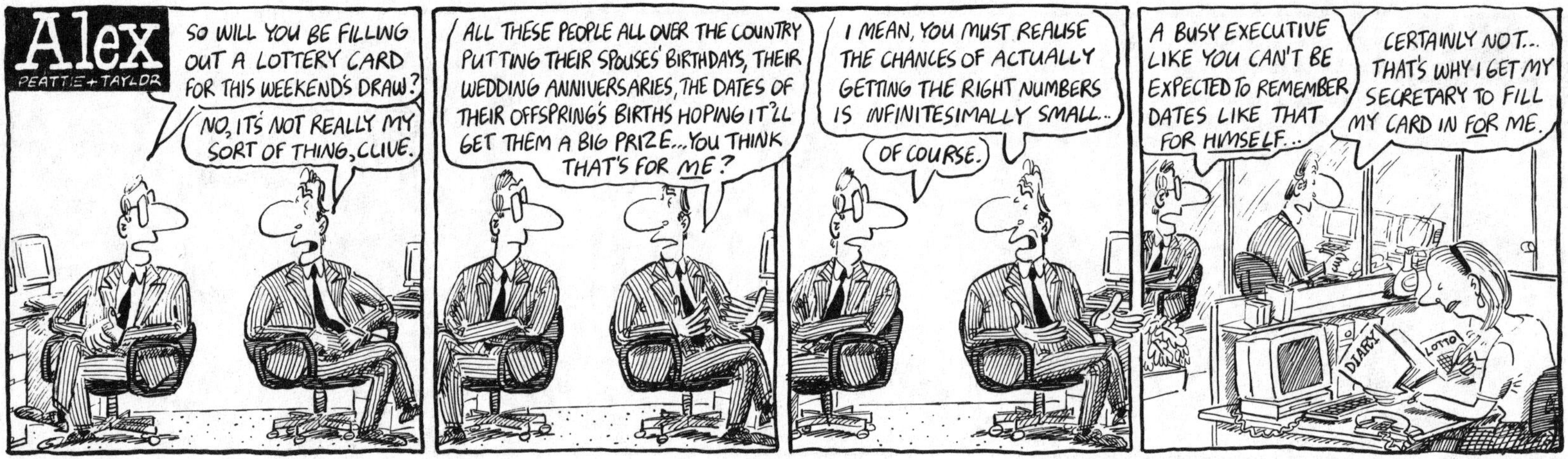
Alex
PEATTIE + TAYLOR
SO WILL YOU BE FILLING OUT A LOTTERY CARD FOR THIS WEEKEND'S DRAW?
NO, IT'S NOT REALLY MY SORT OF THING, CLIVE.
ALL THESE PEOPLE ALL OVER THE COUNTRY PUTTING THEIR SPOUSES' BIRTHDAYS, THEIR WEDDING ANNIVERSARIES, THE DATES OF THEIR OFFSPRING'S BIRTHS HOPING IT'LL GET THEM A BIG PRIZE... YOU THINK THAT'S FOR ME?
I MEAN, YOU MUST REALISE THE CHANCES OF ACTUALLY GETTING THE RIGHT NUMBERS IS INFINITESIMALLY SMALL...
OF COURSE.
A BUSY EXECUTIVE LIKE YOU CAN'T BE EXPECTED TO REMEMBER DATES LIKE THAT FOR HIMSELF...
CERTAINLY NOT... THAT'S WHY I GET MY SECRETARY TO FILL MY CARD IN FOR ME.
DIARY
LOTTO

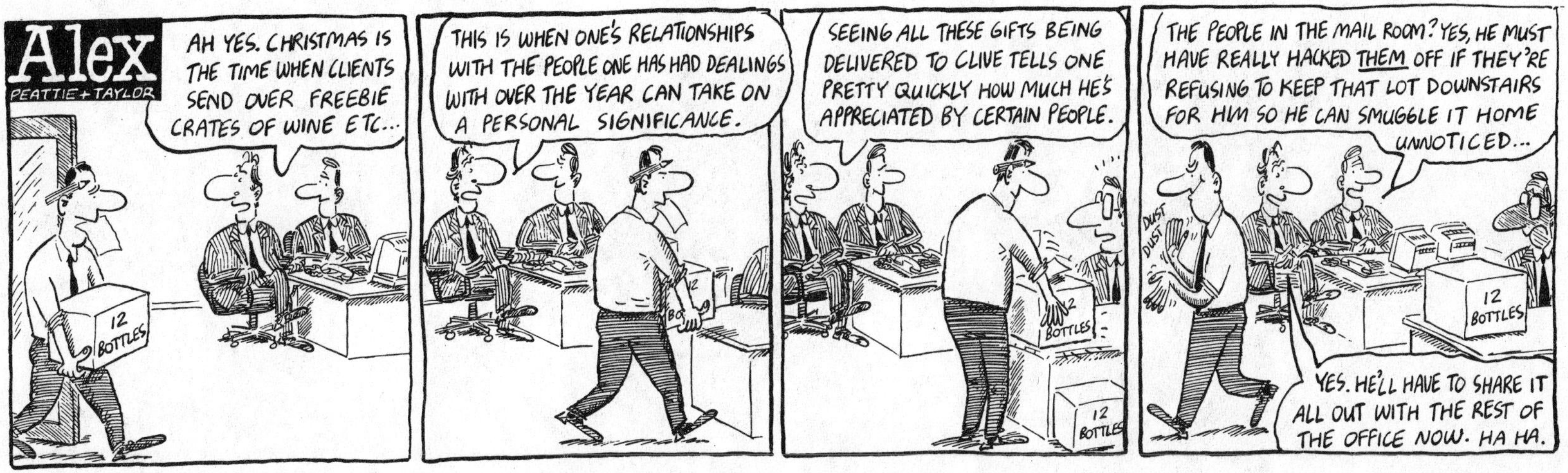
Alex
PEATTIE + TAYLOR
AH YES. CHRISTMAS IS THE TIME WHEN CLIENTS SEND OVER FREEBIE CRATES OF WINE ETC...
12 BOTTLES
THIS IS WHEN ONE'S RELATIONSHIPS WITH THE PEOPLE ONE HAS HAD DEALINGS WITH OVER THE YEAR CAN TAKE ON A PERSONAL SIGNIFICANCE.
SEEING ALL THESE GIFTS BEING DELIVERED TO CLIVE TELLS ONE PRETTY QUICKLY HOW MUCH HE'S APPRECIATED BY CERTAIN PEOPLE.
12 BOTTLES
THE PEOPLE IN THE MAIL ROOM? YES, HE MUST HAVE REALLY HACKED THEM OFF IF THEY'RE REFUSING TO KEEP THAT LOT DOWNSTAIRS FOR HIM SO HE CAN SMUGGLE IT HOME UNNOTICED...
DUST DUST
12 BOTTLES
YES. HE'LL HAVE TO SHARE IT ALL OUT WITH THE REST OF THE OFFICE NOW. HA HA.

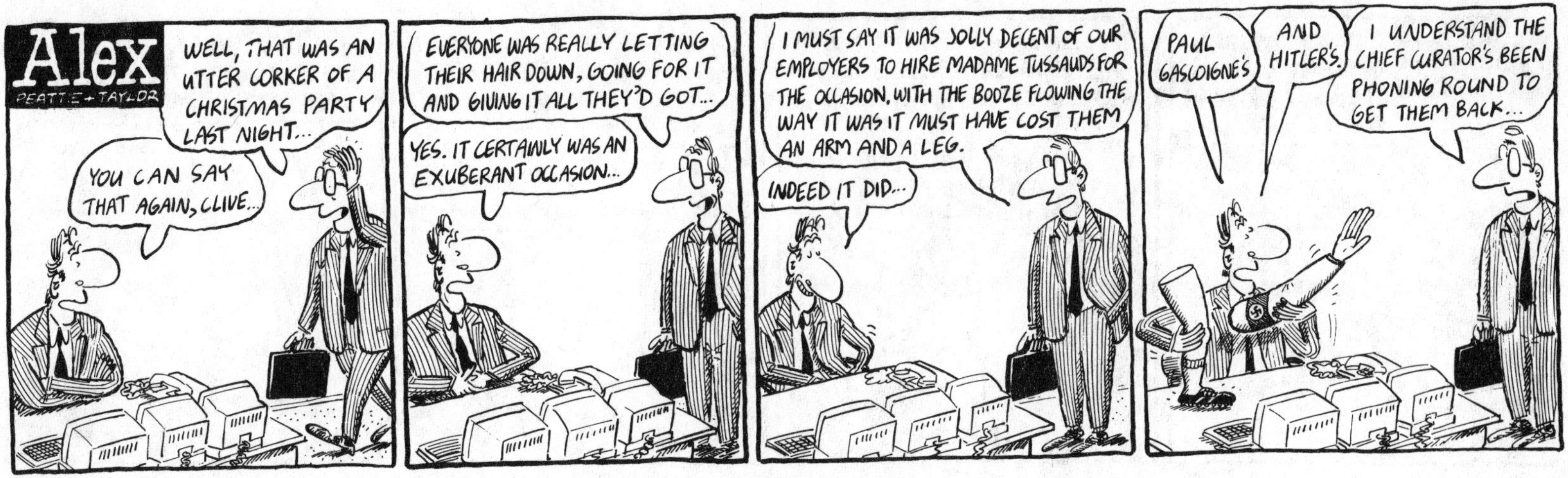
Alex
PEATTIE + TAYLOR
WELL, THAT WAS AN UTTER CORKER OF A CHRISTMAS PARTY LAST NIGHT...
YOU CAN SAY THAT AGAIN, CLIVE...
EVERYONE WAS REALLY LETTING THEIR HAIR DOWN, GOING FOR IT AND GIVING IT ALL THEY'D GOT...
YES. IT CERTAINLY WAS AN EXUBERANT OCCASION...
I MUST SAY IT WAS JOLLY DECENT OF OUR EMPLOYERS TO HIRE MADAME TUSSAUDS FOR THE OCCASION. WITH THE BOOZE FLOWING THE WAY IT WAS IT MUST HAVE COST THEM AN ARM AND A LEG.
INDEED IT DID...
PAUL GASCOIGNE'S
AND HITLER'S.
I UNDERSTAND THE CHIEF CURATOR'S BEEN PHONING ROUND TO GET THEM BACK...

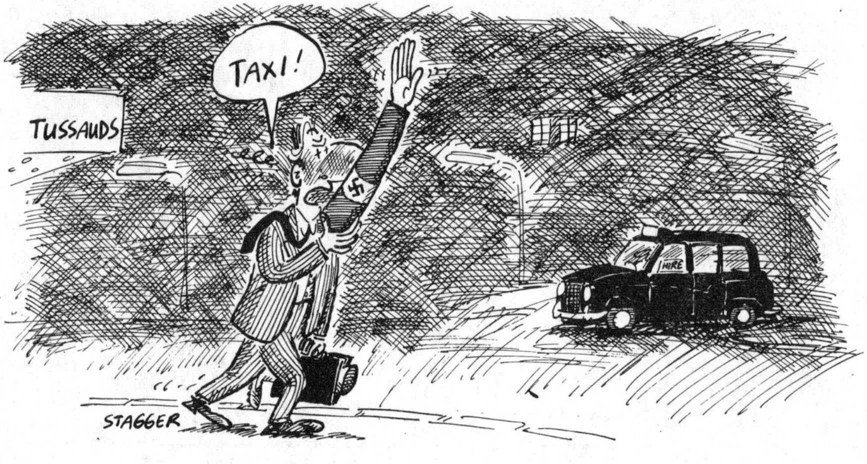
TAXI!
TUSSAUDS
HIRE
STAGGER

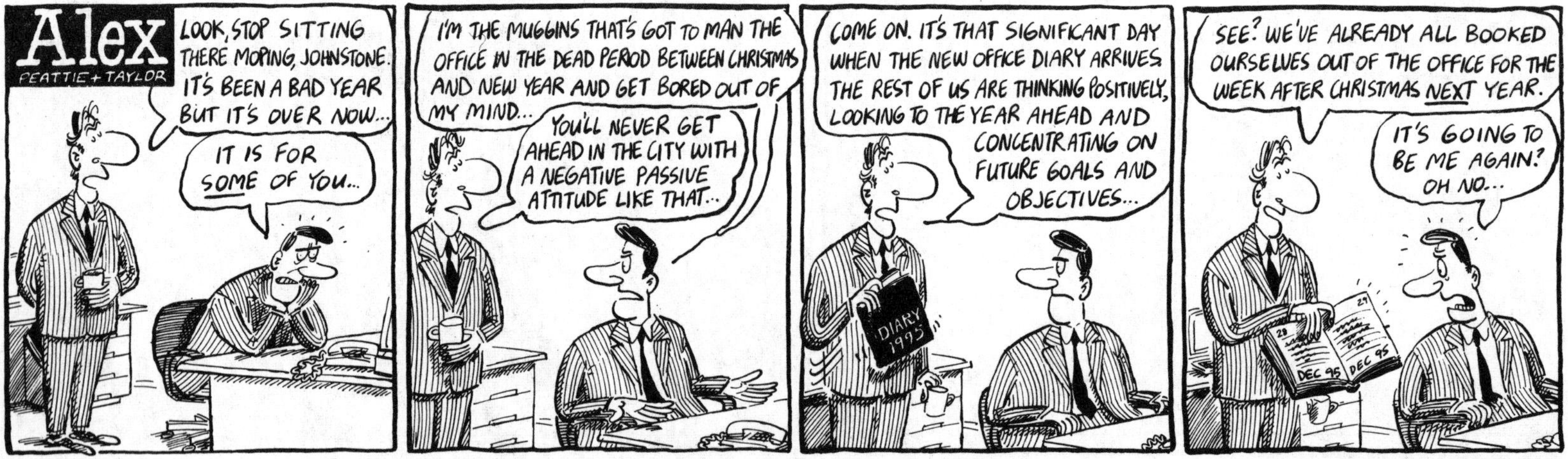
Alex
PEATTIE + TAYLOR
LOOK, STOP SITTING THERE MOPING, JOHNSTONE. IT'S BEEN A BAD YEAR BUT IT'S OVER NOW...
IT IS FOR SOME OF YOU...
I'M THE MUGGINS THAT'S GOT TO MAN THE OFFICE IN THE DEAD PERIOD BETWEEN CHRISTMAS AND NEW YEAR AND GET BORED OUT OF MY MIND...
YOU'LL NEVER GET AHEAD IN THE CITY WITH A NEGATIVE PASSIVE ATTITUDE LIKE THAT...
COME ON. IT'S THAT SIGNIFICANT DAY WHEN THE NEW OFFICE DIARY ARRIVES. THE REST OF US ARE THINKING POSITIVELY, LOOKING TO THE YEAR AHEAD AND CONCENTRATING ON FUTURE GOALS AND OBJECTIVES...
DIARY 1995
SEE? WE'VE ALREADY ALL BOOKED OURSELVES OUT OF THE OFFICE FOR THE WEEK AFTER CHRISTMAS NEXT YEAR.
IT'S GOING TO BE ME AGAIN? OH NO...
DEC 95
DEC 95

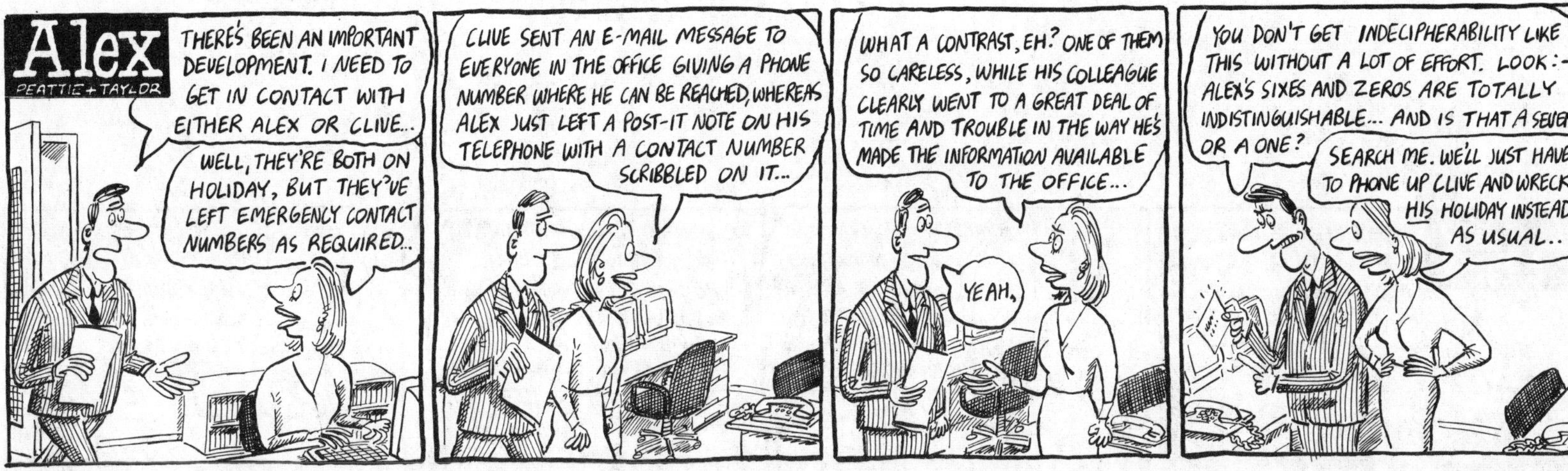
Alex
PEATTIE + TAYLOR
THERE'S BEEN AN IMPORTANT DEVELOPMENT. I NEED TO GET IN CONTACT WITH EITHER ALEX OR CLIVE...
WELL, THEY'RE BOTH ON HOLIDAY, BUT THEY'VE LEFT EMERGENCY CONTACT NUMBERS AS REQUIRED...
CLIVE SENT AN E-MAIL MESSAGE TO EVERYONE IN THE OFFICE GIVING A PHONE NUMBER WHERE HE CAN BE REACHED, WHEREAS ALEX JUST LEFT A POST-IT NOTE ON HIS TELEPHONE WITH A CONTACT NUMBER SCRIBBLED ON IT...
WHAT A CONTRAST, EH? ONE OF THEM SO CARELESS, WHILE HIS COLLEAGUE CLEARLY WENT TO A GREAT DEAL OF TIME AND TROUBLE IN THE WAY HE'S MADE THE INFORMATION AVAILABLE TO THE OFFICE...
YEAH,
YOU DON'T GET INDECIPHERABILITY LIKE THIS WITHOUT A LOT OF EFFORT. LOOK:- ALEX'S SIXES AND ZEROS ARE TOTALLY INDISTINGUISHABLE... AND IS THAT A SEVEN OR A ONE?
SEARCH ME. WE'LL JUST HAVE TO PHONE UP CLIVE AND WRECK HIS HOLIDAY INSTEAD AS USUAL..

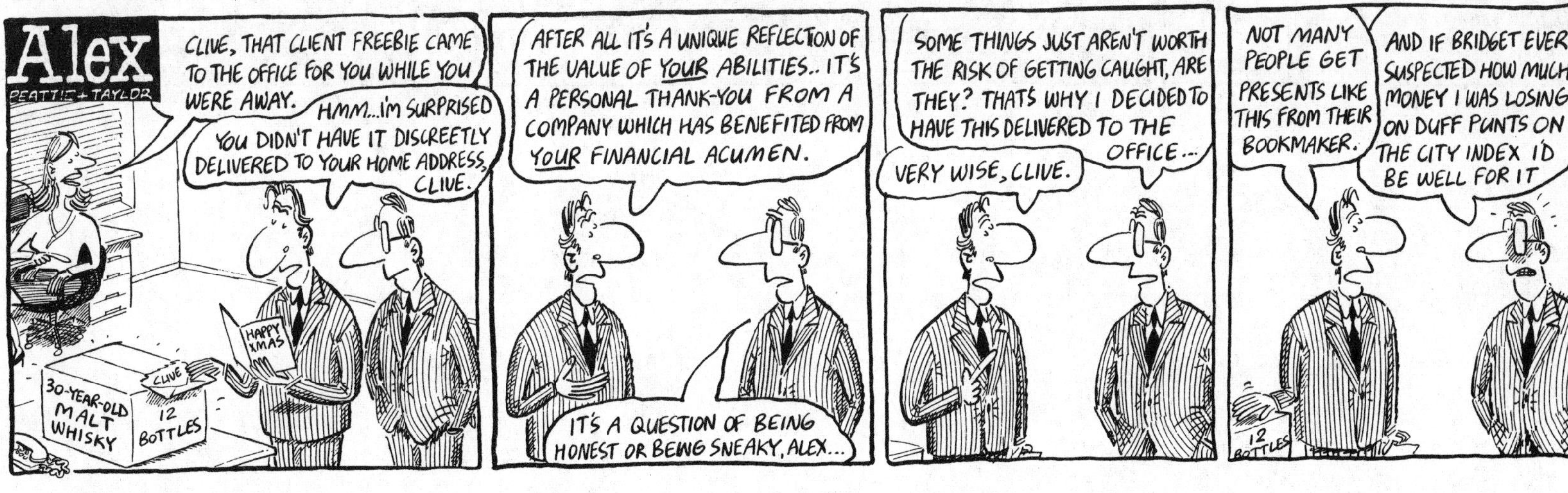
Alex
PEATTIE + TAYLOR
CLIVE, THAT CLIENT FREEBIE CAME TO THE OFFICE FOR YOU WHILE YOU WERE AWAY.
HMM...I'M SURPRISED YOU DIDN'T HAVE IT DISCREETLY DELIVERED TO YOUR HOME ADDRESS, CLIVE.
HAPPY XMAS
CLIVE
30-YEAR-OLD MALT WHISKY
12 BOTTLES
AFTER ALL IT'S A UNIQUE REFLECTION OF THE VALUE OF YOUR ABILITIES.. IT'S A PERSONAL THANK-YOU FROM A COMPANY WHICH HAS BENEFITED FROM YOUR FINANCIAL ACUMEN.
IT'S A QUESTION OF BEING HONEST OR BEING SNEAKY, ALEX...
SOME THINGS JUST AREN'T WORTH THE RISK OF GETTING CAUGHT, ARE THEY? THAT'S WHY I DECIDED TO HAVE THIS DELIVERED TO THE OFFICE...
VERY WISE, CLIVE.
NOT MANY PEOPLE GET PRESENTS LIKE THIS FROM THEIR BOOKMAKER.
AND IF BRIDGET EVER SUSPECTED HOW MUCH MONEY I WAS LOSING ON DUFF PUNTS ON THE CITY INDEX I'D BE WELL FOR IT
12 BOTTLES

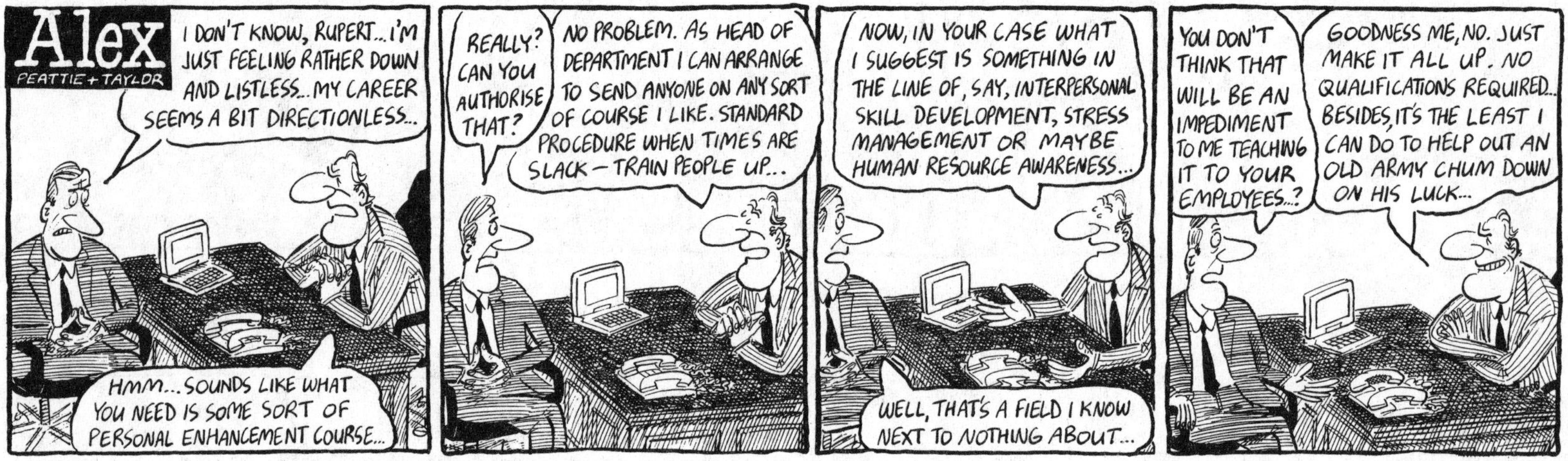
Alex
PEATTIE + TAYLOR
I DON'T KNOW, RUPERT... I'M JUST FEELING RATHER DOWN AND LISTLESS... MY CAREER SEEMS A BIT DIRECTIONLESS...
HMM... SOUNDS LIKE WHAT YOU NEED IS SOME SORT OF PERSONAL ENHANCEMENT COURSE...
REALLY? CAN YOU AUTHORISE THAT?
NO PROBLEM. AS HEAD OF DEPARTMENT I CAN ARRANGE TO SEND ANYONE ON ANY SORT OF COURSE I LIKE. STANDARD PROCEDURE WHEN TIMES ARE SLACK — TRAIN PEOPLE UP...
NOW, IN YOUR CASE WHAT I SUGGEST IS SOMETHING IN THE LINE OF, SAY, INTERPERSONAL SKILL DEVELOPMENT, STRESS MANAGEMENT OR MAYBE HUMAN RESOURCE AWARENESS...
WELL, THAT'S A FIELD I KNOW NEXT TO NOTHING ABOUT...
YOU DON'T THINK THAT WILL BE AN IMPEDIMENT TO ME TEACHING IT TO YOUR EMPLOYEES...?
GOODNESS ME, NO. JUST MAKE IT ALL UP. NO QUALIFICATIONS REQUIRED... BESIDES, IT'S THE LEAST I CAN DO TO HELP OUT AN OLD ARMY CHUM DOWN ON HIS LUCK...

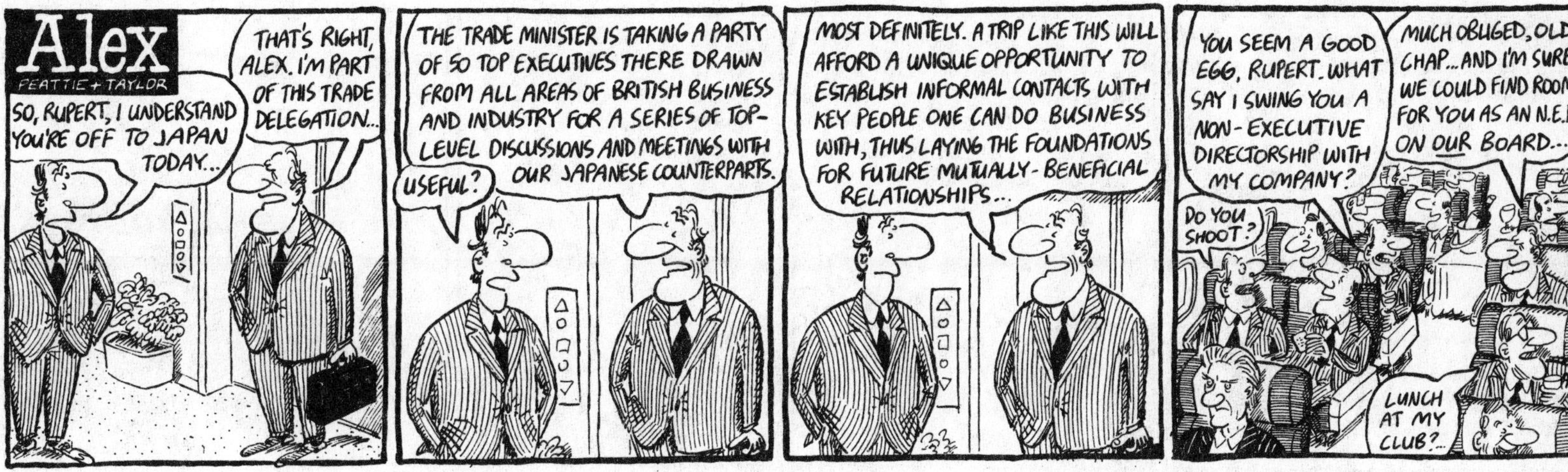
Alex
PEATTIE + TAYLOR
SO, RUPERT, I UNDERSTAND YOU'RE OFF TO JAPAN TODAY...
THAT'S RIGHT, ALEX. I'M PART OF THIS TRADE DELEGATION...
THE TRADE MINISTER IS TAKING A PARTY OF 50 TOP EXECUTIVES THERE DRAWN FROM ALL AREAS OF BRITISH BUSINESS AND INDUSTRY FOR A SERIES OF TOP-LEVEL DISCUSSIONS AND MEETINGS WITH OUR JAPANESE COUNTERPARTS.
USEFUL?
MOST DEFINITELY. A TRIP LIKE THIS WILL AFFORD A UNIQUE OPPORTUNITY TO ESTABLISH INFORMAL CONTACTS WITH KEY PEOPLE ONE CAN DO BUSINESS WITH, THUS LAYING THE FOUNDATIONS FOR FUTURE MUTUALLY-BENEFICIAL RELATIONSHIPS...
YOU SEEM A GOOD EGG, RUPERT. WHAT SAY I SWING YOU A NON-EXECUTIVE DIRECTORSHIP WITH MY COMPANY?
MUCH OBLIGED, OLD CHAP... AND I'M SURE WE COULD FIND ROOM FOR YOU AS AN N.E.D. ON OUR BOARD...
DO YOU SHOOT?
LUNCH AT MY CLUB?...

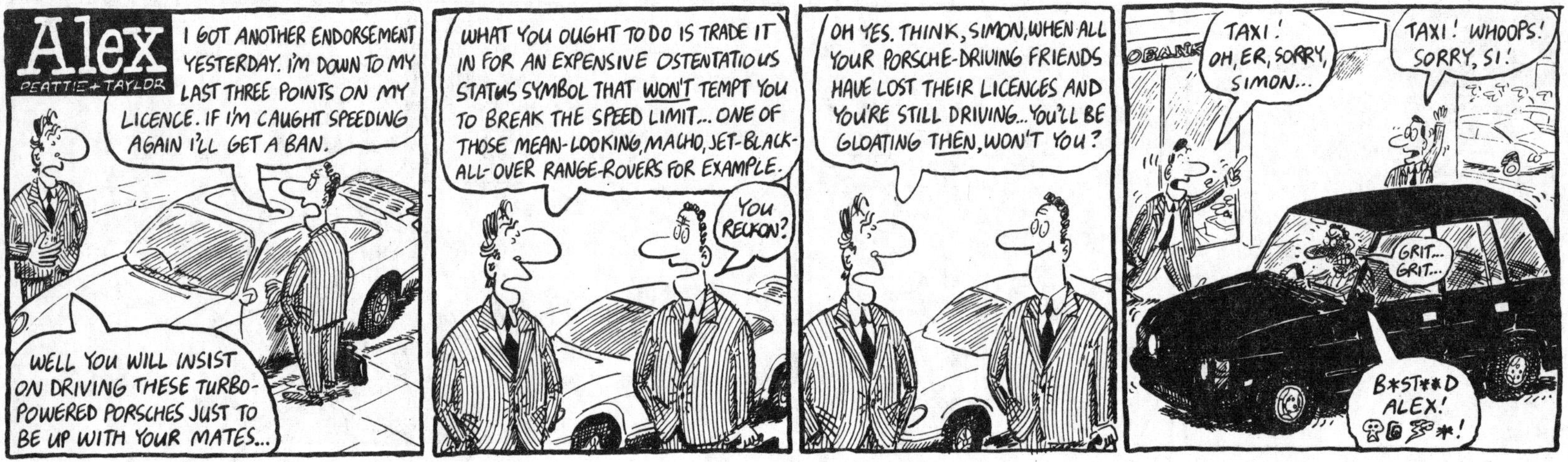
Alex
PEATTIE + TAYLOR
I GOT ANOTHER ENDORSEMENT YESTERDAY. I'M DOWN TO MY LAST THREE POINTS ON MY LICENCE. IF I'M CAUGHT SPEEDING AGAIN I'LL GET A BAN.
WELL YOU WILL INSIST ON DRIVING THESE TURBO-POWERED PORSCHES JUST TO BE UP WITH YOUR MATES...
WHAT YOU OUGHT TO DO IS TRADE IT IN FOR AN EXPENSIVE OSTENTATIOUS STATUS SYMBOL THAT WON'T TEMPT YOU TO BREAK THE SPEED LIMIT... ONE OF THOSE MEAN-LOOKING, MACHO, JET-BLACK-ALL-OVER RANGE-ROVERS FOR EXAMPLE.
YOU RECKON?
OH YES. THINK, SIMON, WHEN ALL YOUR PORSCHE-DRIVING FRIENDS HAVE LOST THEIR LICENCES AND YOU'RE STILL DRIVING... YOU'LL BE GLOATING THEN, WON'T YOU?
BANK
TAXI! OH, ER, SORRY, SIMON...
TAXI! WHOOPS! SORRY, SI!
GRIT... GRIT...
B*ST**D ALEX!

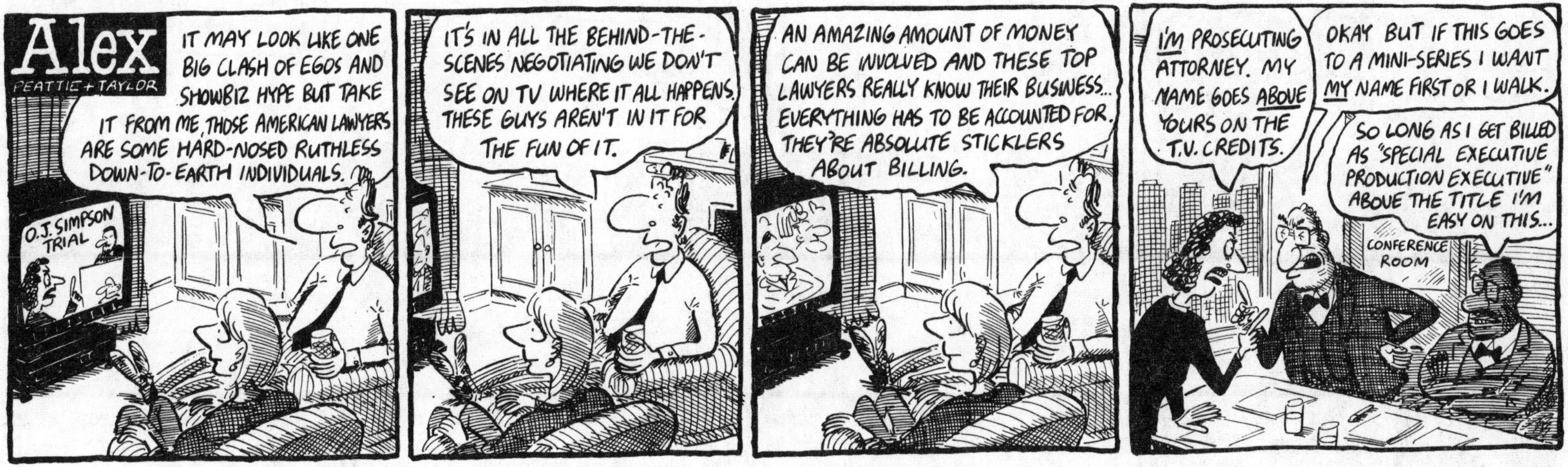
Alex
PEATTIE + TAYLOR
IT MAY LOOK LIKE ONE BIG CLASH OF EGOS AND SHOWBIZ HYPE BUT TAKE IT FROM ME, THOSE AMERICAN LAWYERS ARE SOME HARD-NOSED RUTHLESS DOWN-TO-EARTH INDIVIDUALS.
O.J. SIMPSON TRIAL
IT'S IN ALL THE BEHIND-THE-SCENES NEGOTIATING WE DON'T SEE ON TV WHERE IT ALL HAPPENS. THESE GUYS AREN'T IN IT FOR THE FUN OF IT.
AN AMAZING AMOUNT OF MONEY CAN BE INVOLVED AND THESE TOP LAWYERS REALLY KNOW THEIR BUSINESS... EVERYTHING HAS TO BE ACCOUNTED FOR. THEY'RE ABSOLUTE STICKLERS ABOUT BILLING.
I'M PROSECUTING ATTORNEY. MY NAME GOES ABOVE YOURS ON THE T.V. CREDITS.
OKAY BUT IF THIS GOES TO A MINI-SERIES I WANT MY NAME FIRST OR I WALK.
SO LONG AS I GET BILLED AS "SPECIAL EXECUTIVE PRODUCTION EXECUTIVE" ABOVE THE TITLE I'M EASY ON THIS...
CONFERENCE ROOM

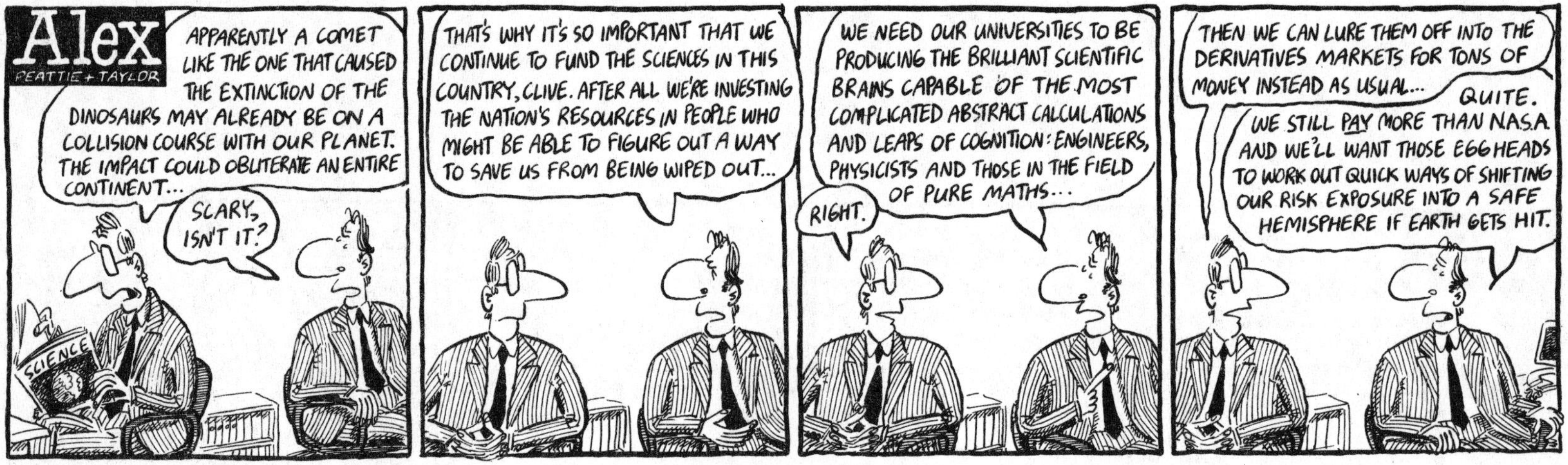
Alex
BEATTIE + TAYLOR
APPARENTLY A COMET LIKE THE ONE THAT CAUSED THE EXTINCTION OF THE DINOSAURS MAY ALREADY BE ON A COLLISION COURSE WITH OUR PLANET. THE IMPACT COULD OBLITERATE AN ENTIRE CONTINENT...
SCARY, ISN'T IT?
SCIENCE
THAT'S WHY IT'S SO IMPORTANT THAT WE CONTINUE TO FUND THE SCIENCES IN THIS COUNTRY, CLIVE. AFTER ALL WE'RE INVESTING THE NATION'S RESOURCES IN PEOPLE WHO MIGHT BE ABLE TO FIGURE OUT A WAY TO SAVE US FROM BEING WIPED OUT...
WE NEED OUR UNIVERSITIES TO BE PRODUCING THE BRILLIANT SCIENTIFIC BRAINS CAPABLE OF THE MOST COMPLICATED ABSTRACT CALCULATIONS AND LEAPS OF COGNITION: ENGINEERS, PHYSICISTS AND THOSE IN THE FIELD OF PURE MATHS...
RIGHT.
THEN WE CAN LURE THEM OFF INTO THE DERIVATIVES MARKETS FOR TONS OF MONEY INSTEAD AS USUAL...
QUITE. WE STILL PAY MORE THAN N.A.S.A. AND WE'LL WANT THOSE EGGHEADS TO WORK OUT QUICK WAYS OF SHIFTING OUR RISK EXPOSURE INTO A SAFE HEMISPHERE IF EARTH GETS HIT.

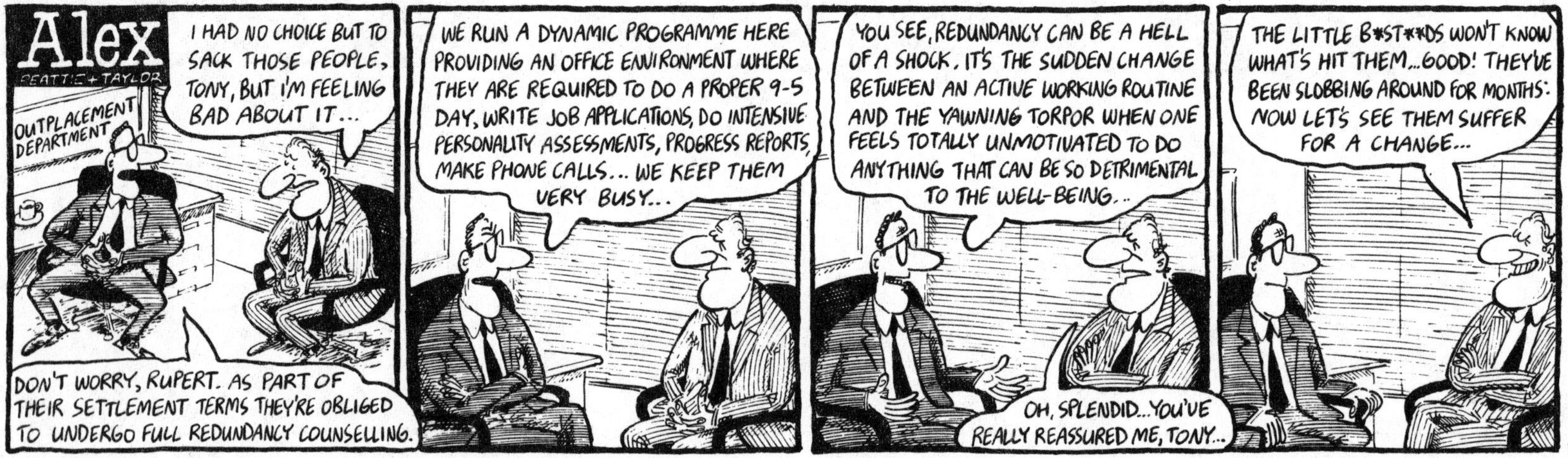
Alex
BEATTIE + TAYLOR
OUTPLACEMENT DEPARTMENT
I HAD NO CHOICE BUT TO SACK THOSE PEOPLE, TONY, BUT I'M FEELING BAD ABOUT IT...
DON'T WORRY, RUPERT. AS PART OF THEIR SETTLEMENT TERMS THEY'RE OBLIGED TO UNDERGO FULL REDUNDANCY COUNSELLING.
WE RUN A DYNAMIC PROGRAMME HERE PROVIDING AN OFFICE ENVIRONMENT WHERE THEY ARE REQUIRED TO DO A PROPER 9-5 DAY, WRITE JOB APPLICATIONS, DO INTENSIVE PERSONALITY ASSESSMENTS, PROGRESS REPORTS, MAKE PHONE CALLS... WE KEEP THEM VERY BUSY...
YOU SEE, REDUNDANCY CAN BE A HELL OF A SHOCK. IT'S THE SUDDEN CHANGE BETWEEN AN ACTIVE WORKING ROUTINE AND THE YAWNING TORPOR WHEN ONE FEELS TOTALLY UNMOTIVATED TO DO ANYTHING THAT CAN BE SO DETRIMENTAL TO THE WELL-BEING...
OH, SPLENDID... YOU'VE REALLY REASSURED ME, TONY...
THE LITTLE B*ST**DS WON'T KNOW WHAT'S HIT THEM...GOOD! THEY'VE BEEN SLOBBING AROUND FOR MONTHS: NOW LET'S SEE THEM SUFFER FOR A CHANGE...

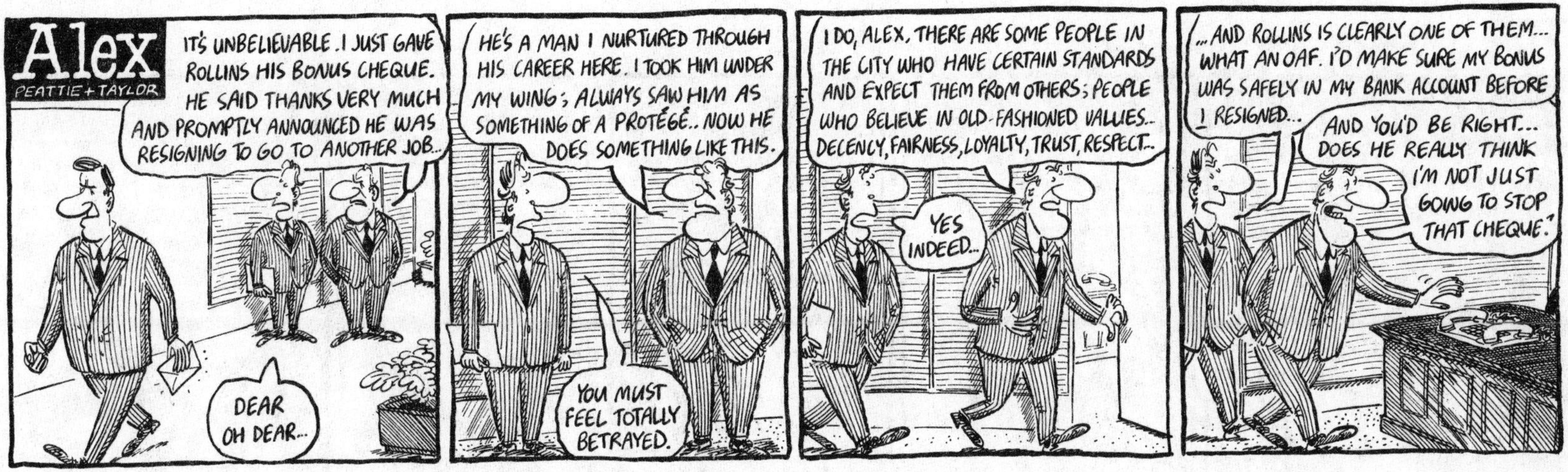
Alex
PEATTIE + TAYLOR
IT'S UNBELIEVABLE. I JUST GAVE ROLLINS HIS BONUS CHEQUE. HE SAID THANKS VERY MUCH AND PROMPTLY ANNOUNCED HE WAS RESIGNING TO GO TO ANOTHER JOB...
DEAR OH DEAR...
HE'S A MAN I NURTURED THROUGH HIS CAREER HERE. I TOOK HIM UNDER MY WING; ALWAYS SAW HIM AS SOMETHING OF A PROTÉGÉ.. NOW HE DOES SOMETHING LIKE THIS.
YOU MUST FEEL TOTALLY BETRAYED.
I DO, ALEX. THERE ARE SOME PEOPLE IN THE CITY WHO HAVE CERTAIN STANDARDS AND EXPECT THEM FROM OTHERS; PEOPLE WHO BELIEVE IN OLD-FASHIONED VALUES.. DECENCY, FAIRNESS, LOYALTY, TRUST, RESPECT...
YES INDEED...
... AND ROLLINS IS CLEARLY ONE OF THEM... WHAT AN OAF. I'D MAKE SURE MY BONUS WAS SAFELY IN MY BANK ACCOUNT BEFORE I RESIGNED...
AND YOU'D BE RIGHT... DOES HE REALLY THINK I'M NOT JUST GOING TO STOP THAT CHEQUE?

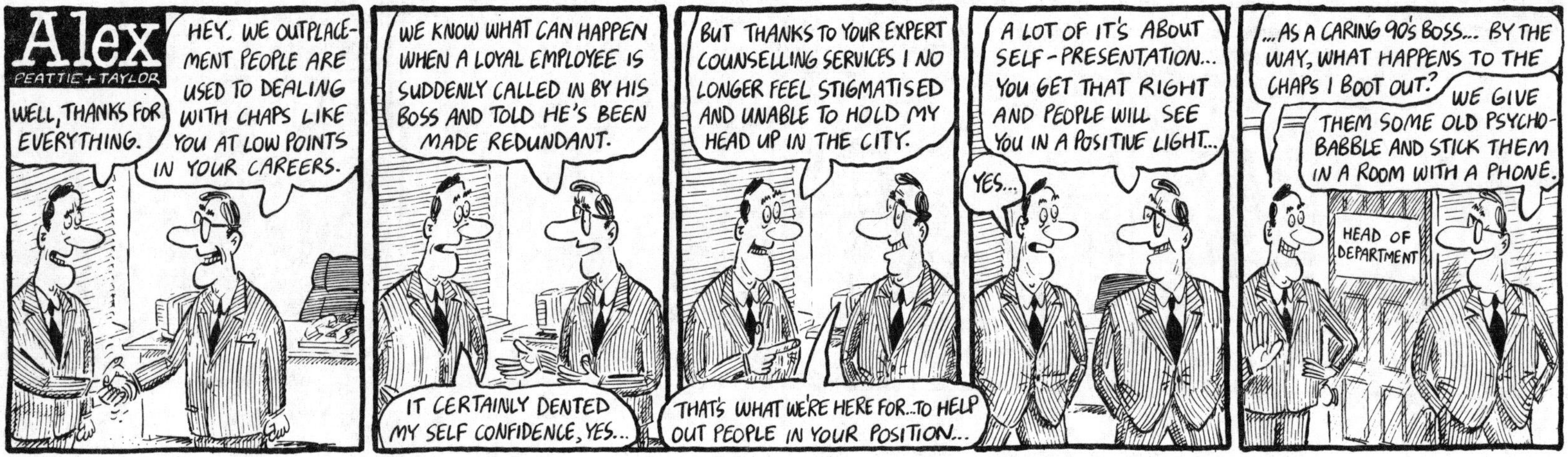
Alex
PEATTIE + TAYLOR
WELL, THANKS FOR EVERYTHING.
HEY. WE OUTPLACEMENT PEOPLE ARE USED TO DEALING WITH CHAPS LIKE YOU AT LOW POINTS IN YOUR CAREERS.
WE KNOW WHAT CAN HAPPEN WHEN A LOYAL EMPLOYEE IS SUDDENLY CALLED IN BY HIS BOSS AND TOLD HE'S BEEN MADE REDUNDANT.
IT CERTAINLY DENTED MY SELF CONFIDENCE, YES...
BUT THANKS TO YOUR EXPERT COUNSELLING SERVICES I NO LONGER FEEL STIGMATISED AND UNABLE TO HOLD MY HEAD UP IN THE CITY.
THAT'S WHAT WE'RE HERE FOR...TO HELP OUT PEOPLE IN YOUR POSITION...
A LOT OF IT'S ABOUT SELF-PRESENTATION... YOU GET THAT RIGHT AND PEOPLE WILL SEE YOU IN A POSITIVE LIGHT...
YES...
...AS A CARING 90'S BOSS... BY THE WAY, WHAT HAPPENS TO THE CHAPS I BOOT OUT?
WE GIVE THEM SOME OLD PSYCHO-BABBLE AND STICK THEM IN A ROOM WITH A PHONE.
HEAD OF DEPARTMENT

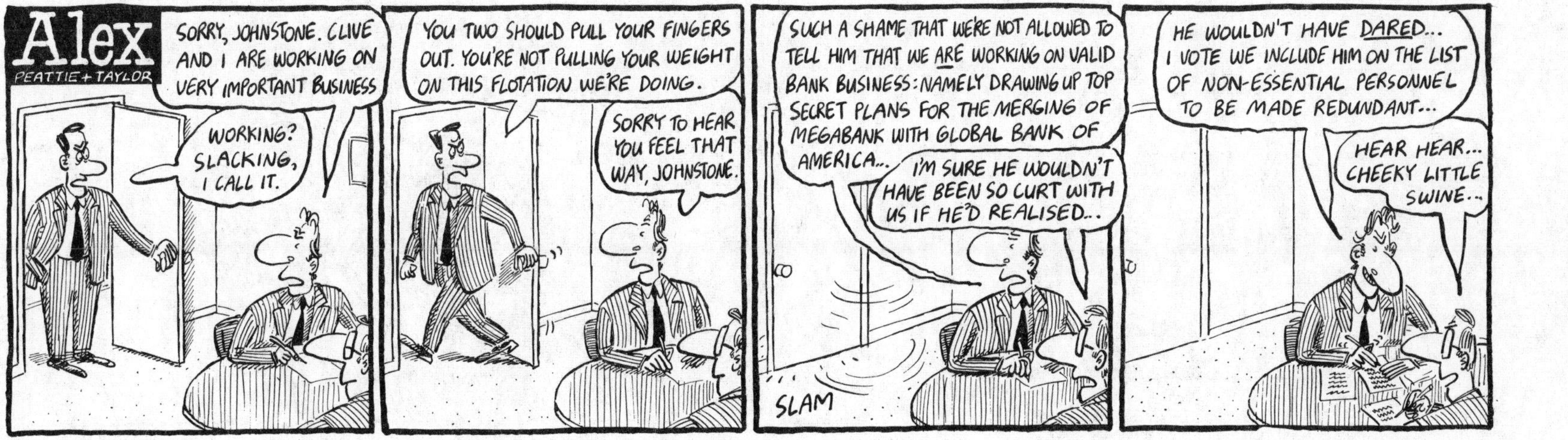
Alex
PEATTIE + TAYLOR
SORRY, JOHNSTONE. CLIVE AND I ARE WORKING ON VERY IMPORTANT BUSINESS
WORKING? SLACKING, I CALL IT.
YOU TWO SHOULD PULL YOUR FINGERS OUT. YOU'RE NOT PULLING YOUR WEIGHT ON THIS FLOTATION WE'RE DOING.
SORRY TO HEAR YOU FEEL THAT WAY, JOHNSTONE.
SLAM
SUCH A SHAME THAT WE'RE NOT ALLOWED TO TELL HIM THAT WE ARE WORKING ON VALID BANK BUSINESS: NAMELY DRAWING UP TOP SECRET PLANS FOR THE MERGING OF MEGABANK WITH GLOBAL BANK OF AMERICA...
I'M SURE HE WOULDN'T HAVE BEEN SO CURT WITH US IF HE'D REALISED...
HE WOULDN'T HAVE DARED... I VOTE WE INCLUDE HIM ON THE LIST OF NON-ESSENTIAL PERSONNEL TO BE MADE REDUNDANT...
HEAR HEAR... CHEEKY LITTLE SWINE...

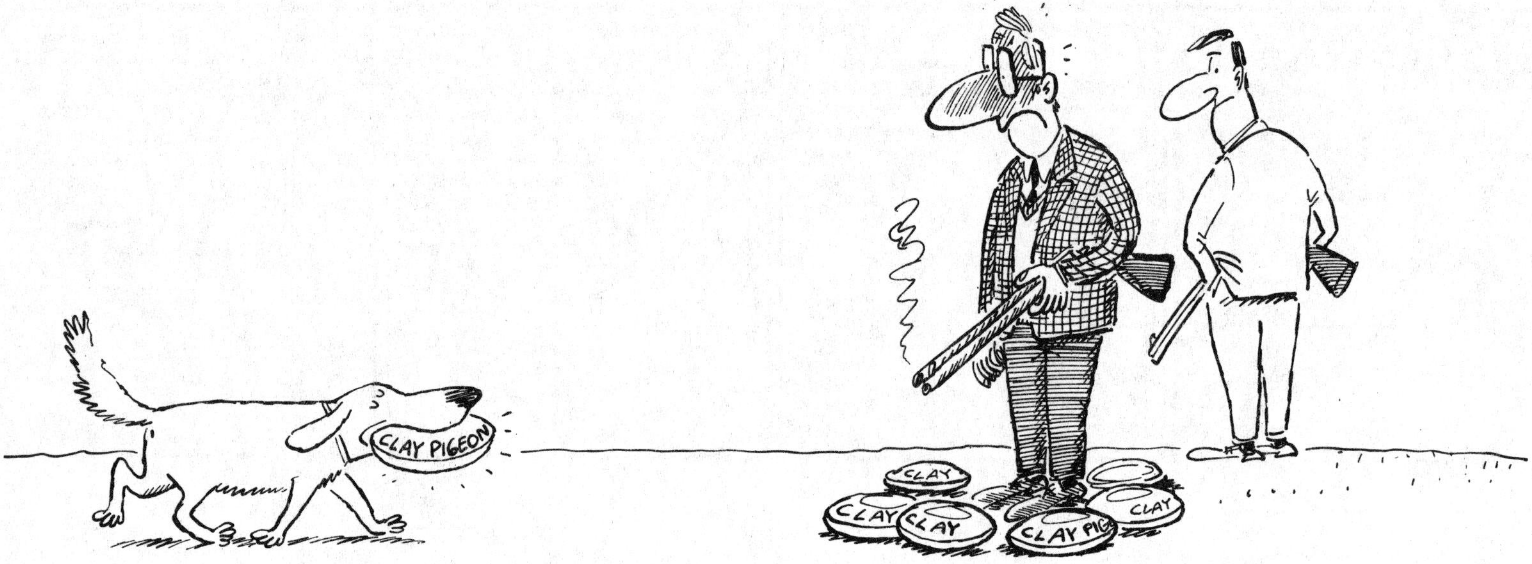
CLAY PIGEON
CLAY
CLAY
CLAY
CLAY
CLAY PIG
CLAY

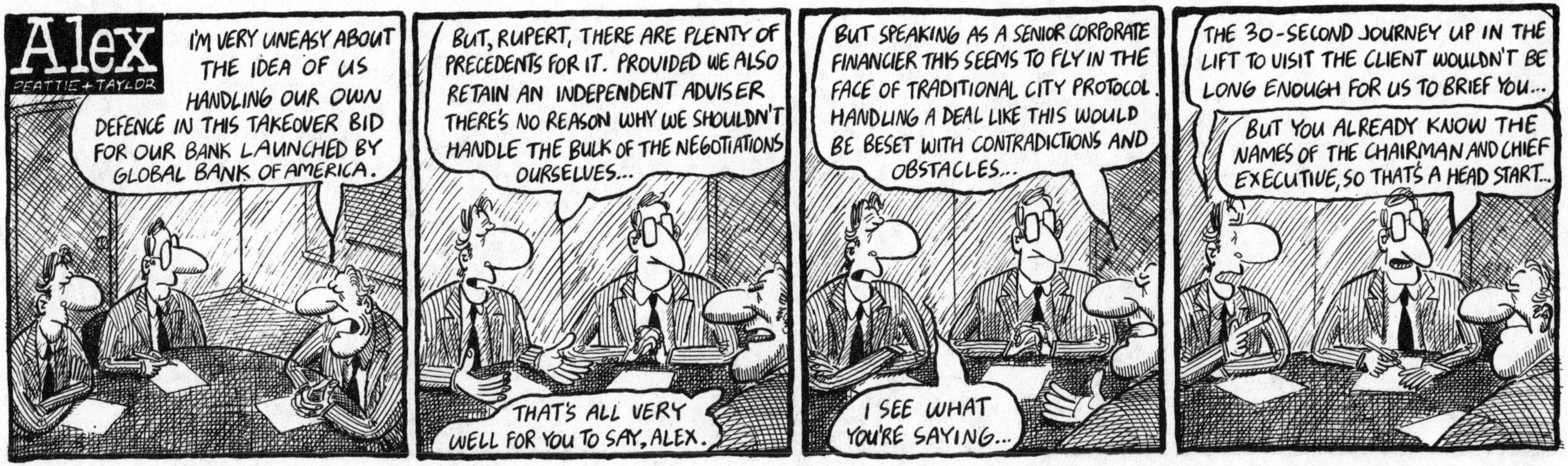
Alex
BEATTIE + TAYLOR
I'M VERY UNEASY ABOUT THE IDEA OF US HANDLING OUR OWN DEFENCE IN THIS TAKEOVER BID FOR OUR BANK LAUNCHED BY GLOBAL BANK OF AMERICA.
BUT, RUPERT, THERE ARE PLENTY OF PRECEDENTS FOR IT. PROVIDED WE ALSO RETAIN AN INDEPENDENT ADVISER THERE'S NO REASON WHY WE SHOULDN'T HANDLE THE BULK OF THE NEGOTIATIONS OURSELVES...
THAT'S ALL VERY WELL FOR YOU TO SAY, ALEX.
BUT SPEAKING AS A SENIOR CORPORATE FINANCIER THIS SEEMS TO FLY IN THE FACE OF TRADITIONAL CITY PROTOCOL. HANDLING A DEAL LIKE THIS WOULD BE BESET WITH CONTRADICTIONS AND OBSTACLES...
I SEE WHAT YOU'RE SAYING...
THE 30-SECOND JOURNEY UP IN THE LIFT TO VISIT THE CLIENT WOULDN'T BE LONG ENOUGH FOR US TO BRIEF YOU...
BUT YOU ALREADY KNOW THE NAMES OF THE CHAIRMAN AND CHIEF EXECUTIVE, SO THAT'S A HEAD START...

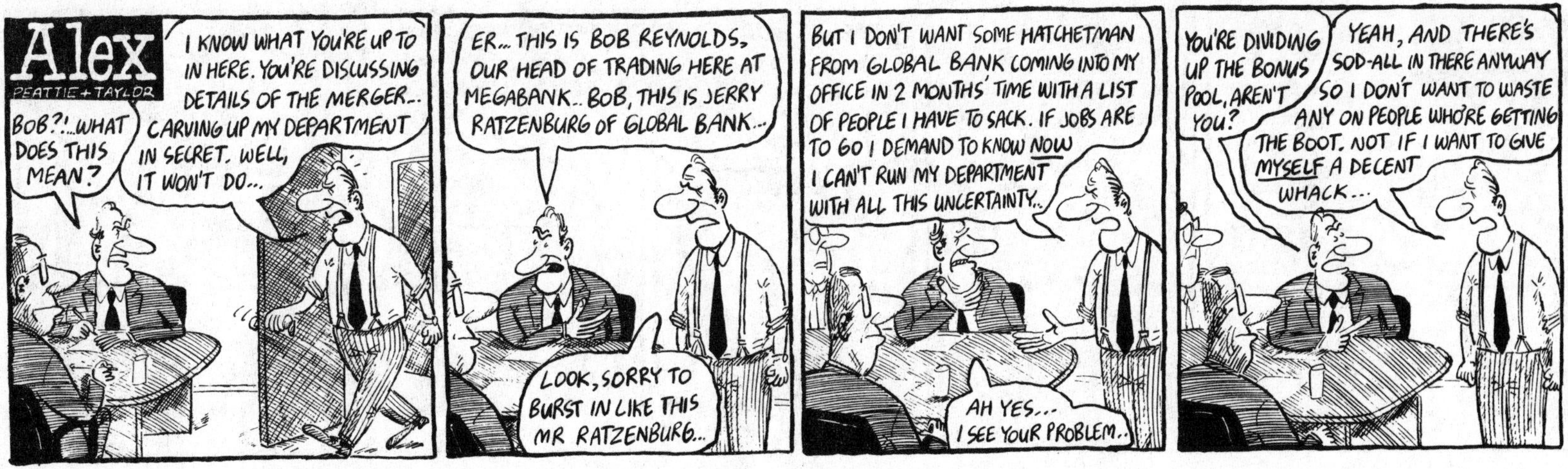
Alex
BEATTIE + TAYLOR
I KNOW WHAT YOU'RE UP TO IN HERE. YOU'RE DISCUSSING DETAILS OF THE MERGER... CARVING UP MY DEPARTMENT IN SECRET. WELL, IT WON'T DO...
BOB?!...WHAT DOES THIS MEAN?
ER... THIS IS BOB REYNOLDS, OUR HEAD OF TRADING HERE AT MEGABANK.. BOB, THIS IS JERRY RATZENBURG OF GLOBAL BANK...
LOOK, SORRY TO BURST IN LIKE THIS MR RATZENBURG...
BUT I DON'T WANT SOME HATCHETMAN FROM GLOBAL BANK COMING INTO MY OFFICE IN 2 MONTHS' TIME WITH A LIST OF PEOPLE I HAVE TO SACK. IF JOBS ARE TO GO I DEMAND TO KNOW NOW I CAN'T RUN MY DEPARTMENT WITH ALL THIS UNCERTAINTY..
AH YES... I SEE YOUR PROBLEM..
YOU'RE DIVIDING UP THE BONUS POOL, AREN'T YOU?
YEAH, AND THERE'S SOD-ALL IN THERE ANYWAY SO I DON'T WANT TO WASTE ANY ON PEOPLE WHO'RE GETTING THE BOOT. NOT IF I WANT TO GIVE MYSELF A DECENT WHACK...

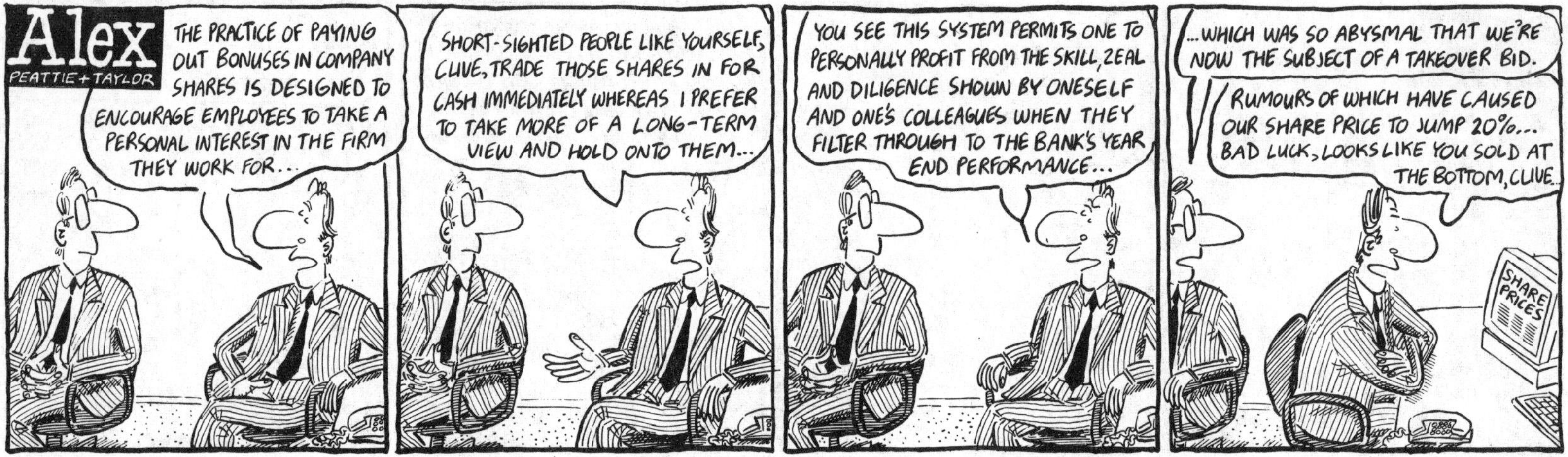
Alex
PEATTIE + TAYLOR
THE PRACTICE OF PAYING OUT BONUSES IN COMPANY SHARES IS DESIGNED TO ENCOURAGE EMPLOYEES TO TAKE A PERSONAL INTEREST IN THE FIRM THEY WORK FOR...
SHORT-SIGHTED PEOPLE LIKE YOURSELF, CLIVE, TRADE THOSE SHARES IN FOR CASH IMMEDIATELY WHEREAS I PREFER TO TAKE MORE OF A LONG-TERM VIEW AND HOLD ONTO THEM...
YOU SEE THIS SYSTEM PERMITS ONE TO PERSONALLY PROFIT FROM THE SKILL, ZEAL AND DILIGENCE SHOWN BY ONESELF AND ONE'S COLLEAGUES WHEN THEY FILTER THROUGH TO THE BANK'S YEAR END PERFORMANCE...
...WHICH WAS SO ABYSMAL THAT WE'RE NOW THE SUBJECT OF A TAKEOVER BID.
RUMOURS OF WHICH HAVE CAUSED OUR SHARE PRICE TO JUMP 20%... BAD LUCK, LOOKS LIKE YOU SOLD AT THE BOTTOM, CLIVE.
SHARE PRICES

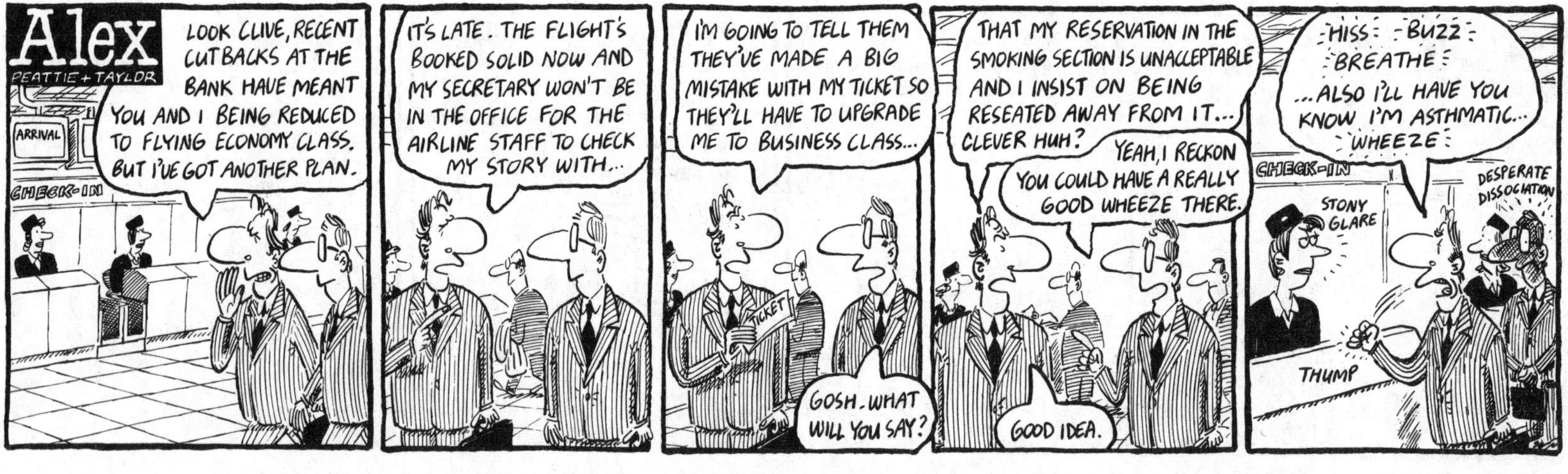
Alex
PEATTIE + TAYLOR
LOOK CLIVE, RECENT CUTBACKS AT THE BANK HAVE MEANT YOU AND I BEING REDUCED TO FLYING ECONOMY CLASS. BUT I'VE GOT ANOTHER PLAN.
ARRIVAL
CHECK-IN
IT'S LATE. THE FLIGHT'S BOOKED SOLID NOW AND MY SECRETARY WON'T BE IN THE OFFICE FOR THE AIRLINE STAFF TO CHECK MY STORY WITH...
I'M GOING TO TELL THEM THEY'VE MADE A BIG MISTAKE WITH MY TICKET SO THEY'LL HAVE TO UPGRADE ME TO BUSINESS CLASS...
TICKET
GOSH. WHAT WILL YOU SAY?
THAT MY RESERVATION IN THE SMOKING SECTION IS UNACCEPTABLE AND I INSIST ON BEING RESEATED AWAY FROM IT... CLEVER HUH?
GOOD IDEA.
YEAH, I RECKON YOU COULD HAVE A REALLY GOOD WHEEZE THERE.
HISS BUZZ
BREATHE
...ALSO I'LL HAVE YOU KNOW I'M ASTHMATIC...
WHEEZE
CHECK-IN
STONY GLARE
DESPERATE DISSOCIATION
THUMP

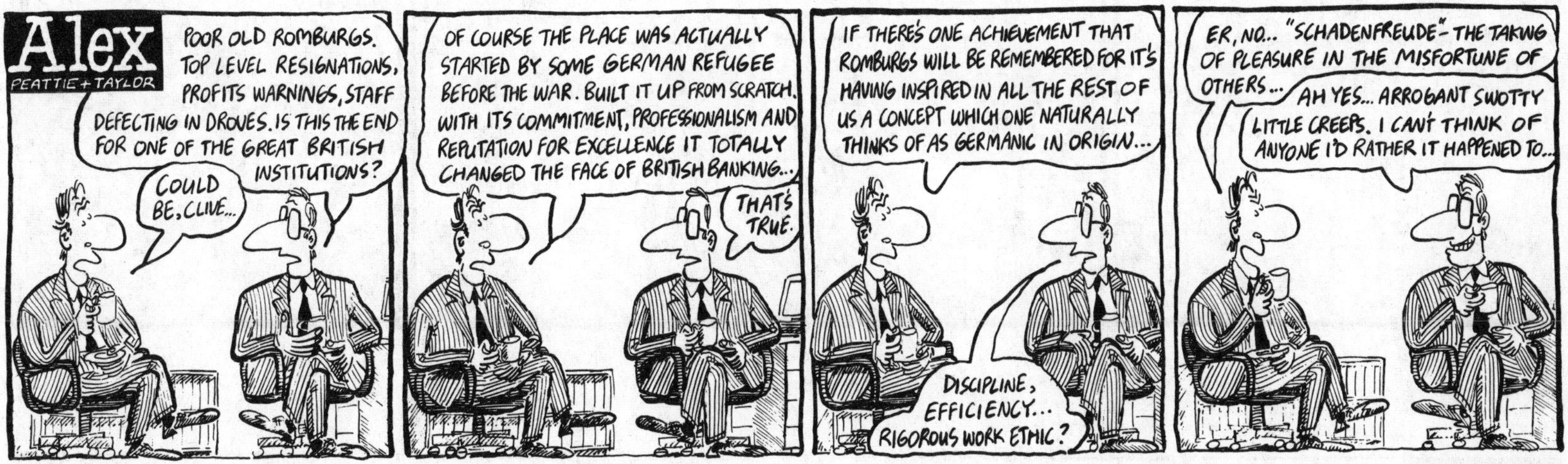
Alex
PEATTIE + TAYLOR
POOR OLD ROMBURGS. TOP LEVEL RESIGNATIONS, PROFITS WARNINGS, STAFF DEFECTING IN DROVES. IS THIS THE END FOR ONE OF THE GREAT BRITISH INSTITUTIONS?
COULD BE, CLIVE...
OF COURSE THE PLACE WAS ACTUALLY STARTED BY SOME GERMAN REFUGEE BEFORE THE WAR. BUILT IT UP FROM SCRATCH. WITH ITS COMMITMENT, PROFESSIONALISM AND REPUTATION FOR EXCELLENCE IT TOTALLY CHANGED THE FACE OF BRITISH BANKING...
THAT'S TRUE.
IF THERE'S ONE ACHIEVEMENT THAT ROMBURGS WILL BE REMEMBERED FOR IT'S HAVING INSPIRED IN ALL THE REST OF US A CONCEPT WHICH ONE NATURALLY THINKS OF AS GERMANIC IN ORIGIN...
DISCIPLINE, EFFICIENCY... RIGOROUS WORK ETHIC?
ER, NO... "SCHADENFREUDE" - THE TAKING OF PLEASURE IN THE MISFORTUNE OF OTHERS...
AH YES... ARROGANT SWOTTY LITTLE CREEPS. I CAN'T THINK OF ANYONE I'D RATHER IT HAPPENED TO...

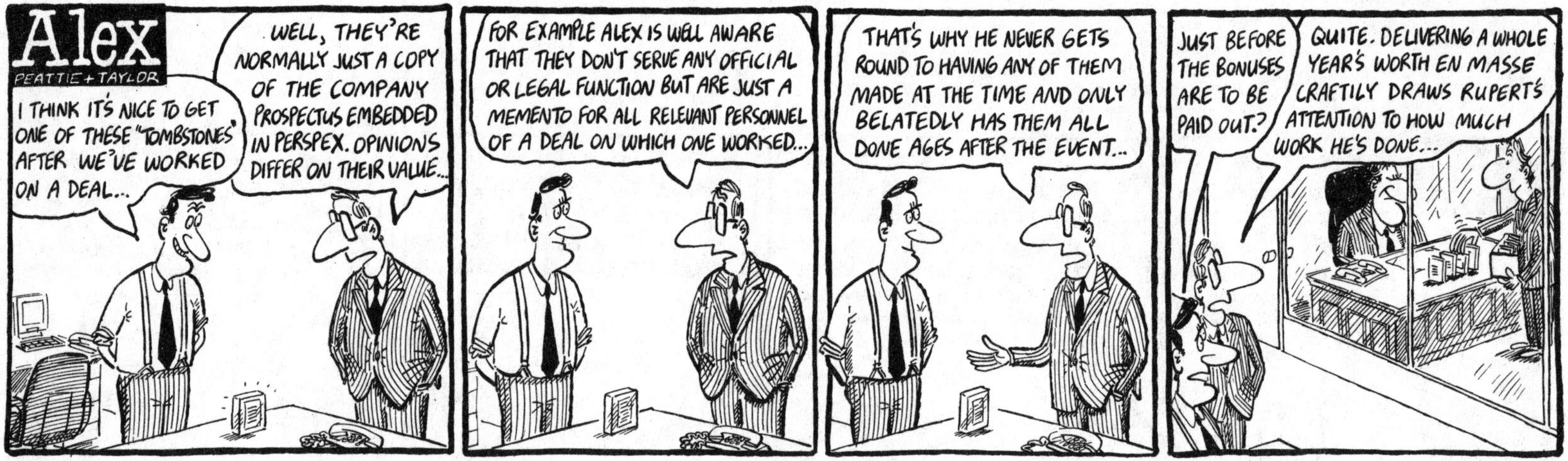
Alex
PEATTIE + TAYLOR
I THINK IT'S NICE TO GET ONE OF THESE "TOMBSTONES" AFTER WE'VE WORKED ON A DEAL...
WELL, THEY'RE NORMALLY JUST A COPY OF THE COMPANY PROSPECTUS EMBEDDED IN PERSPEX. OPINIONS DIFFER ON THEIR VALUE...
FOR EXAMPLE ALEX IS WELL AWARE THAT THEY DON'T SERVE ANY OFFICIAL OR LEGAL FUNCTION BUT ARE JUST A MEMENTO FOR ALL RELEVANT PERSONNEL OF A DEAL ON WHICH ONE WORKED...
THAT'S WHY HE NEVER GETS ROUND TO HAVING ANY OF THEM MADE AT THE TIME AND ONLY BELATEDLY HAS THEM ALL DONE AGES AFTER THE EVENT...
JUST BEFORE THE BONUSES ARE TO BE PAID OUT?
QUITE. DELIVERING A WHOLE YEAR'S WORTH EN MASSE CRAFTILY DRAWS RUPERT'S ATTENTION TO HOW MUCH WORK HE'S DONE...

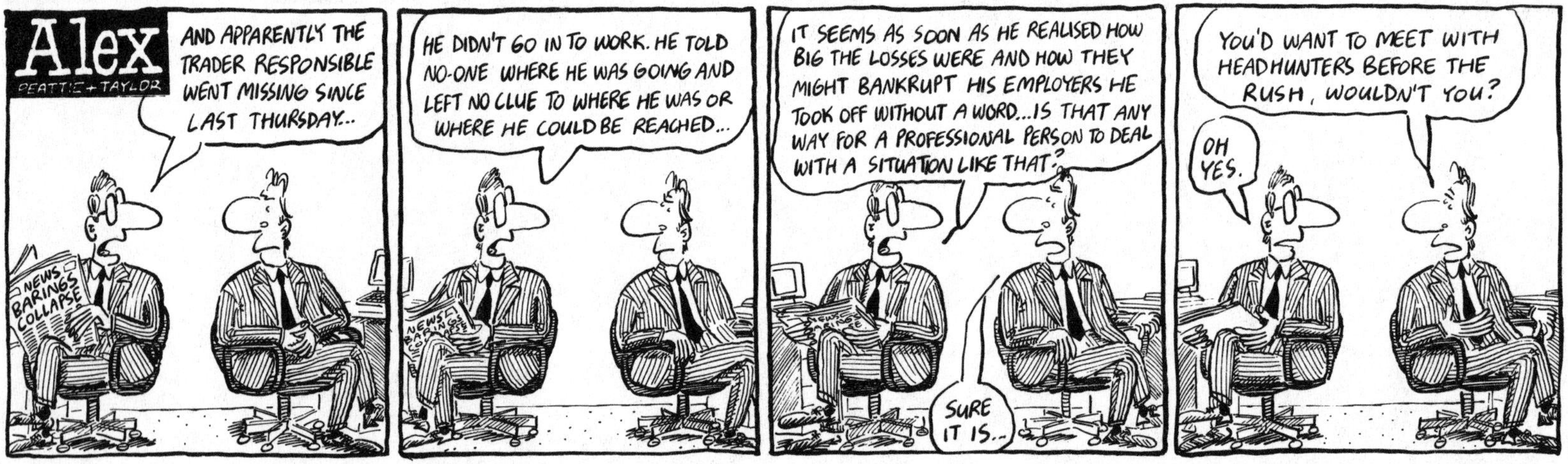
Alex
PEATTIE + TAYLOR
AND APPARENTLY THE TRADER RESPONSIBLE WENT MISSING SINCE LAST THURSDAY...
NEWS BARINGS COLLAPSE
HE DIDN'T GO IN TO WORK. HE TOLD NO-ONE WHERE HE WAS GOING AND LEFT NO CLUE TO WHERE HE WAS OR WHERE HE COULD BE REACHED...
IT SEEMS AS SOON AS HE REALISED HOW BIG THE LOSSES WERE AND HOW THEY MIGHT BANKRUPT HIS EMPLOYERS HE TOOK OFF WITHOUT A WORD... IS THAT ANY WAY FOR A PROFESSIONAL PERSON TO DEAL WITH A SITUATION LIKE THAT?
SURE IT IS...
OH YES.
YOU'D WANT TO MEET WITH HEADHUNTERS BEFORE THE RUSH, WOULDN'T YOU?

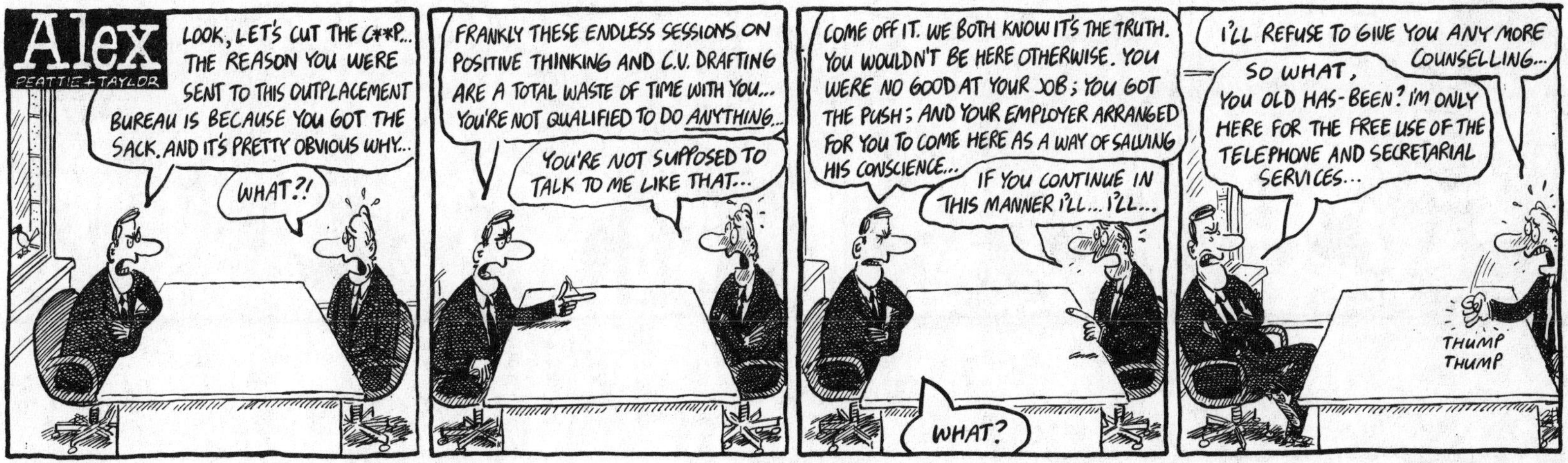
Alex
PEATTIE + TAYLOR
LOOK, LET'S CUT THE C**P... THE REASON YOU WERE SENT TO THIS OUTPLACEMENT BUREAU IS BECAUSE YOU GOT THE SACK. AND IT'S PRETTY OBVIOUS WHY...
WHAT?!
FRANKLY THESE ENDLESS SESSIONS ON POSITIVE THINKING AND C.V. DRAFTING ARE A TOTAL WASTE OF TIME WITH YOU... YOU'RE NOT QUALIFIED TO DO ANYTHING...
YOU'RE NOT SUPPOSED TO TALK TO ME LIKE THAT...
COME OFF IT. WE BOTH KNOW IT'S THE TRUTH. YOU WOULDN'T BE HERE OTHERWISE. YOU WERE NO GOOD AT YOUR JOB; YOU GOT THE PUSH; AND YOUR EMPLOYER ARRANGED FOR YOU TO COME HERE AS A WAY OF SALVING HIS CONSCIENCE...
IF YOU CONTINUE IN THIS MANNER I'LL... I'LL...
WHAT?
I'LL REFUSE TO GIVE YOU ANY MORE COUNSELLING...
SO WHAT, YOU OLD HAS-BEEN? I'M ONLY HERE FOR THE FREE USE OF THE TELEPHONE AND SECRETARIAL SERVICES...
THUMP THUMP

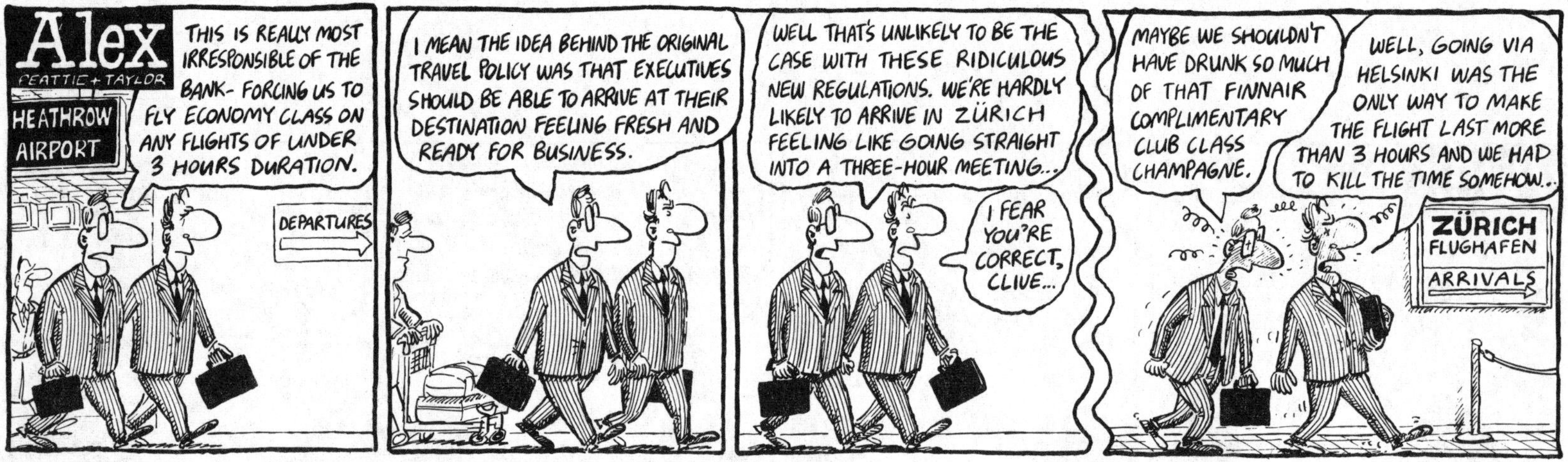

Alex
PEATTIE + TAYLOR
HEATHROW AIRPORT
THIS IS REALLY MOST IRRESPONSIBLE OF THE BANK- FORCING US TO FLY ECONOMY CLASS ON ANY FLIGHTS OF UNDER 3 HOURS DURATION.
DEPARTURES
I MEAN THE IDEA BEHIND THE ORIGINAL TRAVEL POLICY WAS THAT EXECUTIVES SHOULD BE ABLE TO ARRIVE AT THEIR DESTINATION FEELING FRESH AND READY FOR BUSINESS.
WELL THAT'S UNLIKELY TO BE THE CASE WITH THESE RIDICULOUS NEW REGULATIONS. WE'RE HARDLY LIKELY TO ARRIVE IN ZÜRICH FEELING LIKE GOING STRAIGHT INTO A THREE-HOUR MEETING...
I FEAR YOU'RE CORRECT, CLIVE...
MAYBE WE SHOULDN'T HAVE DRUNK SO MUCH OF THAT FINNAIR COMPLIMENTARY CLUB CLASS CHAMPAGNE.
WELL, GOING VIA HELSINKI WAS THE ONLY WAY TO MAKE THE FLIGHT LAST MORE THAN 3 HOURS AND WE HAD TO KILL THE TIME SOMEHOW...
ZÜRICH FLUGHAFEN
ARRIVALS

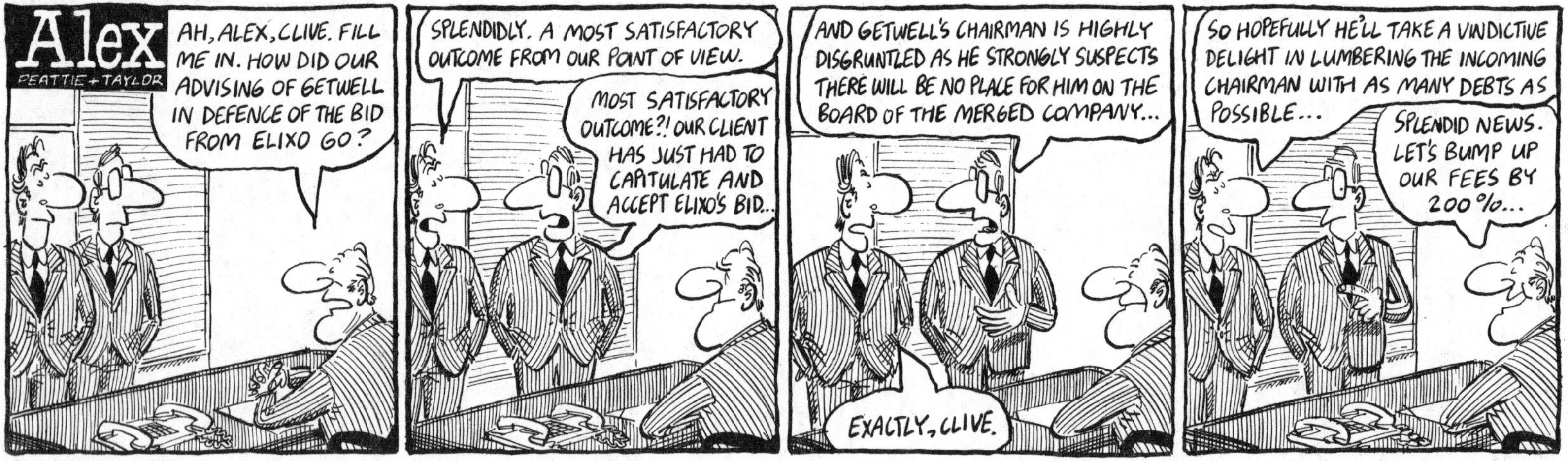

Alex
PEATTIE + TAYLOR
AH, ALEX, CLIVE. FILL ME IN. HOW DID OUR ADVISING OF GETWELL IN DEFENCE OF THE BID FROM ELIXO GO?
SPLENDIDLY. A MOST SATISFACTORY OUTCOME FROM OUR POINT OF VIEW.
MOST SATISFACTORY OUTCOME?! OUR CLIENT HAS JUST HAD TO CAPITULATE AND ACCEPT ELIXO'S BID...
AND GETWELL'S CHAIRMAN IS HIGHLY DISGRUNTLED AS HE STRONGLY SUSPECTS THERE WILL BE NO PLACE FOR HIM ON THE BOARD OF THE MERGED COMPANY...
EXACTLY, CLIVE.
SO HOPEFULLY HE'LL TAKE A VINDICTIVE DELIGHT IN LUMBERING THE INCOMING CHAIRMAN WITH AS MANY DEBTS AS POSSIBLE...
SPLENDID NEWS. LET'S BUMP UP OUR FEES BY 200%...

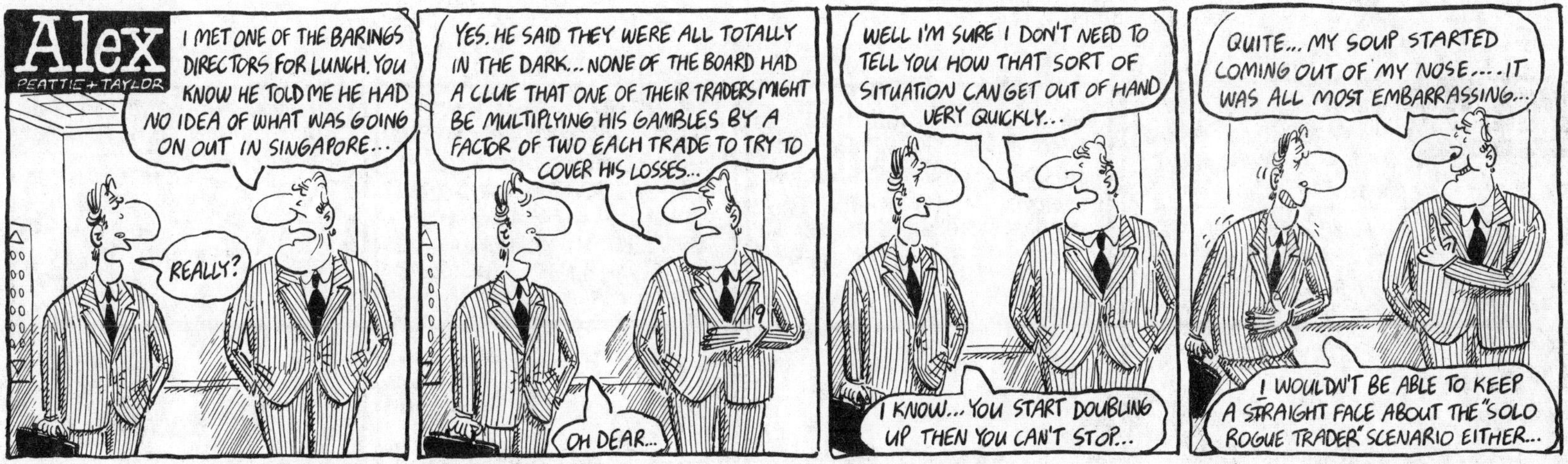
Alex
BEATTIE + TAYLOR
I MET ONE OF THE BARINGS DIRECTORS FOR LUNCH. YOU KNOW HE TOLD ME HE HAD NO IDEA OF WHAT WAS GOING ON OUT IN SINGAPORE...
REALLY?
YES. HE SAID THEY WERE ALL TOTALLY IN THE DARK... NONE OF THE BOARD HAD A CLUE THAT ONE OF THEIR TRADERS MIGHT BE MULTIPLYING HIS GAMBLES BY A FACTOR OF TWO EACH TRADE TO TRY TO COVER HIS LOSSES...
OH DEAR...
WELL I'M SURE I DON'T NEED TO TELL YOU HOW THAT SORT OF SITUATION CAN GET OUT OF HAND VERY QUICKLY...
I KNOW... YOU START DOUBLING UP THEN YOU CAN'T STOP...
QUITE... MY SOUP STARTED COMING OUT OF MY NOSE.... IT WAS ALL MOST EMBARRASSING...
I WOULDN'T BE ABLE TO KEEP A STRAIGHT FACE ABOUT THE "SOLO ROGUE TRADER" SCENARIO EITHER...

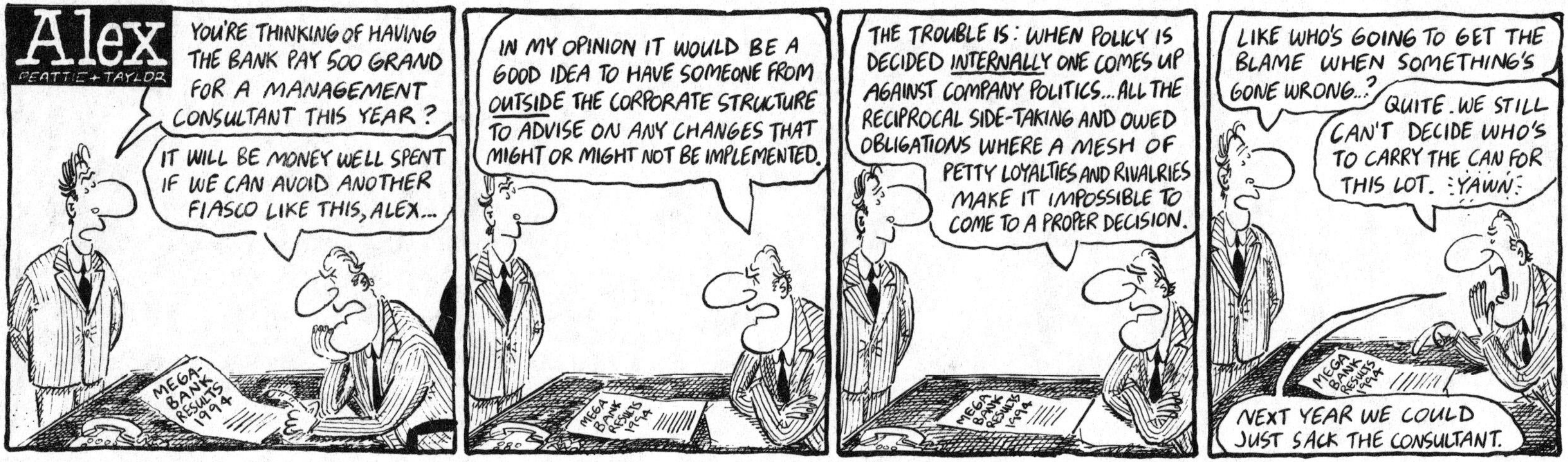
Alex
BEATTIE + TAYLOR
YOU'RE THINKING OF HAVING THE BANK PAY 500 GRAND FOR A MANAGEMENT CONSULTANT THIS YEAR?
IT WILL BE MONEY WELL SPENT IF WE CAN AVOID ANOTHER FIASCO LIKE THIS, ALEX...
MEGA-BANK RESULTS 1994
IN MY OPINION IT WOULD BE A GOOD IDEA TO HAVE SOMEONE FROM OUTSIDE THE CORPORATE STRUCTURE TO ADVISE ON ANY CHANGES THAT MIGHT OR MIGHT NOT BE IMPLEMENTED.
MEGA BANK RESULTS 1994
THE TROUBLE IS: WHEN POLICY IS DECIDED INTERNALLY ONE COMES UP AGAINST COMPANY POLITICS... ALL THE RECIPROCAL SIDE-TAKING AND OWED OBLIGATIONS WHERE A MESH OF PETTY LOYALTIES AND RIVALRIES MAKE IT IMPOSSIBLE TO COME TO A PROPER DECISION.
MEGA BANK RESULTS 1994
LIKE WHO'S GOING TO GET THE BLAME WHEN SOMETHING'S GONE WRONG..?
QUITE. WE STILL CAN'T DECIDE WHO'S TO CARRY THE CAN FOR THIS LOT. YAWN
MEGA BANK RESULTS 1994
NEXT YEAR WE COULD JUST SACK THE CONSULTANT.

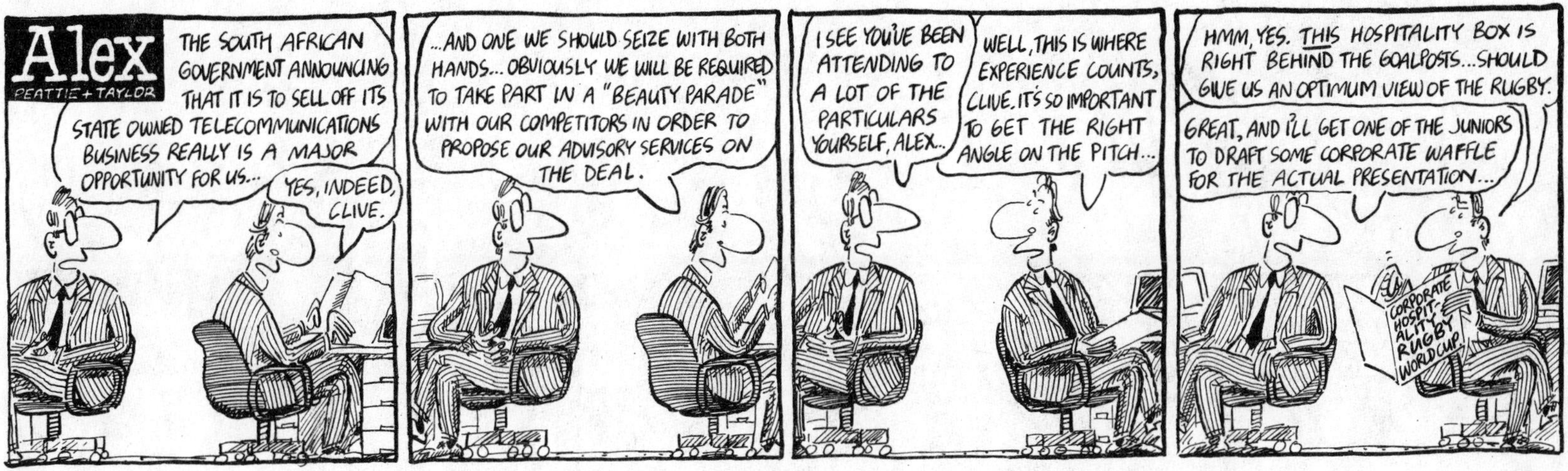
Alex
PEATTIE + TAYLOR
THE SOUTH AFRICAN GOVERNMENT ANNOUNCING THAT IT IS TO SELL OFF ITS STATE OWNED TELECOMMUNICATIONS BUSINESS REALLY IS A MAJOR OPPORTUNITY FOR US...
YES, INDEED, CLIVE.
...AND ONE WE SHOULD SEIZE WITH BOTH HANDS... OBVIOUSLY WE WILL BE REQUIRED TO TAKE PART IN A "BEAUTY PARADE" WITH OUR COMPETITORS IN ORDER TO PROPOSE OUR ADVISORY SERVICES ON THE DEAL.
I SEE YOU'VE BEEN ATTENDING TO A LOT OF THE PARTICULARS YOURSELF, ALEX...
WELL, THIS IS WHERE EXPERIENCE COUNTS, CLIVE. IT'S SO IMPORTANT TO GET THE RIGHT ANGLE ON THE PITCH...
HMM, YES. THIS HOSPITALITY BOX IS RIGHT BEHIND THE GOALPOSTS...SHOULD GIVE US AN OPTIMUM VIEW OF THE RUGBY.
GREAT, AND I'LL GET ONE OF THE JUNIORS TO DRAFT SOME CORPORATE WAFFLE FOR THE ACTUAL PRESENTATION...
CORPORATE HOSPIT-ALITY RUGBY WORLD CUP

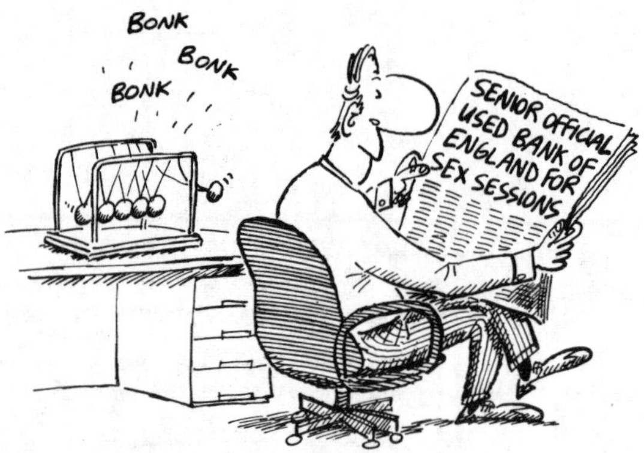
BONK
BONK
BONK
SENIOR OFFICIAL USED BANK OF ENGLAND FOR SEX SESSIONS

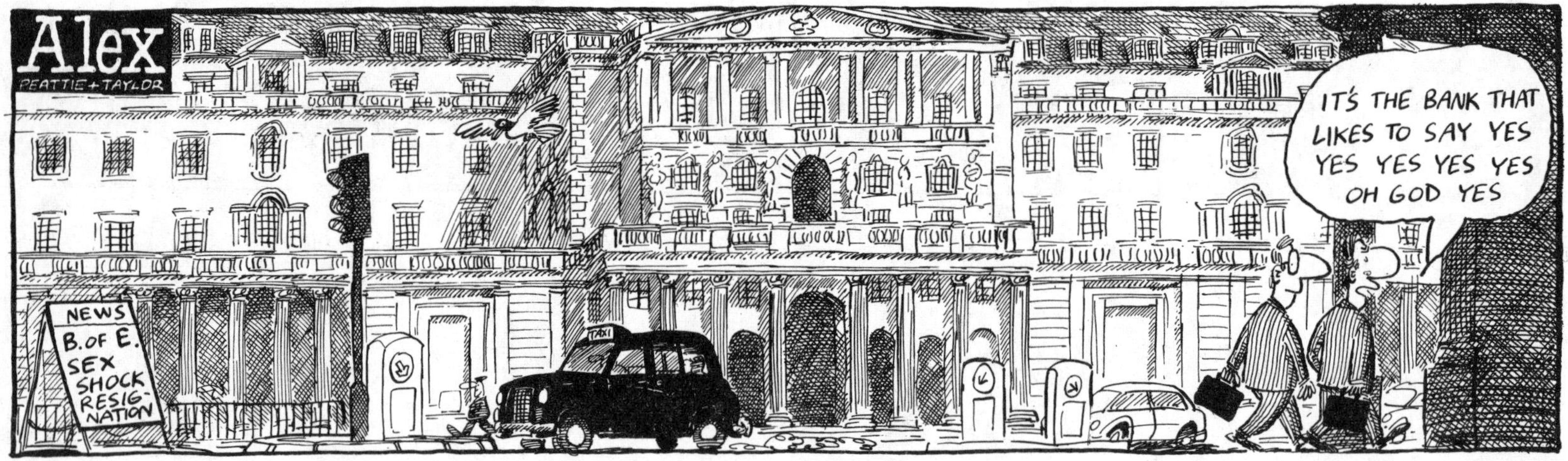
Alex
PEATTIE + TAYLOR
NEWS
B. OF E. SEX SHOCK RESIG-NATION
TAXI
IT'S THE BANK THAT LIKES TO SAY YES YES YES YES YES OH GOD YES

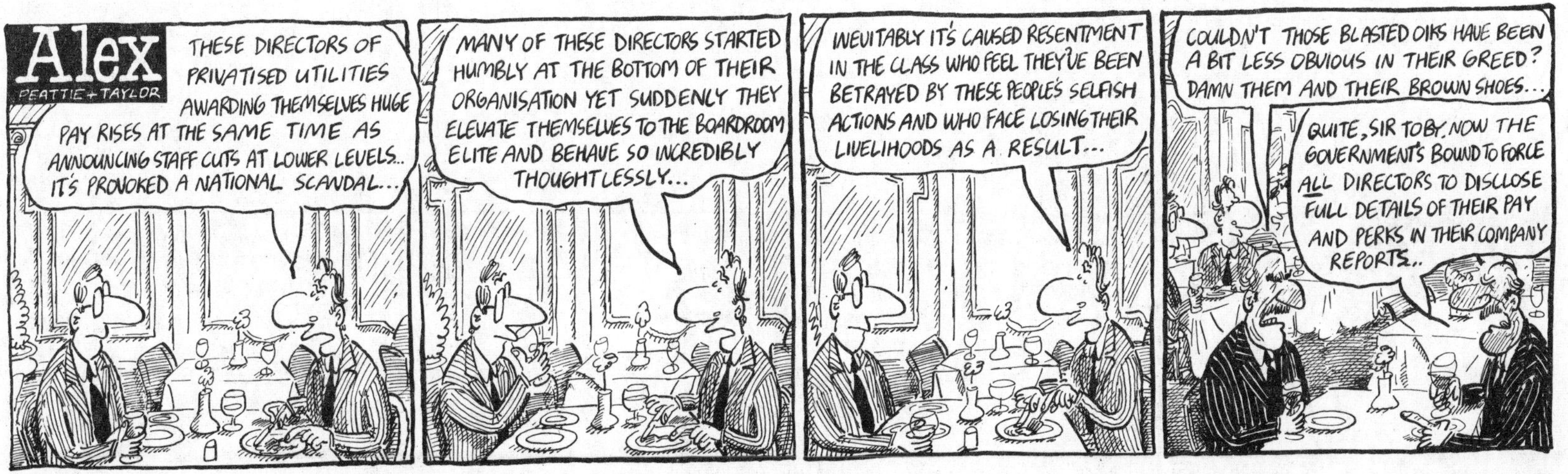
Alex
PEATTIE + TAYLOR
THESE DIRECTORS OF PRIVATISED UTILITIES AWARDING THEMSELVES HUGE PAY RISES AT THE SAME TIME AS ANNOUNCING STAFF CUTS AT LOWER LEVELS.. IT'S PROVOKED A NATIONAL SCANDAL...
MANY OF THESE DIRECTORS STARTED HUMBLY AT THE BOTTOM OF THEIR ORGANISATION YET SUDDENLY THEY ELEVATE THEMSELVES TO THE BOARDROOM ELITE AND BEHAVE SO INCREDIBLY THOUGHTLESSLY...
INEVITABLY IT'S CAUSED RESENTMENT IN THE CLASS WHO FEEL THEY'VE BEEN BETRAYED BY THESE PEOPLE'S SELFISH ACTIONS AND WHO FACE LOSING THEIR LIVELIHOODS AS A RESULT...
COULDN'T THOSE BLASTED OIKS HAVE BEEN A BIT LESS OBVIOUS IN THEIR GREED? DAMN THEM AND THEIR BROWN SHOES...
QUITE, SIR TOBY. NOW THE GOVERNMENT'S BOUND TO FORCE ALL DIRECTORS TO DISCLOSE FULL DETAILS OF THEIR PAY AND PERKS IN THEIR COMPANY REPORTS..

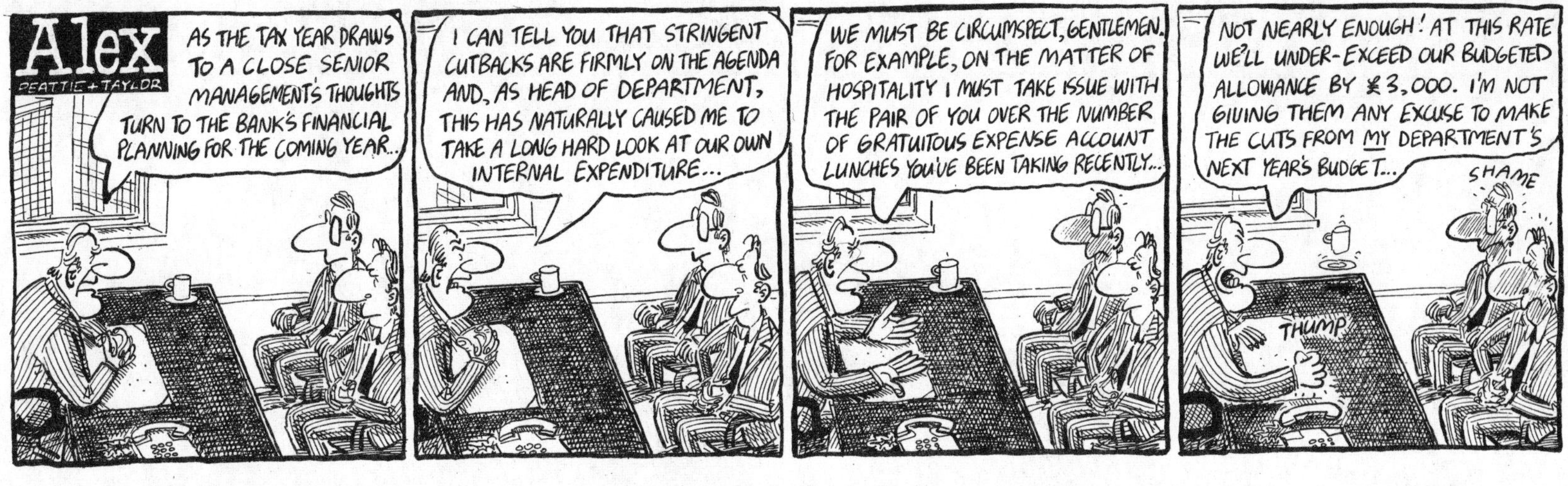
Alex
PEATTIE + TAYLOR
AS THE TAX YEAR DRAWS TO A CLOSE SENIOR MANAGEMENT'S THOUGHTS TURN TO THE BANK'S FINANCIAL PLANNING FOR THE COMING YEAR...
I CAN TELL YOU THAT STRINGENT CUTBACKS ARE FIRMLY ON THE AGENDA AND, AS HEAD OF DEPARTMENT, THIS HAS NATURALLY CAUSED ME TO TAKE A LONG HARD LOOK AT OUR OWN INTERNAL EXPENDITURE...
WE MUST BE CIRCUMSPECT, GENTLEMEN. FOR EXAMPLE, ON THE MATTER OF HOSPITALITY I MUST TAKE ISSUE WITH THE PAIR OF YOU OVER THE NUMBER OF GRATUITOUS EXPENSE ACCOUNT LUNCHES YOU'VE BEEN TAKING RECENTLY...
NOT NEARLY ENOUGH! AT THIS RATE WE'LL UNDER-EXCEED OUR BUDGETED ALLOWANCE BY £3,000. I'M NOT GIVING THEM ANY EXCUSE TO MAKE THE CUTS FROM MY DEPARTMENT'S NEXT YEAR'S BUDGET...
SHAME
THUMP

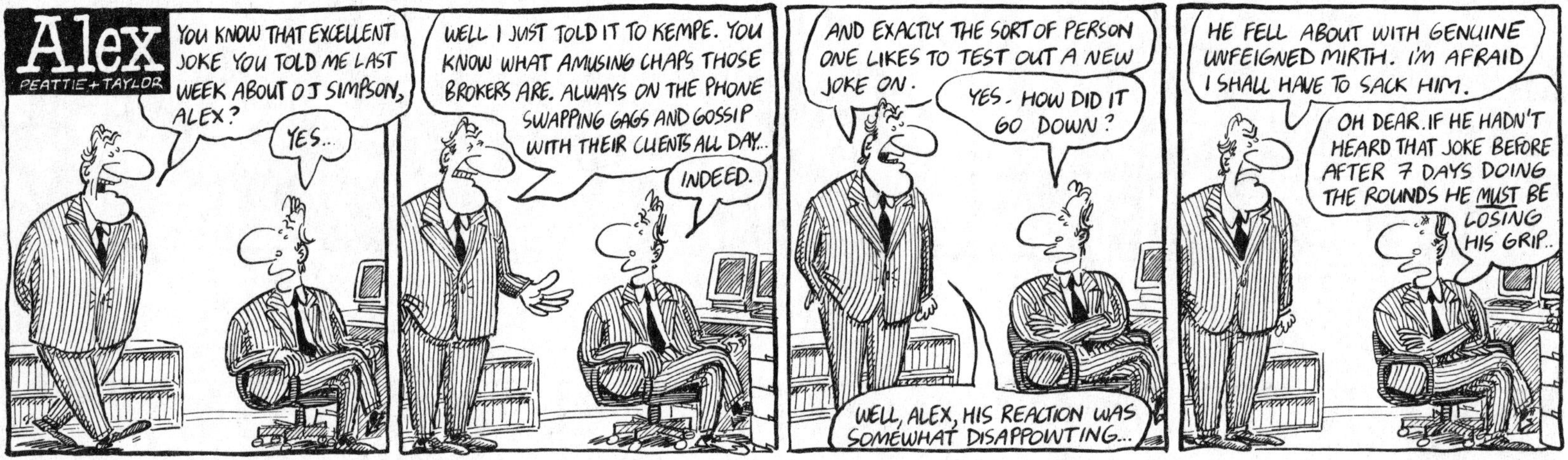
Alex
PEATTIE + TAYLOR
YOU KNOW THAT EXCELLENT JOKE YOU TOLD ME LAST WEEK ABOUT O J SIMPSON, ALEX?
YES...
WELL I JUST TOLD IT TO KEMPE. YOU KNOW WHAT AMUSING CHAPS THOSE BROKERS ARE. ALWAYS ON THE PHONE SWAPPING GAGS AND GOSSIP WITH THEIR CLIENTS ALL DAY...
INDEED.
AND EXACTLY THE SORT OF PERSON ONE LIKES TO TEST OUT A NEW JOKE ON.
YES. HOW DID IT GO DOWN?
WELL, ALEX, HIS REACTION WAS SOMEWHAT DISAPPOINTING...
HE FELL ABOUT WITH GENUINE UNFEIGNED MIRTH. I'M AFRAID I SHALL HAVE TO SACK HIM.
OH DEAR. IF HE HADN'T HEARD THAT JOKE BEFORE AFTER 7 DAYS DOING THE ROUNDS HE MUST BE LOSING HIS GRIP..

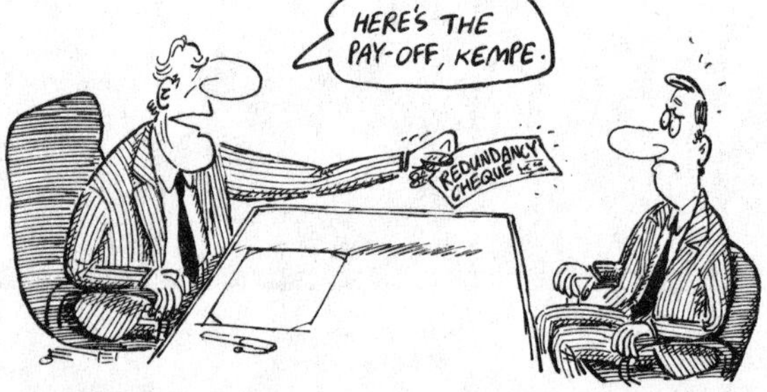
HERE'S THE PAY-OFF, KEMPE.
REDUNDANCY CHEQUE

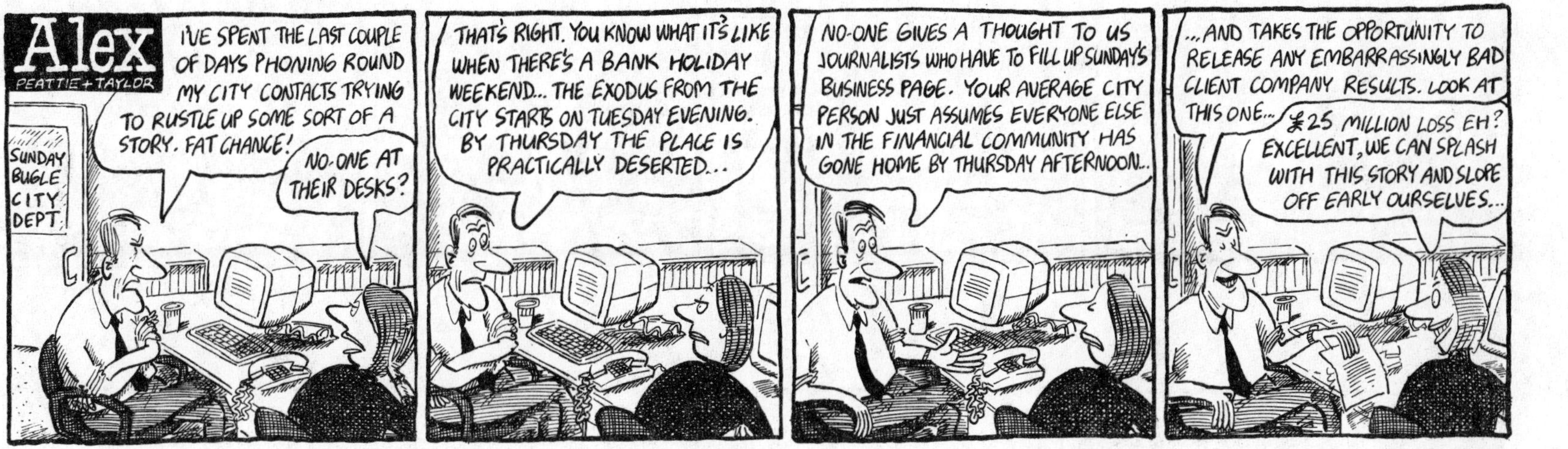
Alex
PEATTIE + TAYLOR
I'VE SPENT THE LAST COUPLE OF DAYS PHONING ROUND MY CITY CONTACTS TRYING TO RUSTLE UP SOME SORT OF A STORY. FAT CHANCE!
SUNDAY BUGLE CITY DEPT
NO-ONE AT THEIR DESKS?
THAT'S RIGHT. YOU KNOW WHAT IT'S LIKE WHEN THERE'S A BANK HOLIDAY WEEKEND... THE EXODUS FROM THE CITY STARTS ON TUESDAY EVENING. BY THURSDAY THE PLACE IS PRACTICALLY DESERTED...
NO-ONE GIVES A THOUGHT TO US JOURNALISTS WHO HAVE TO FILL UP SUNDAY'S BUSINESS PAGE. YOUR AVERAGE CITY PERSON JUST ASSUMES EVERYONE ELSE IN THE FINANCIAL COMMUNITY HAS GONE HOME BY THURSDAY AFTERNOON...
...AND TAKES THE OPPORTUNITY TO RELEASE ANY EMBARRASSINGLY BAD CLIENT COMPANY RESULTS. LOOK AT THIS ONE...
£25 MILLION LOSS EH? EXCELLENT, WE CAN SPLASH WITH THIS STORY AND SLOPE OFF EARLY OURSELVES...

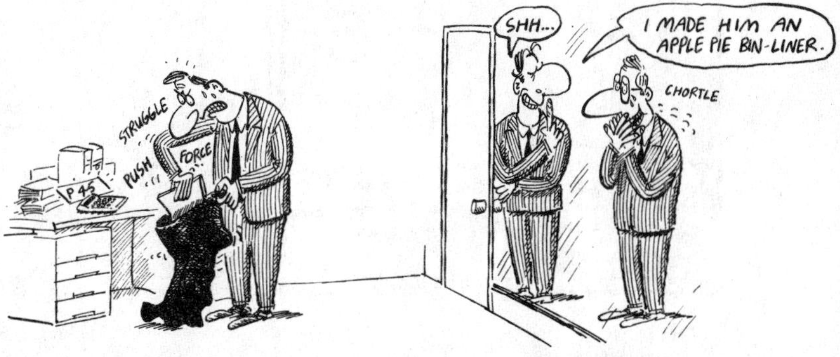
STRUGGLE
PUSH
FORCE
P45
SHH...
I MADE HIM AN APPLE PIE BIN-LINER.
CHORTLE

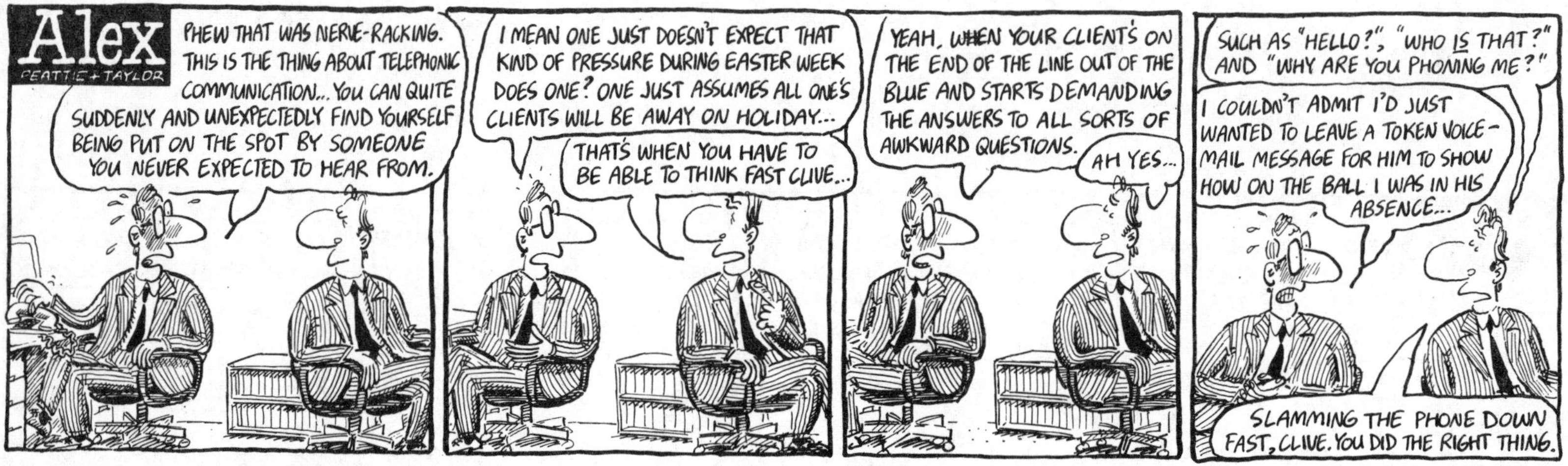
Alex
BEATTIE + TAYLOR
PHEW THAT WAS NERVE-RACKING. THIS IS THE THING ABOUT TELEPHONIC COMMUNICATION... YOU CAN QUITE SUDDENLY AND UNEXPECTEDLY FIND YOURSELF BEING PUT ON THE SPOT BY SOMEONE YOU NEVER EXPECTED TO HEAR FROM.
I MEAN ONE JUST DOESN'T EXPECT THAT KIND OF PRESSURE DURING EASTER WEEK DOES ONE? ONE JUST ASSUMES ALL ONE'S CLIENTS WILL BE AWAY ON HOLIDAY...
THAT'S WHEN YOU HAVE TO BE ABLE TO THINK FAST CLIVE...
YEAH, WHEN YOUR CLIENT'S ON THE END OF THE LINE OUT OF THE BLUE AND STARTS DEMANDING THE ANSWERS TO ALL SORTS OF AWKWARD QUESTIONS.
AH YES...
SUCH AS "HELLO?", "WHO IS THAT?" AND "WHY ARE YOU PHONING ME?"
I COULDN'T ADMIT I'D JUST WANTED TO LEAVE A TOKEN VOICE-MAIL MESSAGE FOR HIM TO SHOW HOW ON THE BALL I WAS IN HIS ABSENCE...
SLAMMING THE PHONE DOWN FAST, CLIVE. YOU DID THE RIGHT THING.

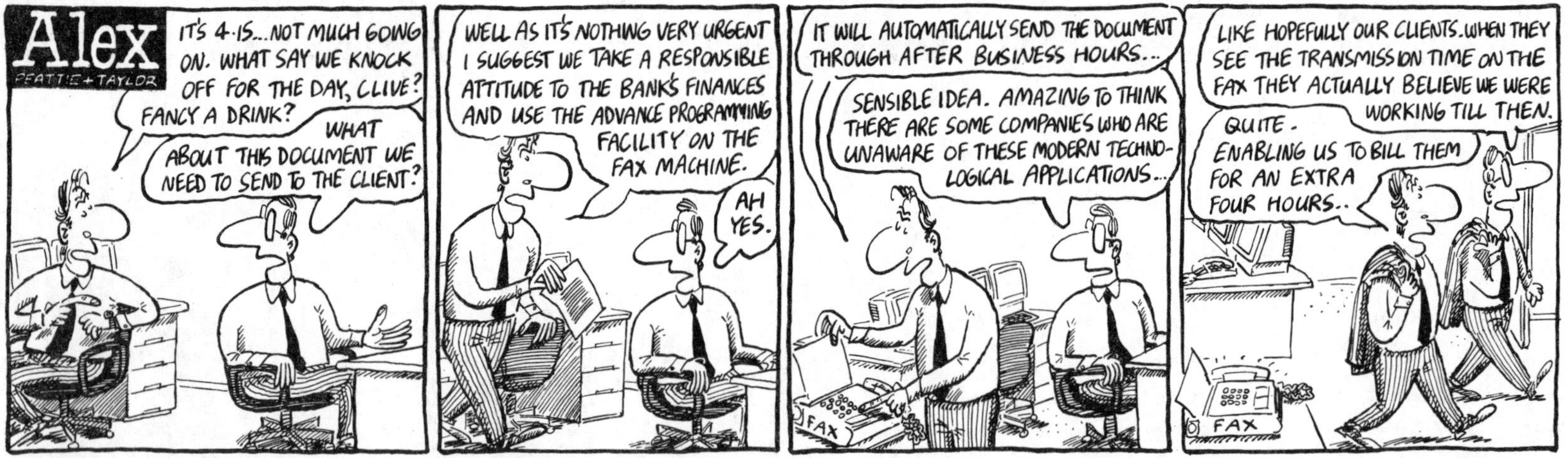
Alex
BEATTIE + TAYLOR
IT'S 4.15...NOT MUCH GOING ON. WHAT SAY WE KNOCK OFF FOR THE DAY, CLIVE? FANCY A DRINK?
WHAT ABOUT THIS DOCUMENT WE NEED TO SEND TO THE CLIENT?
WELL AS IT'S NOTHING VERY URGENT I SUGGEST WE TAKE A RESPONSIBLE ATTITUDE TO THE BANK'S FINANCES AND USE THE ADVANCE PROGRAMMING FACILITY ON THE FAX MACHINE.
AH YES.
IT WILL AUTOMATICALLY SEND THE DOCUMENT THROUGH AFTER BUSINESS HOURS...
SENSIBLE IDEA. AMAZING TO THINK THERE ARE SOME COMPANIES WHO ARE UNAWARE OF THESE MODERN TECHNOLOGICAL APPLICATIONS...
FAX
LIKE HOPEFULLY OUR CLIENTS. WHEN THEY SEE THE TRANSMISSION TIME ON THE FAX THEY ACTUALLY BELIEVE WE WERE WORKING TILL THEN.
QUITE - ENABLING US TO BILL THEM FOR AN EXTRA FOUR HOURS..
FAX

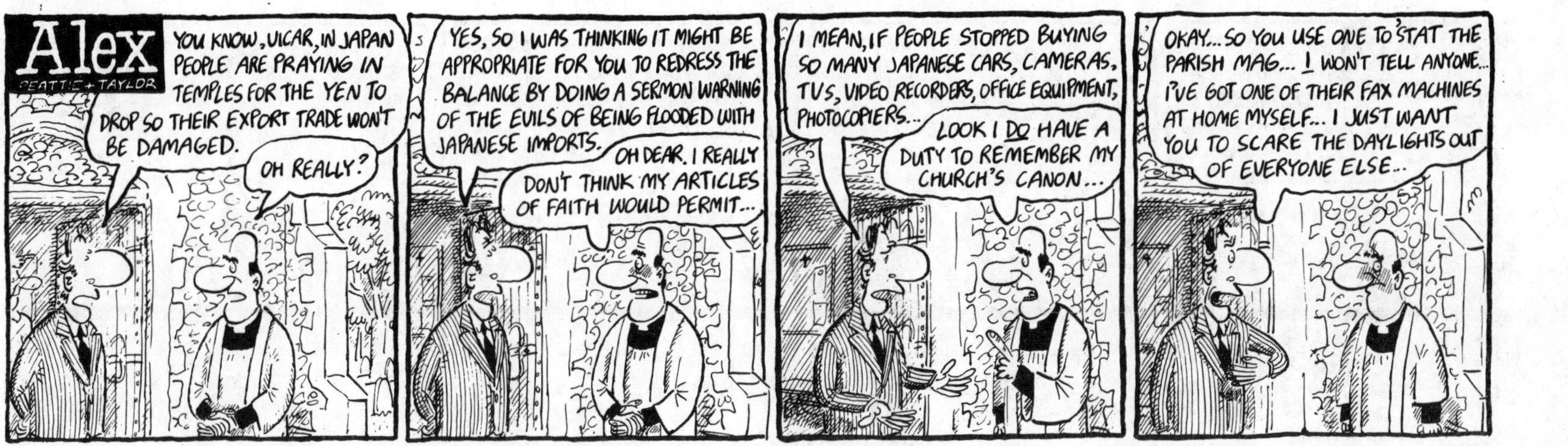
Alex
BEATTIE + TAYLOR
YOU KNOW, VICAR, IN JAPAN PEOPLE ARE PRAYING IN TEMPLES FOR THE YEN TO DROP SO THEIR EXPORT TRADE WON'T BE DAMAGED.
OH REALLY?
YES, SO I WAS THINKING IT MIGHT BE APPROPRIATE FOR YOU TO REDRESS THE BALANCE BY DOING A SERMON WARNING OF THE EVILS OF BEING FLOODED WITH JAPANESE IMPORTS.
OH DEAR. I REALLY DON'T THINK MY ARTICLES OF FAITH WOULD PERMIT...
I MEAN, IF PEOPLE STOPPED BUYING SO MANY JAPANESE CARS, CAMERAS, TV'S, VIDEO RECORDERS, OFFICE EQUIPMENT, PHOTOCOPIERS...
LOOK I DO HAVE A DUTY TO REMEMBER MY CHURCH'S CANON...
OKAY... SO YOU USE ONE TO 'STAT THE PARISH MAG... I WON'T TELL ANYONE... I'VE GOT ONE OF THEIR FAX MACHINES AT HOME MYSELF... I JUST WANT YOU TO SCARE THE DAYLIGHTS OUT OF EVERYONE ELSE...

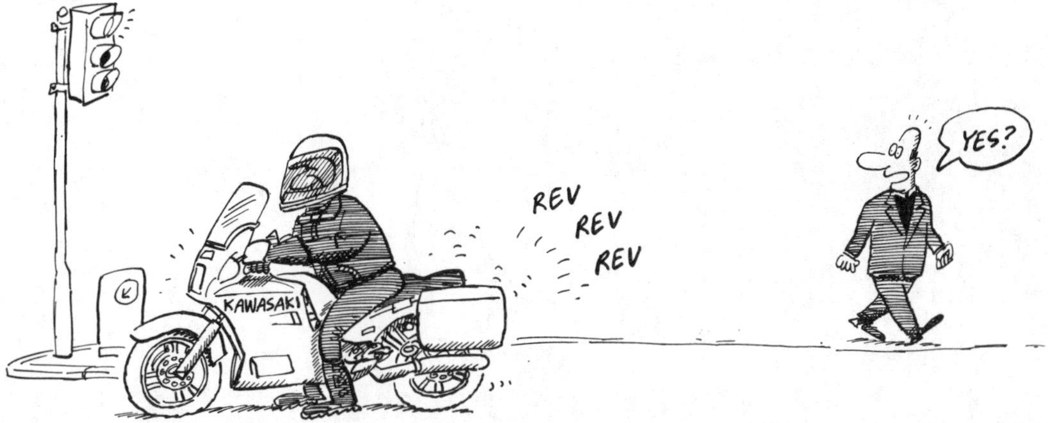
KAWASAKI
REV
REV
REV
YES?

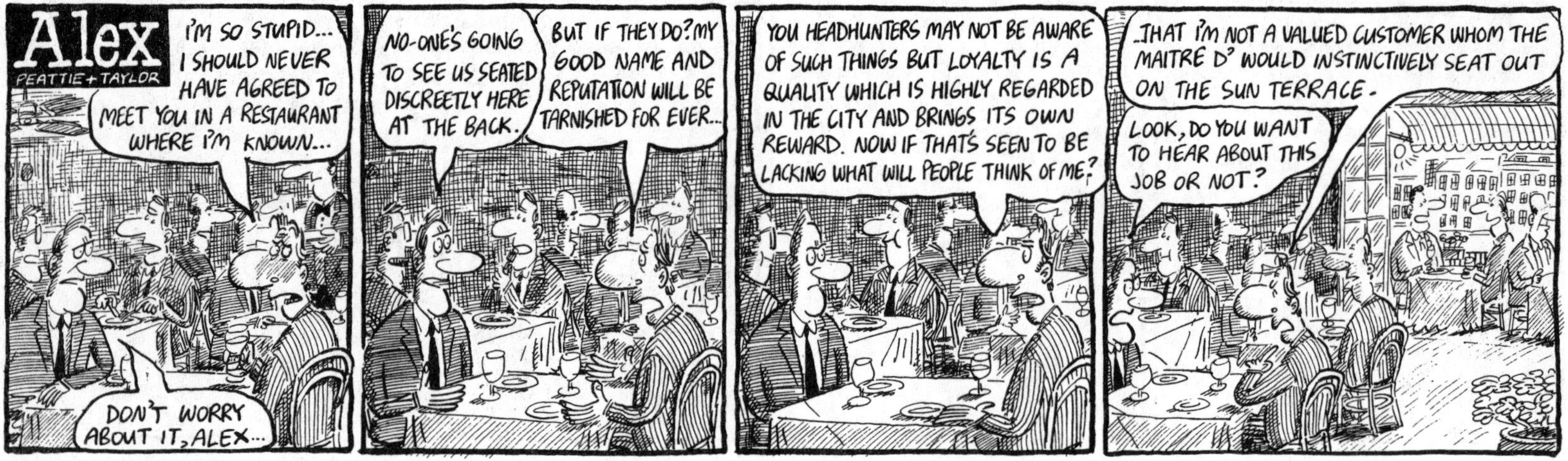
Alex
PEATTIE + TAYLOR
I'M SO STUPID... I SHOULD NEVER HAVE AGREED TO MEET YOU IN A RESTAURANT WHERE I'M KNOWN...
DON'T WORRY ABOUT IT, ALEX...
NO-ONE'S GOING TO SEE US SEATED DISCREETLY HERE AT THE BACK.
BUT IF THEY DO? MY GOOD NAME AND REPUTATION WILL BE TARNISHED FOR EVER...
YOU HEADHUNTERS MAY NOT BE AWARE OF SUCH THINGS BUT LOYALTY IS A QUALITY WHICH IS HIGHLY REGARDED IN THE CITY AND BRINGS ITS OWN REWARD. NOW IF THAT'S SEEN TO BE LACKING WHAT WILL PEOPLE THINK OF ME?
..THAT I'M NOT A VALUED CUSTOMER WHOM THE MAITRE D' WOULD INSTINCTIVELY SEAT OUT ON THE SUN TERRACE.
LOOK, DO YOU WANT TO HEAR ABOUT THIS JOB OR NOT?

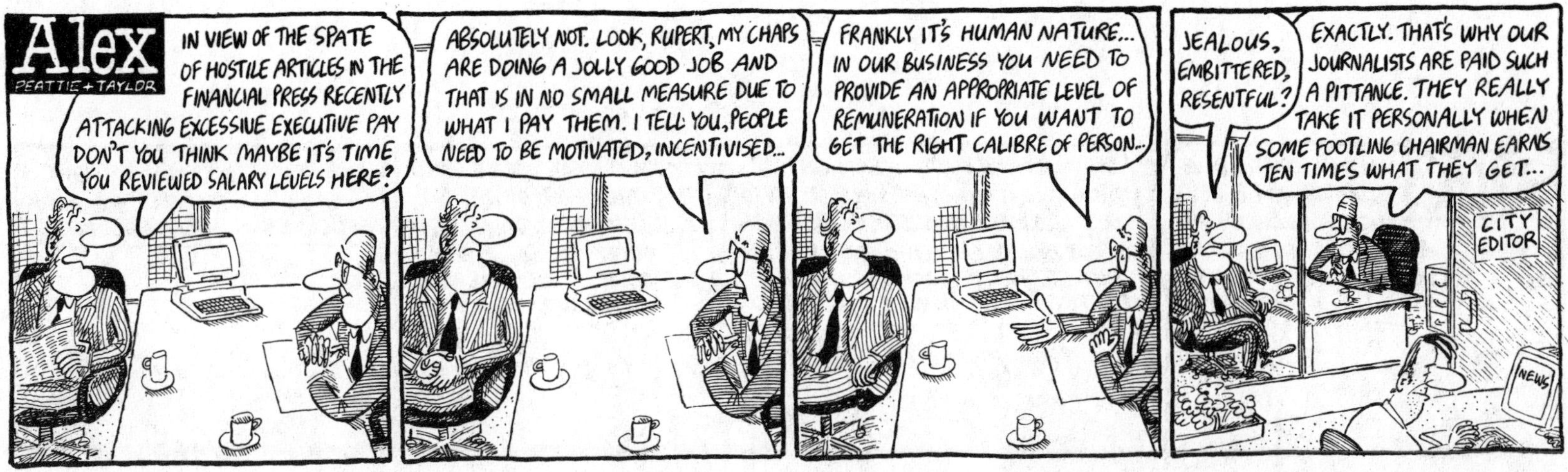
Alex
PEATTIE + TAYLOR
IN VIEW OF THE SPATE OF HOSTILE ARTICLES IN THE FINANCIAL PRESS RECENTLY ATTACKING EXCESSIVE EXECUTIVE PAY DON'T YOU THINK MAYBE IT'S TIME YOU REVIEWED SALARY LEVELS HERE?
ABSOLUTELY NOT. LOOK, RUPERT, MY CHAPS ARE DOING A JOLLY GOOD JOB AND THAT IS IN NO SMALL MEASURE DUE TO WHAT I PAY THEM. I TELL YOU, PEOPLE NEED TO BE MOTIVATED, INCENTIVISED...
FRANKLY IT'S HUMAN NATURE... IN OUR BUSINESS YOU NEED TO PROVIDE AN APPROPRIATE LEVEL OF REMUNERATION IF YOU WANT TO GET THE RIGHT CALIBRE OF PERSON...
JEALOUS, EMBITTERED, RESENTFUL?
EXACTLY. THAT'S WHY OUR JOURNALISTS ARE PAID SUCH A PITTANCE. THEY REALLY TAKE IT PERSONALLY WHEN SOME FOOTLING CHAIRMAN EARNS TEN TIMES WHAT THEY GET...
CITY EDITOR
NEWS

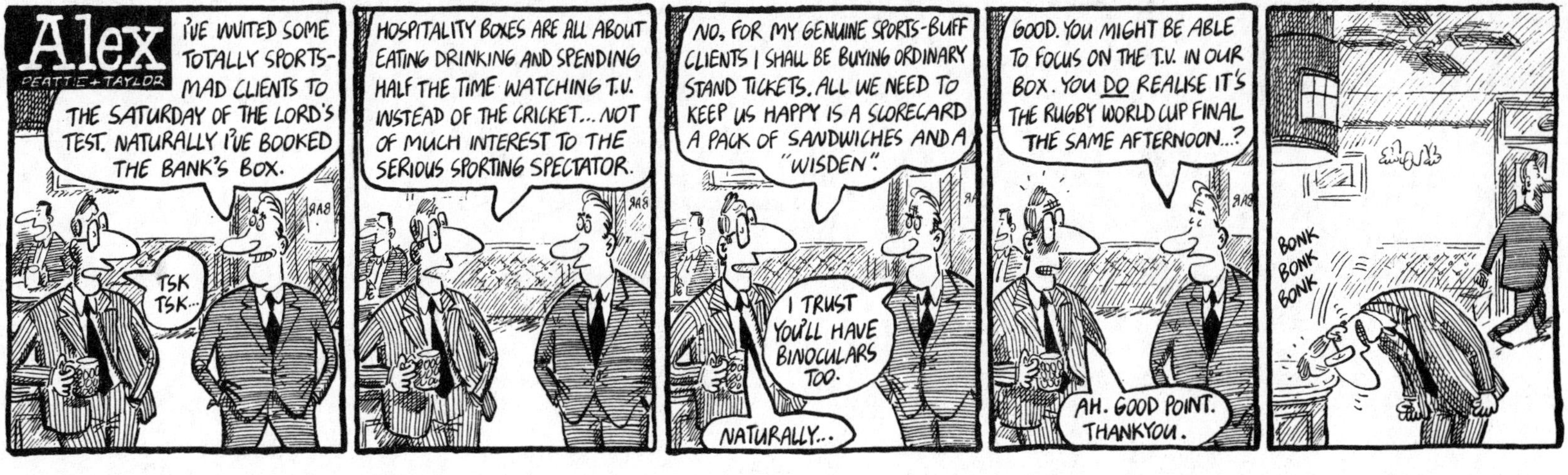
Alex
PEATTIE + TAYLOR
I'VE INVITED SOME TOTALLY SPORTS-MAD CLIENTS TO THE SATURDAY OF THE LORD'S TEST. NATURALLY I'VE BOOKED THE BANK'S BOX.
TSK TSK...
HOSPITALITY BOXES ARE ALL ABOUT EATING DRINKING AND SPENDING HALF THE TIME WATCHING T.V. INSTEAD OF THE CRICKET... NOT OF MUCH INTEREST TO THE SERIOUS SPORTING SPECTATOR.
NO, FOR MY GENUINE SPORTS-BUFF CLIENTS I SHALL BE BUYING ORDINARY STAND TICKETS. ALL WE NEED TO KEEP US HAPPY IS A SCORECARD A PACK OF SANDWICHES AND A "WISDEN".
I TRUST YOU'LL HAVE BINOCULARS TOO.
NATURALLY...
GOOD. YOU MIGHT BE ABLE TO FOCUS ON THE T.V. IN OUR BOX. YOU DO REALISE IT'S THE RUGBY WORLD CUP FINAL THE SAME AFTERNOON...?
AH. GOOD POINT. THANKYOU.
BONK
BONK
BONK

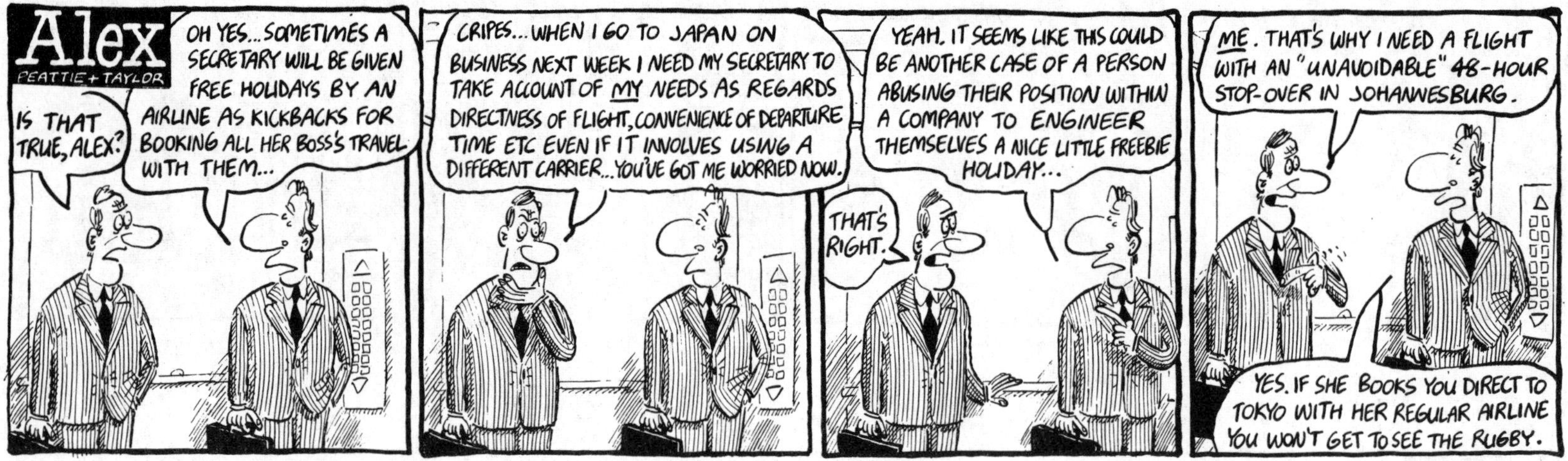
Alex
PEATTIE + TAYLOR
IS THAT TRUE, ALEX?
OH YES... SOMETIMES A SECRETARY WILL BE GIVEN FREE HOLIDAYS BY AN AIRLINE AS KICKBACKS FOR BOOKING ALL HER BOSS'S TRAVEL WITH THEM...
CRIPES... WHEN I GO TO JAPAN ON BUSINESS NEXT WEEK I NEED MY SECRETARY TO TAKE ACCOUNT OF MY NEEDS AS REGARDS DIRECTNESS OF FLIGHT, CONVENIENCE OF DEPARTURE TIME ETC EVEN IF IT INVOLVES USING A DIFFERENT CARRIER... YOU'VE GOT ME WORRIED NOW.
YEAH. IT SEEMS LIKE THIS COULD BE ANOTHER CASE OF A PERSON ABUSING THEIR POSITION WITHIN A COMPANY TO ENGINEER THEMSELVES A NICE LITTLE FREEBIE HOLIDAY...
THAT'S RIGHT.
ME. THAT'S WHY I NEED A FLIGHT WITH AN "UNAVOIDABLE" 48-HOUR STOP-OVER IN JOHANNESBURG.
YES. IF SHE BOOKS YOU DIRECT TO TOKYO WITH HER REGULAR AIRLINE YOU WON'T GET TO SEE THE RUGBY.

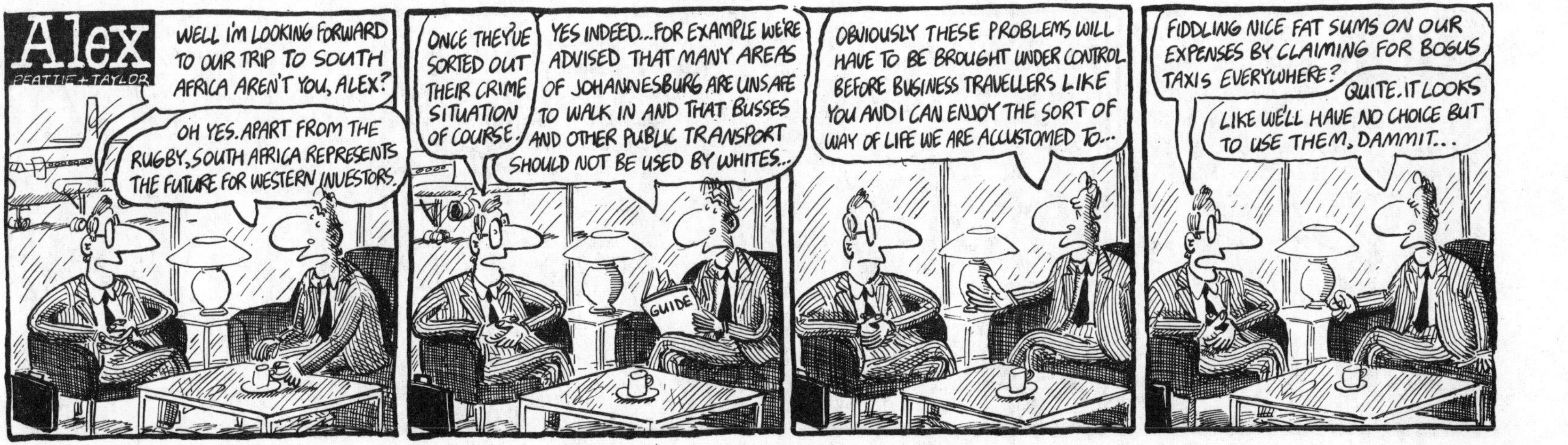
Alex
PEATTIE + TAYLOR
WELL I'M LOOKING FORWARD TO OUR TRIP TO SOUTH AFRICA AREN'T YOU, ALEX?
OH YES. APART FROM THE RUGBY, SOUTH AFRICA REPRESENTS THE FUTURE FOR WESTERN INVESTORS.
ONCE THEY'VE SORTED OUT THEIR CRIME SITUATION OF COURSE.
YES INDEED... FOR EXAMPLE WE'RE ADVISED THAT MANY AREAS OF JOHANNESBURG ARE UNSAFE TO WALK IN AND THAT BUSSES AND OTHER PUBLIC TRANSPORT SHOULD NOT BE USED BY WHITES...
GUIDE
OBVIOUSLY THESE PROBLEMS WILL HAVE TO BE BROUGHT UNDER CONTROL BEFORE BUSINESS TRAVELLERS LIKE YOU AND I CAN ENJOY THE SORT OF WAY OF LIFE WE ARE ACCUSTOMED TO...
FIDDLING NICE FAT SUMS ON OUR EXPENSES BY CLAIMING FOR BOGUS TAXIS EVERYWHERE?
QUITE. IT LOOKS LIKE WE'LL HAVE NO CHOICE BUT TO USE THEM, DAMMIT...

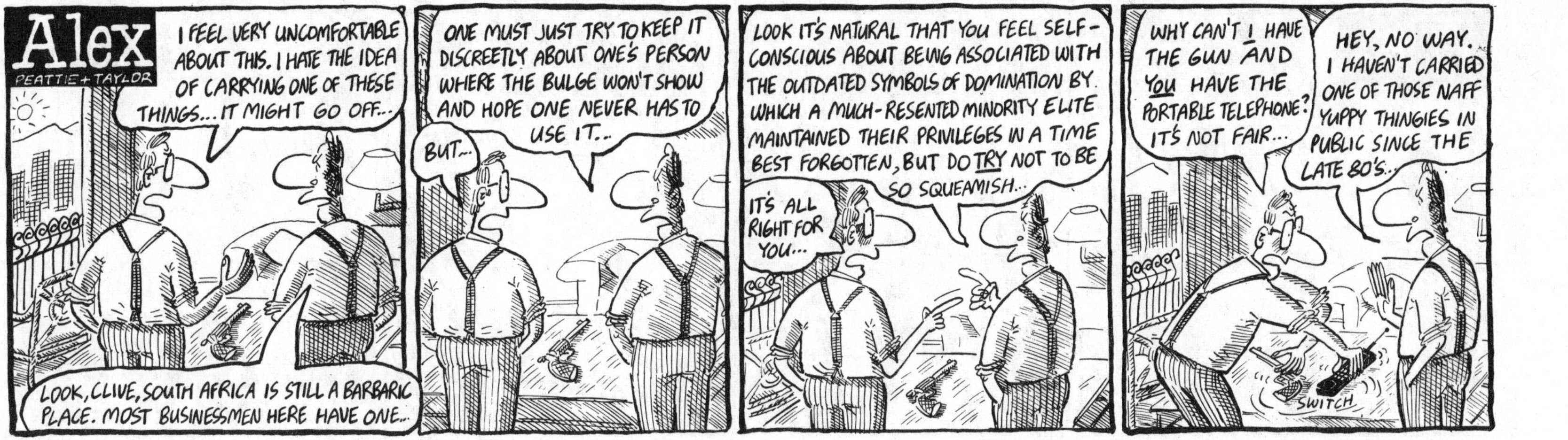
Alex
PEATTIE + TAYLOR
I FEEL VERY UNCOMFORTABLE ABOUT THIS. I HATE THE IDEA OF CARRYING ONE OF THESE THINGS... IT MIGHT GO OFF...
LOOK, CLIVE, SOUTH AFRICA IS STILL A BARBARIC PLACE. MOST BUSINESSMEN HERE HAVE ONE...
ONE MUST JUST TRY TO KEEP IT DISCREETLY ABOUT ONE'S PERSON WHERE THE BULGE WON'T SHOW AND HOPE ONE NEVER HAS TO USE IT...
BUT...
LOOK IT'S NATURAL THAT YOU FEEL SELF-CONSCIOUS ABOUT BEING ASSOCIATED WITH THE OUTDATED SYMBOLS OF DOMINATION BY WHICH A MUCH-RESENTED MINORITY ELITE MAINTAINED THEIR PRIVILEGES IN A TIME BEST FORGOTTEN, BUT DO TRY NOT TO BE SO SQUEAMISH...
IT'S ALL RIGHT FOR YOU...
WHY CAN'T I HAVE THE GUN AND YOU HAVE THE PORTABLE TELEPHONE? IT'S NOT FAIR...
HEY, NO WAY. I HAVEN'T CARRIED ONE OF THOSE NAFF YUPPY THINGIES IN PUBLIC SINCE THE LATE 80'S...
SWITCH

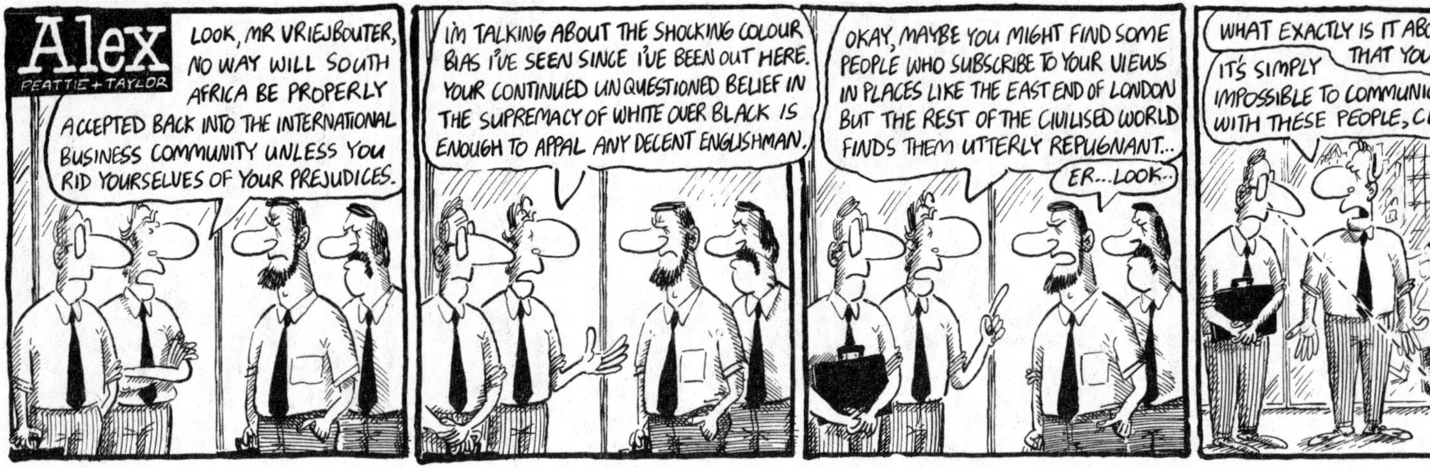
Alex
PEATTIE + TAYLOR
LOOK, MR VRIEJBOUTER, NO WAY WILL SOUTH AFRICA BE PROPERLY ACCEPTED BACK INTO THE INTERNATIONAL BUSINESS COMMUNITY UNLESS YOU RID YOURSELVES OF YOUR PREJUDICES.
I'M TALKING ABOUT THE SHOCKING COLOUR BIAS I'VE SEEN SINCE I'VE BEEN OUT HERE. YOUR CONTINUED UNQUESTIONED BELIEF IN THE SUPREMACY OF WHITE OVER BLACK IS ENOUGH TO APPAL ANY DECENT ENGLISHMAN.
OKAY, MAYBE YOU MIGHT FIND SOME PEOPLE WHO SUBSCRIBE TO YOUR VIEWS IN PLACES LIKE THE EAST END OF LONDON BUT THE REST OF THE CIVILISED WORLD FINDS THEM UTTERLY REPUGNANT...
ER... LOOK...
WHAT EXACTLY IS IT ABOUT WHITE SOCKS THAT YOU DON'T LIKE?
IT'S SIMPLY IMPOSSIBLE TO COMMUNICATE WITH THESE PEOPLE, CLIVE...

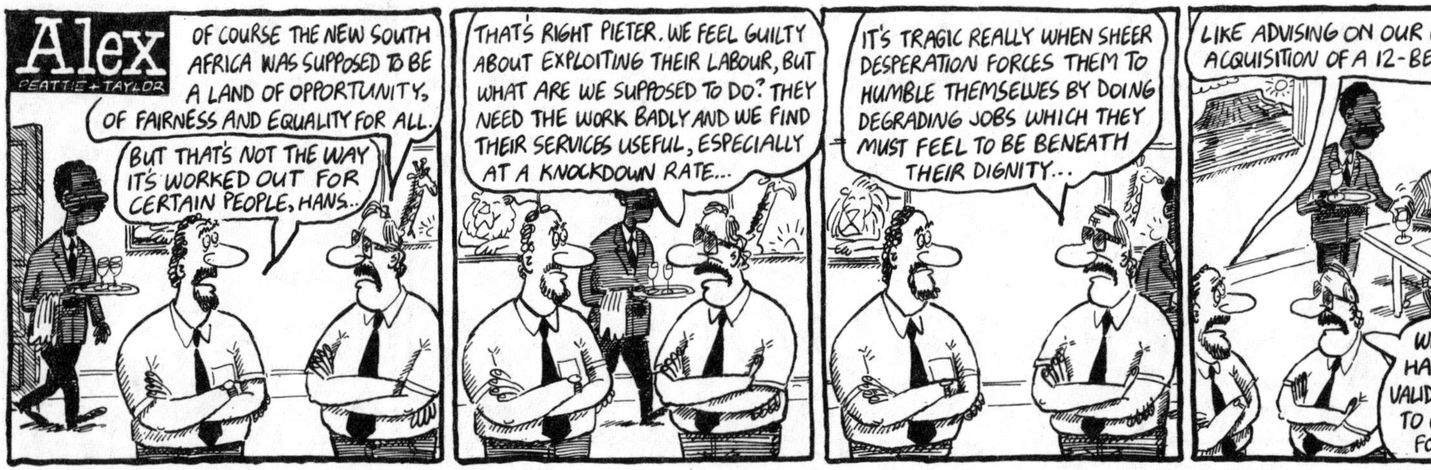
Alex
PEATTIE + TAYLOR
OF COURSE THE NEW SOUTH AFRICA WAS SUPPOSED TO BE A LAND OF OPPORTUNITY, OF FAIRNESS AND EQUALITY FOR ALL.
BUT THAT'S NOT THE WAY IT'S WORKED OUT FOR CERTAIN PEOPLE, HANS...
THAT'S RIGHT PIETER. WE FEEL GUILTY ABOUT EXPLOITING THEIR LABOUR, BUT WHAT ARE WE SUPPOSED TO DO? THEY NEED THE WORK BADLY AND WE FIND THEIR SERVICES USEFUL, ESPECIALLY AT A KNOCKDOWN RATE...
IT'S TRAGIC REALLY WHEN SHEER DESPERATION FORCES THEM TO HUMBLE THEMSELVES BY DOING DEGRADING JOBS WHICH THEY MUST FEEL TO BE BENEATH THEIR DIGNITY...
LIKE ADVISING ON OUR COMPANY'S ACQUISITION OF A 12-BEDROOM MOTEL?
WELL, THEY WERE HAPPY TO FIND ANY VALID BUSINESS EXCUSE TO GET OUT HERE FOR THE RUGBY.

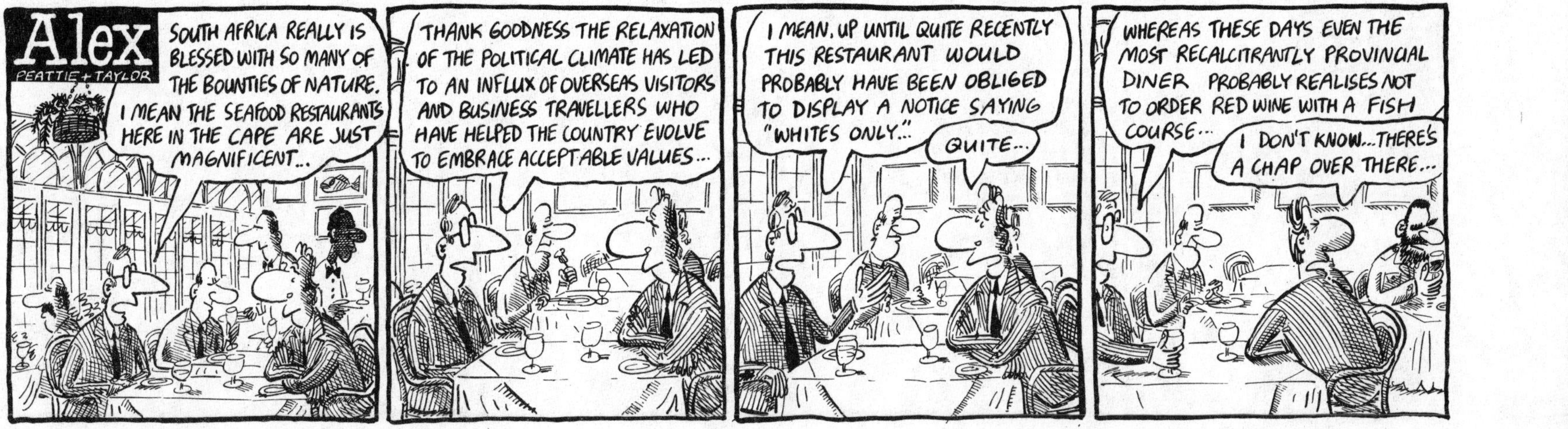
Alex
PEATTIE + TAYLOR
SOUTH AFRICA REALLY IS BLESSED WITH SO MANY OF THE BOUNTIES OF NATURE. I MEAN THE SEAFOOD RESTAURANTS HERE IN THE CAPE ARE JUST MAGNIFICENT...
THANK GOODNESS THE RELAXATION OF THE POLITICAL CLIMATE HAS LED TO AN INFLUX OF OVERSEAS VISITORS AND BUSINESS TRAVELLERS WHO HAVE HELPED THE COUNTRY EVOLVE TO EMBRACE ACCEPTABLE VALUES...
I MEAN, UP UNTIL QUITE RECENTLY THIS RESTAURANT WOULD PROBABLY HAVE BEEN OBLIGED TO DISPLAY A NOTICE SAYING "WHITES ONLY."
QUITE...
WHEREAS THESE DAYS EVEN THE MOST RECALCITRANTLY PROVINCIAL DINER PROBABLY REALISES NOT TO ORDER RED WINE WITH A FISH COURSE...
I DON'T KNOW... THERE'S A CHAP OVER THERE...

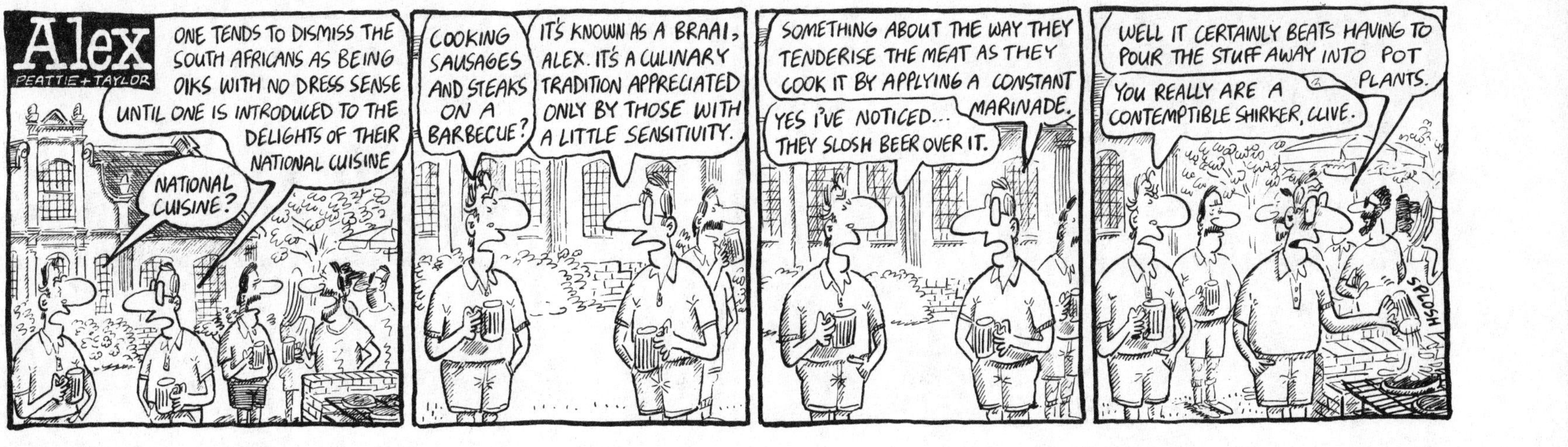
Alex
PEATTIE + TAYLOR
ONE TENDS TO DISMISS THE SOUTH AFRICANS AS BEING OIKS WITH NO DRESS SENSE UNTIL ONE IS INTRODUCED TO THE DELIGHTS OF THEIR NATIONAL CUISINE
NATIONAL CUISINE?
COOKING SAUSAGES AND STEAKS ON A BARBECUE?
IT'S KNOWN AS A BRAAI, ALEX. IT'S A CULINARY TRADITION APPRECIATED ONLY BY THOSE WITH A LITTLE SENSITIVITY.
SOMETHING ABOUT THE WAY THEY TENDERISE THE MEAT AS THEY COOK IT BY APPLYING A CONSTANT MARINADE.
YES I'VE NOTICED... THEY SLOSH BEER OVER IT.
WELL IT CERTAINLY BEATS HAVING TO POUR THE STUFF AWAY INTO POT PLANTS.
YOU REALLY ARE A CONTEMPTIBLE SHIRKER, CLIVE.
SPLOSH

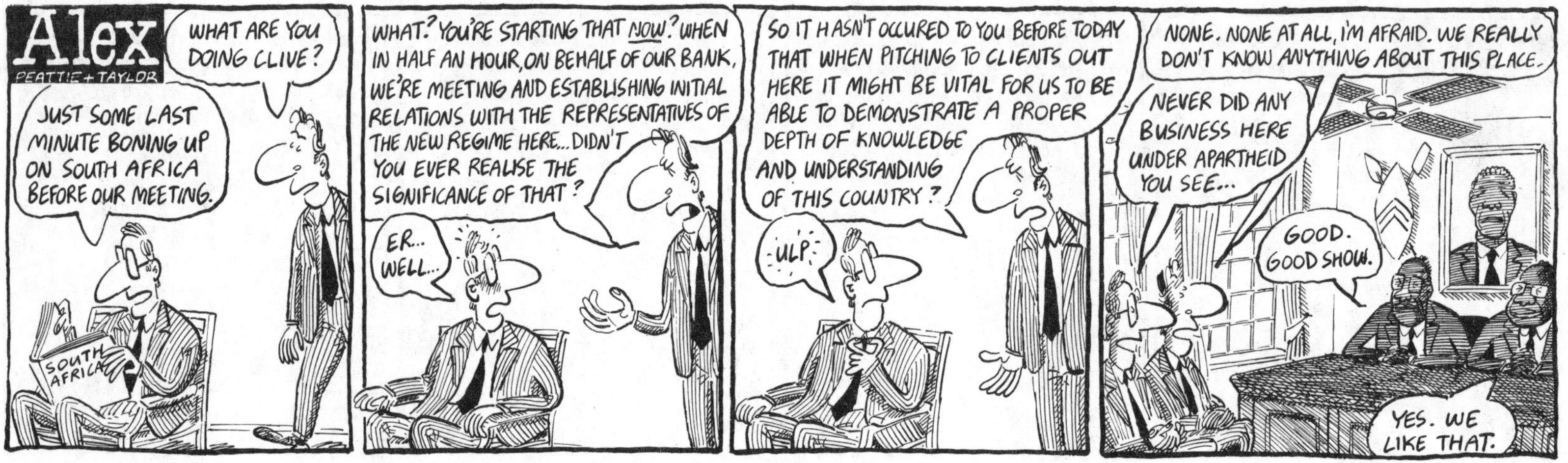
Alex
PEATTIE + TAYLOR
WHAT ARE YOU DOING CLIVE?
JUST SOME LAST MINUTE BONING UP ON SOUTH AFRICA BEFORE OUR MEETING.
SOUTH AFRICA
WHAT? YOU'RE STARTING THAT NOW? WHEN IN HALF AN HOUR, ON BEHALF OF OUR BANK, WE'RE MEETING AND ESTABLISHING INITIAL RELATIONS WITH THE REPRESENTATIVES OF THE NEW REGIME HERE... DIDN'T YOU EVER REALISE THE SIGNIFICANCE OF THAT?
ER... WELL...
SO IT HASN'T OCCURED TO YOU BEFORE TODAY THAT WHEN PITCHING TO CLIENTS OUT HERE IT MIGHT BE VITAL FOR US TO BE ABLE TO DEMONSTRATE A PROPER DEPTH OF KNOWLEDGE AND UNDERSTANDING OF THIS COUNTRY?
ULP
NONE. NONE AT ALL, I'M AFRAID. WE REALLY DON'T KNOW ANYTHING ABOUT THIS PLACE.
NEVER DID ANY BUSINESS HERE UNDER APARTHEID YOU SEE...
GOOD. GOOD SHOW.
YES. WE LIKE THAT.

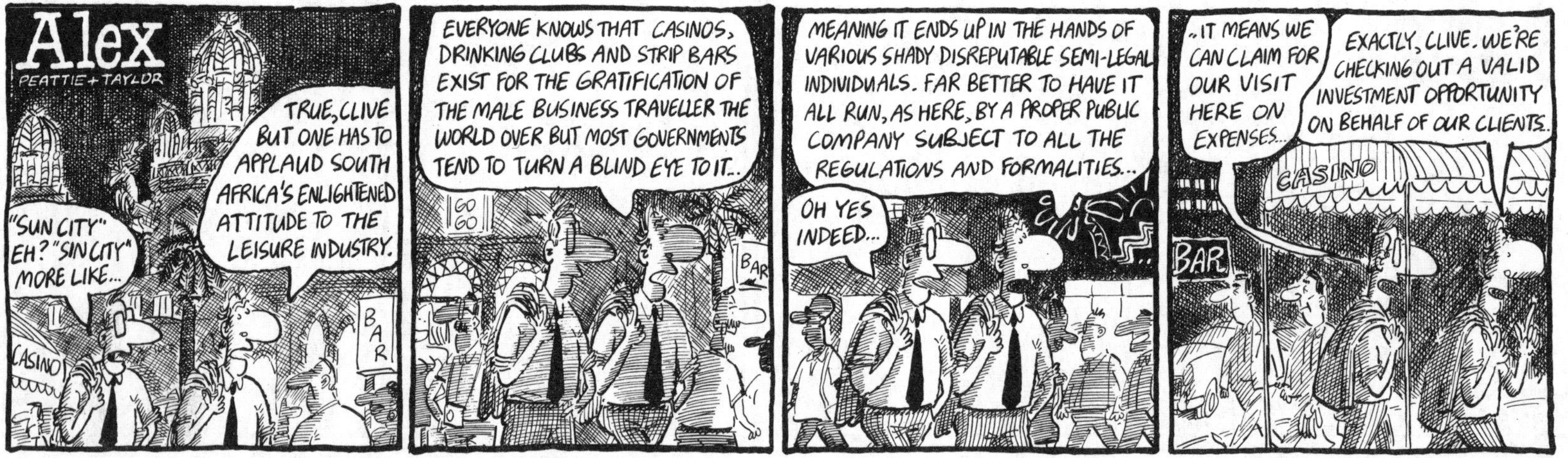
Alex
PEATTIE + TAYLOR
"SUN CITY" EH? "SIN CITY" MORE LIKE...
TRUE, CLIVE BUT ONE HAS TO APPLAUD SOUTH AFRICA'S ENLIGHTENED ATTITUDE TO THE LEISURE INDUSTRY.
CASINO
BAR
EVERYONE KNOWS THAT CASINOS, DRINKING CLUBS AND STRIP BARS EXIST FOR THE GRATIFICATION OF THE MALE BUSINESS TRAVELLER THE WORLD OVER BUT MOST GOVERNMENTS TEND TO TURN A BLIND EYE TO IT...
GO GO
BAR
MEANING IT ENDS UP IN THE HANDS OF VARIOUS SHADY DISREPUTABLE SEMI-LEGAL INDIVIDUALS. FAR BETTER TO HAVE IT ALL RUN, AS HERE, BY A PROPER PUBLIC COMPANY SUBJECT TO ALL THE REGULATIONS AND FORMALITIES...
OH YES INDEED...
..IT MEANS WE CAN CLAIM FOR OUR VISIT HERE ON EXPENSES...
EXACTLY, CLIVE. WE'RE CHECKING OUT A VALID INVESTMENT OPPORTUNITY ON BEHALF OF OUR CLIENTS..
CASINO
BAR

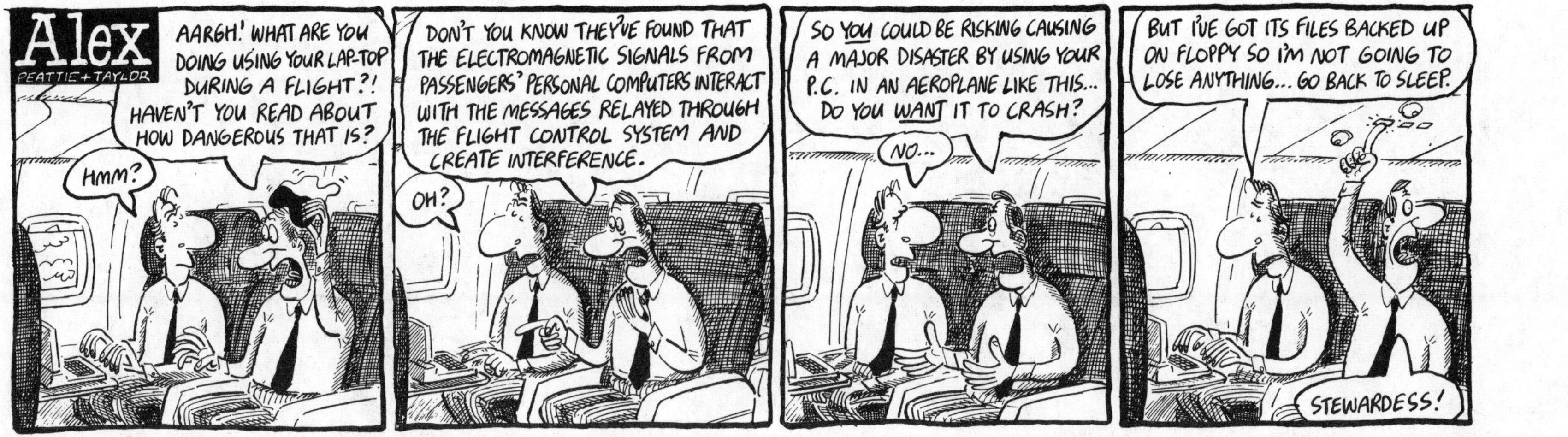
Alex
PEATTIE + TAYLOR
AARGH! WHAT ARE YOU DOING USING YOUR LAP-TOP DURING A FLIGHT?! HAVEN'T YOU READ ABOUT HOW DANGEROUS THAT IS?
HMM?
DON'T YOU KNOW THEY'VE FOUND THAT THE ELECTROMAGNETIC SIGNALS FROM PASSENGERS' PERSONAL COMPUTERS INTERACT WITH THE MESSAGES RELAYED THROUGH THE FLIGHT CONTROL SYSTEM AND CREATE INTERFERENCE.
OH?
SO YOU COULD BE RISKING CAUSING A MAJOR DISASTER BY USING YOUR P.C. IN AN AEROPLANE LIKE THIS... DO YOU WANT IT TO CRASH?
NO...
BUT I'VE GOT ITS FILES BACKED UP ON FLOPPY SO I'M NOT GOING TO LOSE ANYTHING... GO BACK TO SLEEP.
STEWARDESS!

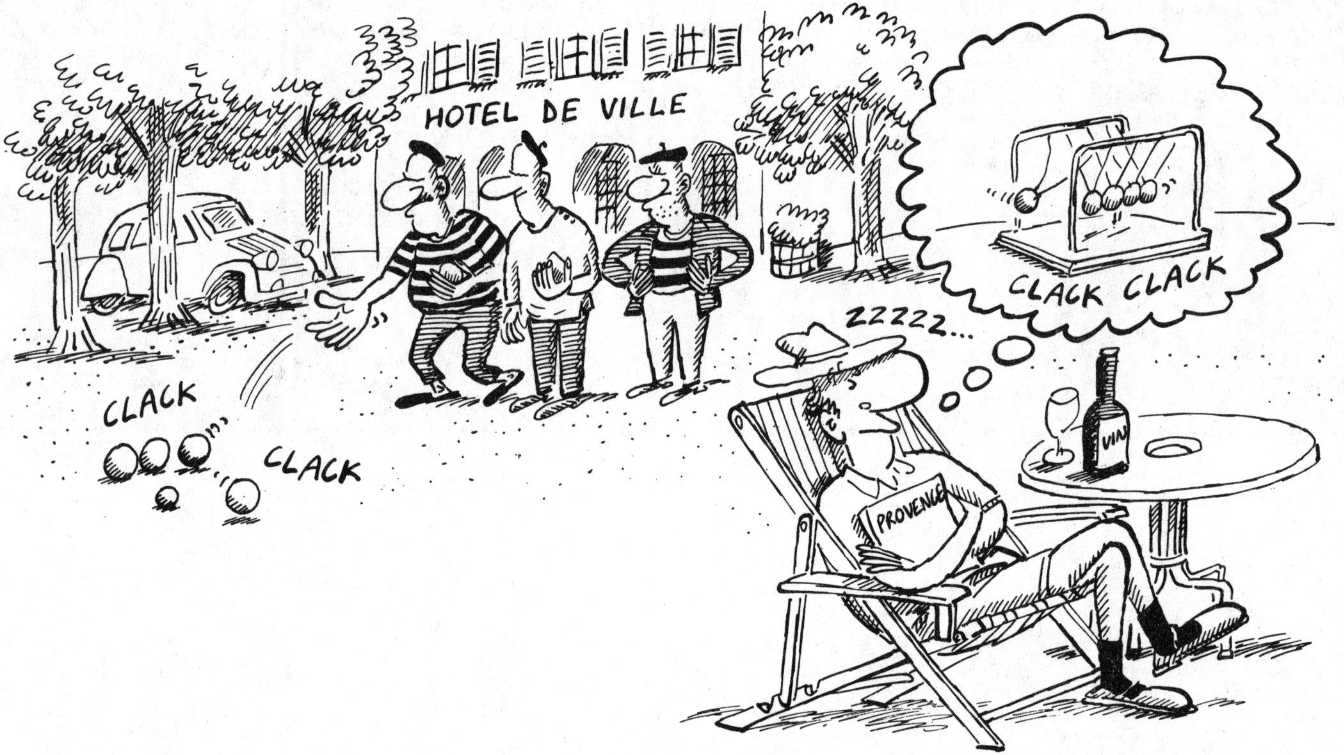
HOTEL DE VILLE
CLACK
CLACK
ZZZZZ...
CLACK CLACK
PROVENCE
VIN